Ne

Business

“Creating a new theory is not like destroying an old barn and erecting a skyscraper in its place. It is rather like climbing a mountain, gaining new and wider views, discovering unexpected connections between our starting point and its rich environment. ”

ALBERT EINSTEIN, *THE EVOLUTION OF PHYSICS* (1938)

Over 325 people contributed to this comprehensive publication including cases and visions from around the globe.

INTERVIEWS WITH

75+

CEOS, DIRECTORS AND SENIOR EXECUTIVES

THE CRITICAL INPUT FROM

40+

INTERNATIONAL SCIENTISTS

THE REFRESHING INTERVENTION OF

50+

STUDENTS

CONTRIBUTIONS THROUGH CROWDSOURCING FROM

175+

PROFESSIONALS FROM BUSINESSES, NON-PROFIT ORGANIZATIONS, GOVERNMENTS AND CREATIVE INDUSTRIES

Watch the introduction movie
'New Economy Business' on our website
www.neweconomybusiness.world

New Economy Business

Seven windows of opportunity

Marga Hoek

NEW ECONOMY PUBLICATIONS

Amsterdam, 2016

Editors: Amie de Jeu, Felix de Fijter

Colophon

MIX
Paper from responsible sources
FSC® C006253

Recycled paper
Made from recycled materials.

This publication is fully CO_2 and climate neutral.

Author: Marga Hoek
Editors: Felix de Fijter, Tekstbureau Vakmaten & Amie de Jeu, AdeJeu English Language Services
Translator: Amie de Jeu, AdeJeu English Language Services
Design, cover and illustrations: AnneMarie Adriaans, I AM creative
Infographics and figures: Dorus Galama
Printing: Ecodrukkers
Publisher: New Economy Publications, 2016

ISBN 978 90 8237 852 8 (folio)
ISBN 978 90 8237 853 5 (e-book)

Table of contents

Icons

The content of this book is enhanced with illustrations, infographics, details, examples, and business cases. They are shown clearly using the following seven icons:

Case	Facts & Figures	Infographic	New Framework	Quote	Shortcut	Wrap up

Case	More than 50 business cases are presented in this book to give practical examples of the content discussed in the different chapters.
Facts & Figures	Relevant background information giving quantitative support to the content presented.
Infographic	The infographics give informative, visual background information.
New Framework	In each chapter, we introduce one or more new practical management models.
Quote	Citations from CEOs, scientists or other experts enrich and clarify the information presented.
Shortcut	The shortcuts concisely show contrasts and differences.
Wrap up	Each chapter ends with a Wrap up. A succinct summary of the chapter.

Business cases around the globe

cal motion, United States San Mateo • Rolls-Royce, Europe, England, London • Spotify, Europe, England, Europe, Sweden, Stock
ates, Ann Arbor • Primark, Europe, Ireland, Dublin • Mud Jeans, Europe, Netherlands, Rhenen • Nudie Jeans co., Europe, Sweden
ited States, Green Island, New York • Panasonic Eco, Technology Center, Asia, Japan, Kato City • Recover E, RHDHV, Europe, Neth
rth America, United States, Atlanta • Nike, North America, United States, Beaverton • Skanska, Europe, Sweden, Stockholm •
iker Unie, Europe, Netherlands, Dinteloord • Graz, Europe, Austria • Better Place, North America, United States, Palo Alto • Za
Starbucks, North America, United States, Seattle Veolia Europe, France, Paris • LEGO, Europe, Denmark, Billund • Kraft Foods, No
rope, Netherlands, Eindhoven • General Electric, North America, United States, Fairfield • Quirky North America, United States
uth America, Colombia, Bogotá • Naked Wines, Europe, England, Norwich • Silva Nova, Europe, Sweden, Stockholm • Buraph
akaWaka, Europe, Netherlands, Haarlem • BAM, Europe, Netherlands, Bunnik • PGGM, Europe, Netherlands, Zeist • Zweite Spark
ndon • Fidor Bank, Europe, Germany, Munich • KKR, North America, United States, New York • Puma Europe, Germany, Herzogena

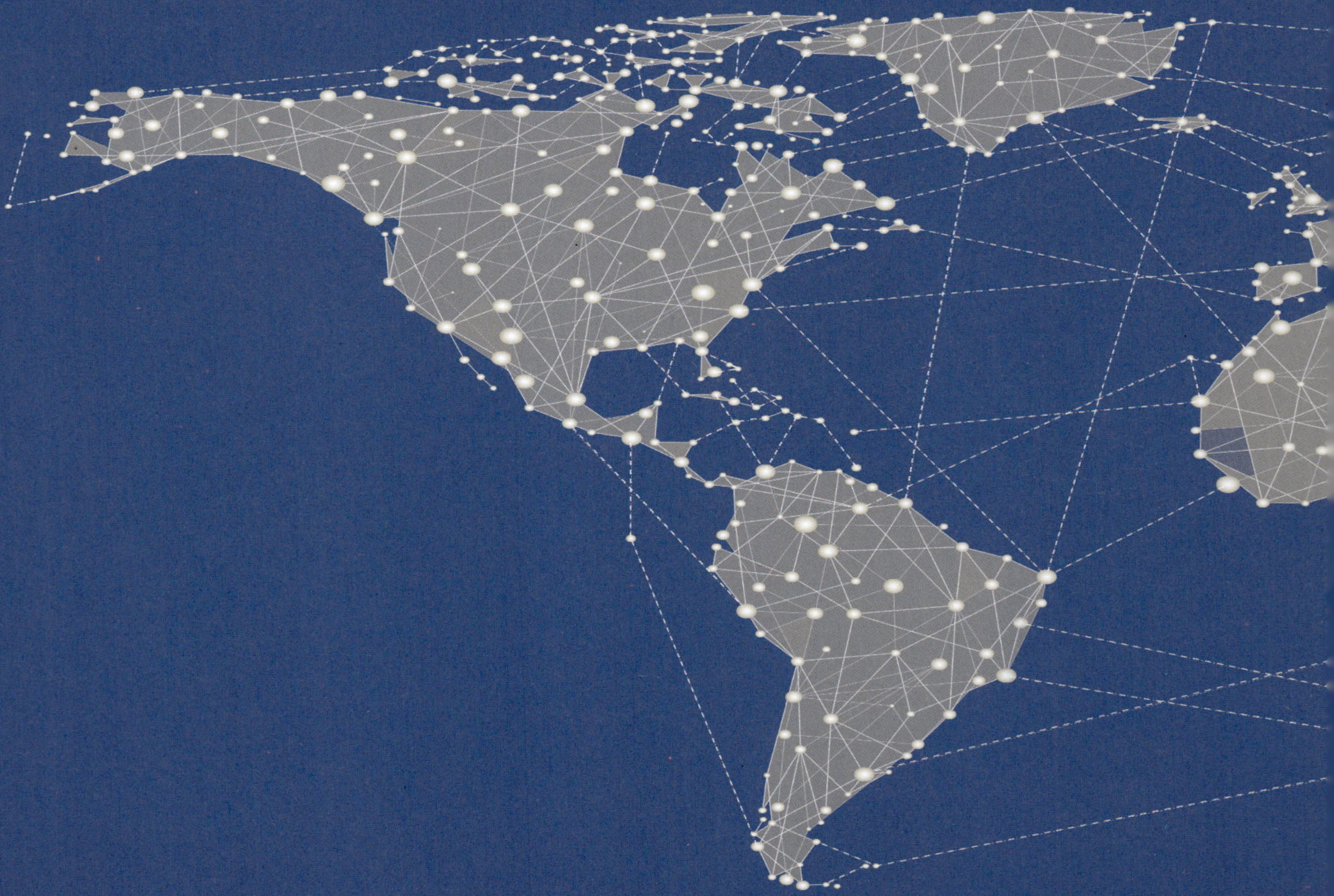

• Netflix, North America, United States, Los Gatos • Off Grid Electric, Africa, Tanzania, Arusha • ReCelular, North America, Unit
enburg • Wear2 Europe, England, • Chester • Active Disassembly Research, Europe, England, London • Ecovative , North Americ
ds, Amersfoort • ASML, Europe, Netherlands, Veldhoven • Intel, North America, United States, Santa Clara, California • Interfac
Foods, North America, United States, New York • Fujifilm, Europe, Netherlands, Tilburg • SCOPE insight, Africa, Kenya , Nairob
ica, Madagascar, Ankorondrano • Unilever, Europe, England, London, Asia, India, Mumbai • Simgas, Africa, Tanzania, Dar es Salaa
erica, United States, Chicago • Zelfo, Europe, Germany, Brandenburg • Unilever, Europe, England, London • Dutch Polymer Institut
York • IKEA, Europe, Netherlands, Leiden • Optiledge, Europe, Netherlands, Eindhoven • Mahindra, Asia, India, Mumbai • Bavar
forestry, Asia, Laos, Ban Phonesaat • Time/bank, Europe, Netherlands, The Hague • Liquor Store, Europe, Netherlands, Sluis
Europe, Austria, Graz • TransferWise Europe, England, London • North America, United States, New York • Iwoca Europe, Englan
• Botanique, South America, Brazil, Bairro dos Mellos •

Forewords

Forewords: Paul Polman, Dan Hendrix, Peter Bakker, Bertrand van Ee, Ton Büchner, Dr Maurits van Rooijen, Jens Birgersson, Frank Heemskerk, Gunter Pauli

Paul Polman

We all have a role to play

In this timely new book, a new form of business is advocated, i.e. one which serves the needs of the world and the population at large. As Marga Hoek succinctly puts it, "The economy is there for the world, the world is not here for the economy." This is a principle I strongly believe in.

The necessity for transformation is supported by simply looking at the numbers: we are currently producing and consuming at rates which are not sustainable. This challenge needs to be addressed, and we all have a role to play.

My company has therefore adopted 'The Unilever Sustainable Living Plan' which forms the foundation for a new sustainable business model focused on creating long-term value. New and great business opportunities are presenting themselves as a consequence.

At the same time however, it is clear that the current group of frontrunners is still too small. We therefore need to form coalitions and partnerships with other businesses, governments and civil society to scale-up.

This book will provide ample inspiration to everyone willing to join this important journey.

Paul Polman
CEO Unilever, England

Dan Hendrix

So right and so smart

Twenty years ago, when Interface began its bold climb up what our founder and visionary pioneer called "Mount Sustainability," we did so without a compass and without a map. Today, with tools like Marga Hoek's book, businesses that wish to engage in the sustainable economy need only read this book.

New Economy Business contains a rich history and is written in an accessible style. Hoek makes a compelling case for not only pursuing sustainable goals in sync with the environment, but also aligned with our social, intellectual, and financial assets. She makes a relevant argument for the idea that the new economy revolves around value creation. Hoek also advocates for 'glocalization' which is focused localization in a context of global connectedness. Additionally, she makes a strong case for an increasing need for corporate transparency, an attunement to changing consumer values, and adaptation to the ever and quickly-evolving digital and mobile revolutions.

Looking at your company through the lens of a new paradigm –this new economy – will give you a new and profound way to view not only what you do, but how you do it, with whom you partner and employ, and where you invest your capital and R&D/innovation funds. If that is not the recipe for building a unique value proposition that will rapidly become a competitive advantage, I don't know what is!

In memory of our late founder and chairman, Ray Anderson, I would propose to you that the ideas shared in *New Economy Business* are, in his words, "so right and so smart."

Dan Hendrix
Chairman & CEO Interface, USA

Peter Bakker

Fascinating frame of reference

This book's title, *New Economy Business*, implies we are about to encounter economic changes leading to a truly new economy. Is it a correct prediction? There's no doubt about it as far as I'm concerned. However, the road leading to this new economy is not an easy one. We have to work towards a new form of capitalism in which we secure, as Marga Hoek rightly states, financial, social and ecological assets.

Businesses, leading ones especially, have a huge impact on the transition to that new economy. An impact that, for the most part, is not being utilised. The fact that this book addresses doing business in this new economy is, of course, progress. Hoek presents a fascinating frame of reference for doing business that will inspire every entrepreneur. I also urge scholars, politicians and other interested parties to read this spectrum of new insights and, more importantly, to let it sink in.

The interpretation of an economy based on the creation of value for the three assets must be made on all system levels. This is elaborated on in the book. What fascinates me is the power of accounting. As I often argue: this is the ideal place to realize and secure the vision of the new economy. Marga Hoek introduces the concept of the Chief Financial Officer becoming the Chief Value Officer which is logical, yet innovative at the same time.

This ground-breaking management book translates a clear vision into solid management models, with over fifty specific cases. And all of that in a very readable book which I strongly recommend.

Peter Bakker
President World Business Council for Sustainable Development (WBCSD), Switzerland

Bertrand van Ee

It is vital to spread the word

The world is moving at a pace that's unprecedented. The internet has made the world more accessible, global and local at the same time. In her book, Hoek provides a razor-sharp analysis of classic theories that are no longer applicable in our present times.

The book offers a stimulating overview of current innovation and relates it to a paradigm shift in the global economy, giving illuminating examples of business models that are flourishing. The broad sector and geographic coverage is impressive and educational to executive thinking. But this book is not only for corporations, it is a must-read for a larger audience including NGOs, policymakers, academics and the public sector, as the solution to our global challenges is often in co-creation.

Climate-KIC, EU's initiative focused on climate change and largest public-private partnership, supports collaboration across countries and companies by providing ground-breaking ideas and technologies. We also work with graduates from top universities to create a legion of change agents, and invest in start-ups through our Acceleration Program, where Hoek chairs the jury of the best cleantech ventures from across Europe.

To meet our global challenges, leaders must think differently and creatively about risks and continuity, combined with a broader responsibility to build awareness of the challenges and the solutions. It is therefore vital to spread the word and engage more companies in order to achieve greater impact. This book will help set the wheels in motion. It is a feast for the mind and for the boardrooms and is bound to provoke some disruptive executive thinking.

Bertrand van Ee CEO *Climate-KIC, England*

Ton Büchner

Lead the change

At AkzoNobel we believe businesses can inspire and lead the change that's needed. But radical transformations are needed across a range of industry sectors if the planet is to be able to support the lives of nine billion people by 2050. Businesses need to be bold, think differently and act differently. Thanks to Marga Hoek's book, *New Economy Business*, companies now have a fascinating guide to do just that.

New Economy Business is written in an accessible way and contains the kind of practical examples that we at AkzoNobel believe are so powerful. Hoek makes a compelling case for a new economic model based on value creation. According to this model, businesses should not only pursue goals that are sympathetic to the environment, but should also take into account social, intellectual, and financial aims.

Perhaps more importantly though, Hoek takes readers back to the core element of business – the customer. And she reveals how companies can grasp the opportunities of the sustainable economy to create business success.

As we say as part of our Planet Possible strategy, just because the world's resources are limited doesn't mean businesses have to limit their ambition and limit their chances of future success.

Ton Büchner
CEO *AkzoNobel, The Netherlands*

Professor Dr Maurits van Rooijen

A new economy based on a new education

In this book Marga Hoek presents the reality of an emerging new economy, based on innovation and sustainability, and the need to challenge old paradigms. The old economy, by definition, is not fit for the future. We may not like it, but new challenges at macro level and new opportunities demand a new economy. This book provides the reader with valuable insights on how the new economy could – and should – look like.

As an educator, this is of crucial importance. The new economy is not a concept, it is an action plan, to be created by a new generation of leaders. This is where education plays an important role. We need to prepare new generations to function effectively and responsibly. The new economy is at the core of this challenge. But the education task is not just about teaching new generations. It is equally about implementing education as part of the ongoing transformation, also at organisational level. In addition to providing learners with work-integrated learning opportunities, our task as educators is to also supply working professionals with learning-integrated work. Sustainable innovation and organisational transformation cannot happen without learning.

All this needs to be approached with a truly global mindset. I am very pleased to be working with Marga Hoek on the development of a new academic programme completely based on the findings of this book. We not only applaud the author for such an insightful work, but we want to be an active part of the emerging global society and help graduates to be a force for good in that process.

Professor Dr. Maurits van Rooijen
Chief Academic Officer Global University Systems, England

Jens Birgersson

Social value requires a different mindset

The insulation industry has a clear and pressing target: significant improvement of energy efficiency. It is a high priority because of the environmental impact of using 40% of the world's energy to heat and cool buildings.

With her book *New Economy Business*, Marga Hoek sets the focus on another important opportunity: the social value. As she says, it is one of the most unchartered areas.

The World Green Building Council (in their 2014 report) explains that 90% of operating costs for an office building are related to staff; 9% are building related costs such as rent, and only 1% are energy costs. It goes without saying that every effort should be made to reduce energy consumption, but attention should also be given to the impact of the building's design on users. As an example, if more attention is paid to the acoustics, thus improving speech intelligibility, this could have a positive influence on stress levels and absenteeism.

This approach requires a different mindset when designing and renovating. It also requires the building industry to be able to justify the investment. It is, in other words, one of the epitomes of value creation, as illustrated by Hoek in this book.

The ambition of ROCKWOOL is not only to keep improving our own processes but also to support our stakeholders in order to create a sustainable society. We have at least one element to investigate further - the social impact, and we will certainly use this book as a source of inspiration to help us deliver the benefits of the triple bottom line.

Jens Birgersson
CEO ROCKWOOL Group, Denmark

Frank Heemskerk

We need to scale up

Marga Hoek has been dedicated to sustainable entrepreneurship for years. She consistently shows how sustainability can be profitable for business and society by conveying her vision and translating it into concrete examples.
In this highly accessible business book she clearly describes both analytical frameworks as well as many best practices. She gives examples of entrepreneurs and successful companies that are both driven by sustainable values as well as creating them.

Unfortunately, sustainable business is still not common. The number of progressive leaders is still too low. We all need to do more so we can remain sustainable. We need to scale up. It is therefore crucial for pioneers in this movement to share their insights with other business leaders, politicians, scientists and consumers.

I am convinced that entrepreneurs and all other readers will gain knowledge and inspiration from *New Economy Business*. If companies, investors, citizens and consumers take actions in the spirit of this book, we will be able to hand over a better and fairer world to future generations. Because that is what it is all about.

Frank Heemskerk
Dutch Executive Director World Bank, USA

Gunter Pauli

Back to the basis of the economy

There is no doubt about it, our current economic system cannot be sustained. More of the same, less of the bad, tightening the belts and hoping for a decrease in unemployment... this is not the way to sustain our society. This is not a plea for rebellion or the building of barricades, but a recognition that things could be a lot better. To answer the question, "How?" Marga Hoek offers a clear vision which is more than welcome – it is essential.

She brings us back to the basis of the economy: The customer. Philip Kotler argued that companies should sell what the client wants. This principle has been adopted by business studies, but not in the business world. In practice, companies sell what they make, what they invent and what they want to promote by large scale production and standardization. They are always looking for a better profit margin and cash flow. The sale of inventory – based on supply chain management – leaves little room to guarantee added value to the customer.

The idea of transforming the Chief Financial Officer into the Chief Value Officer is not only refreshing, it shows how bold the transition to the new economy would be when the customer is king once again.

Gunter Pauli
Author of The Blue Economy and Chairman Novamont, Japan.

Co-creation and Cooperation

This book was not created by me alone. It was in fact the result of a collaborative effort by many people. When the book won the Management Book of the Year award in the Netherlands, many people won, which was truly a great achievement.

The development of this global book has been a co-production with an international team. It has been enhanced from intensive crowdsourcing, numerous interviews with CEOs and input from leading scientists and opinion leaders. This process is in accordance with the integral vision of the new economy, and I am truly grateful for the time over 325 people have spent contributing to this publication, and for the trust given by sharing their insights, sources and knowledge.

Global businesses and knowledge networks were crucial in the development of the content and the identification of business cases throughout the world. They will be just as crucial in helping to spread the messages and knowledge provided here. Since this book is a means to a higher end, I am thankful for their help in giving this book its impact and for their commitment towards realizing the higher goal of making 'business for good' the norm in today's new economy.

Sharing the knowledge

The content of this book is meant to be shared with as many as possible. For this reason *New Economy Business* is licensed by the innovative American licensing organization Creative Commons under the license: Name registration – Non-commercial. This particular license was purposefully chosen in order to permit and encourage readers to share the visions, thoughts, knowledge and examples presented in this book. This also applies to the written text, figures and infographics. High resolution images may be obtained by writing to: info@neweconomypublications.world. Readers are requested to consider the intellectual integrity of the author. For further information on the license terms and conditions, please visit: www.creativecommons.org.

Global business & knowledge networks

wbcsd global network

eit Climate-KIC

forum for the future
action for a sustainable world

GLOBAL UNIVERSITY SYSTEMS

Cordaid

Sustainable Business
entrepreneurs for a new economy

Preface

Every entrepreneur should want to save the world. Businesses should aim to make a positive impact on our planet and protect our primary assets. I feel very strongly about this mission as it touches me deeply when I see the damage that our current economy and business models have caused, and continue to cause. Our resources are becoming more scarce while we continue to waste them, the climate is changing and threatening us all, health and prosperity is being chipped away at while we export health threatening food around the globe. I cannot ignore the oceans becoming more polluted with plastics and chemicals, nor deny the ongoing deforestation and destruction of land. I cannot close my eyes to the dramatically inequitable way capital and wealth is divided with one percent of the poplulation having a hold on 99 percent of the total wealth, or the way debts and underlying values are separated, threatening our economy and well-being. Neither business nor the world can survive this unsustainable global business model. There is just no future in it. It is a dead end street for business and the world.

Therefore, I have endeavored to reinvent myself and redefine my business. As an entrepreneur, I feel the call to change the world. In that quest, I speak and write about the new economy and new economy business based on an economic model that takes all assets (ecological, social and financial) into account, and strives to make a positive impact. It is a journey. The insights and urgency for this transformation sank in over time, to the point where I recognize that we must aim for nothing less than conducting business as a force for good. It has also become clear that businesses who set out to contribute towards finding solutions to our major global challenges are on a mission. And mission driven businesses are more successful and connect better with customers. Business for good is, in fact, a profitable proposition.

Our world needs this transition and we need to combine these high ambitions with scale. The planet's assets are in the red, therefore positive impact must be made on a large scale to stabilize and restore our climate, natural resources, public health and to ensure safe living conditions for nine billion people. Since over 50 of the world's top 100 economies are in fact corporations, if businesses grasp the opportunities and follow the path of positive impact, these challenges can be met rather quickly. Large and small companies around the world are already showing the courage and innovative leadership to move in this direction. Thousands of innovative start-ups appear every day, bringing in transformantive ideas with great potential. Large multinational corporations are able to create impact on a large scale. Unilever, for example, has announced that they are aiming for a CO_2 positive result in operations by 2030. Imagine the impact. That goes for all our challenges. Consider that 750 billion dollars' worth of food is wasted each year while it would take just 80 billion dollars to feed all who go hungry. The costs resulting from the damage to the world are also tremendous. In the last decade alone, the world economy suffered an estimated loss of 2.7 trillion dollars because of natural disasters. It is quite clear that things need to change. And they need to change on a large scale.

The turning point is there. It is not a matter of *if* but *when*. The climate deal in Paris at the end of 2015 marks that tipping point. The world has chosen the direction towards an economy that is there for the world. Leaving behind a world that merely served the economy. The message from the climate conference in Paris and from leading entrepreneurs is that it is time to undertake the biggest business challenge ever, to fight climate change and venture to restore all other assets in keeping with a mission and vision towards the future. Thus, initiatives and collaborations are emerging all around the world. Politicians are also starting to realize that there needs to be a tremendous system change: what we called externalities - the price for resources, pollution and damage - will have to become internalities, consistent with the asset approach I describe in this book. Profit and loss will be about value creation and devaluation of those assets. Public policy and tax systems will need to be transformed accordingly.

Aiming for a positive impact on our world is not only the moral thing to do, it is good business at the same time. The low carbon market is worth more than 5.5 trillion dollars today. Innovations in energy efficiency have the potential to reach 18 trillion dollars by 2035. The circular economy shows the potential to produce 1.8 trillion dollars' worth of revenue and create two million jobs in the EU alone. This potential is demonstrated by investors buying green bonds and it is predicted that this will triple by 2018 to a total of 300 billion dollars. Investments in sustainable businesses have seen a rise of 61% in the last two years and impact investing has also gone up by 132% in just two years.

I am both grateful and hopeful to say that the momentum is there and the course is clear to redefine and repurpose business and our economy. This book is intended as a road-map to help guide and outline the path to the new economy. In the near future, business for good will not be an exception, but the norm. I believe this with all my heart, mind and soul. Let the pioneers in over 50 cases around the world inspire you to take this journey yourself and take with you as many people as you possibly can.

Enjoy the book. Spread the word, but most importantly, spread the deeds.

Let's get down to business.

Marga Hoek

"The economy is there for the world, the world is not here for the economy."

Marga Hoek

Chapter 0
The New Economy

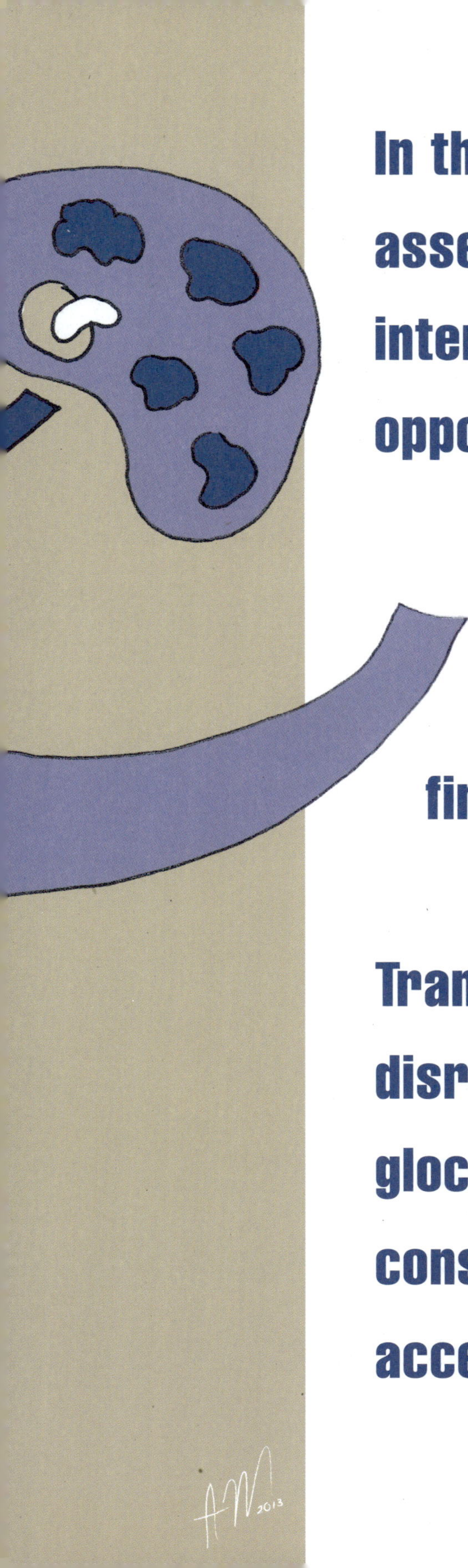

In the new economy our primary assets and transformative trends interact, creating significant opportunities for sustainability.

Value is created for all our assets: ecological, social, and financial.

Transformative trends including disruptive innovative technology, glocalization, and changing consumer values are shaping and accelerating the new economy.

Introduction

The global challenges of our time require a radical shift in our economic perspective. The linear take-make-waste paradigm is no longer valid. We must bid farewell to the traditional economy built on exploitation and short-term perspectives. A new economic design must emerge if we are to build a sustainable future. It is not enough to strive towards minimizing the 'bad', the new economic model must boldly aim towards achieving good.

The new economy is a broadly defined economy, including all assets, in order to create maximum value and growth. Our assets are utilized in the new economy but without permanently exhausting them. Instead, they are cherished, and value is added when possible. This new course is changing the face of the economy in a way that cohesively corresponds with the current transformative trends and the new economic order.

Transformative trends including disruptive technological advances, glocalization, and changing social values have a huge effect on our world and our economy. Societies are utilizing innovative technology and new socio-economic movements are emerging. It is the integration of these transformative trends, together with the creation of value for our three primary assets, that form the essence of the new economy.

The current socio-economic developments present opportunities to integrate sustainability in daily practice. While civic society and the scientific community play pivotal roles in moving our world towards a sustainable future, it is business explorers that will lead the way towards the new economy. Businesses are, after all, unique in their ubiquitous nature; they can transcend borders; they can be local and global at the same time; and they have far-reaching networks and enormous power. Therefore, in *New Economy Business*, we zoom in on this group and explore how businesses are engaged in the new economy.

Businesses are working towards creating a positive impact on the world in the new economy. They recognize that the economic transformation creates great opportunities. There are new markets and customer propositions to explore and greater continuity can be achieved.

Seven windows of opportunity

To demonstrate where these opportunities can be found and give example cases depicting successful business endeavors, the chapters in this book are divided into seven management themes that are as old as business itself: Customers, Scale, Innovation, Business Case, Financing, and Leadership. Although the chapter on Value Cycle may seem unknown, this is the new economy approach to what has been known as the supply chain. While these themes are familiar, the approach may not be. This book will guide you through the familiar terrain and show you how the landscape is changing.

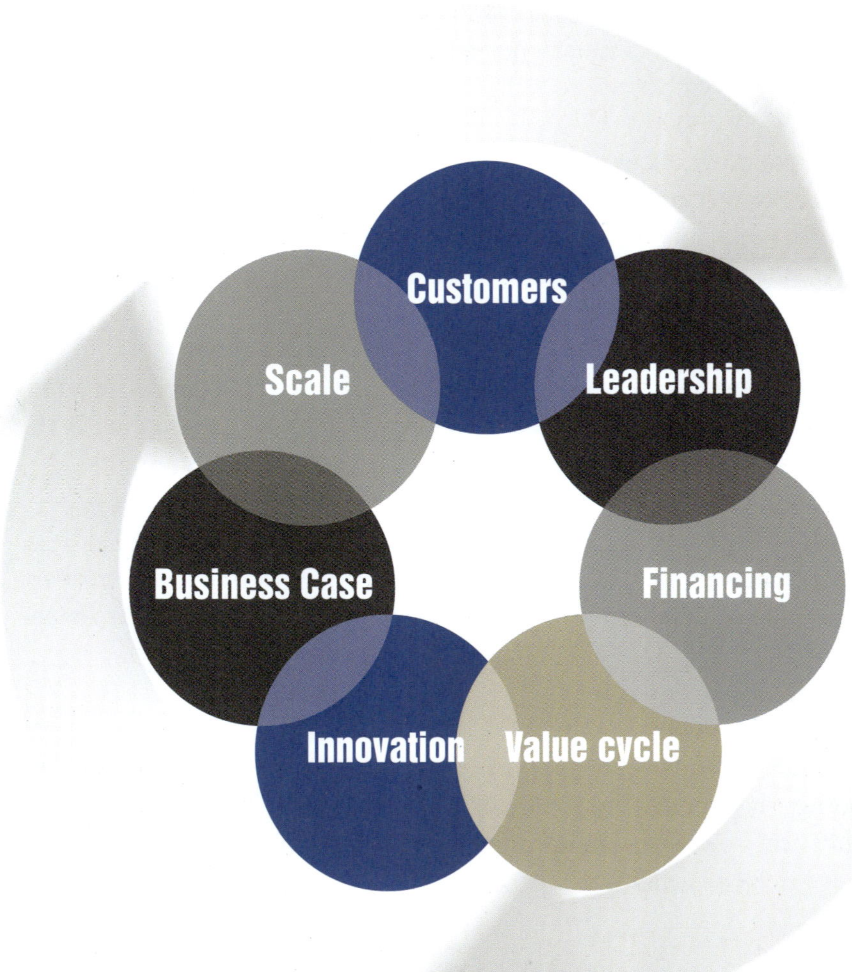

Illustration 1
Seven Windows of Opportunity

Business can be profitable and sustainable at the same time. We do not need to exploit people and the environment in order to succeed. We can learn lessons from the economic models that are outlined in this chapter and incorporate the positive motives with practical methods to achieve sustainability for our environment, population, and economy. As Robert F. Kennedy Jr. recently said in a presentation, "The premise that you need to choose between economic prosperity on the one hand and environmental protection on the other is a false choice." With innovation, appropriate leadership and the drive to promote a value-adding perspective, we most certainly can achieve both.

This chapter sheds light on the foundations of the new economy and the way the various players within it operate. The following points will be discussed:

1. The new economy revolution
The new economy is the culmination of the evolution of economic revolutions and sustainability revolutions.

2. The new economy; all assets count
The new economy is comprehensive and focuses on all our assets: ecological, social, and financial. At its core, the new economy is value driven, sustainable, and circular.

3. Interacting transformative trends shape the new economy
Current transformative trends, including digitalization and global internet use, as well as changing consumer values, harmoniously interact with the principles of the new economy.

4. Pioneers
Today's trailblazers are shaping tomorrow's economy. Visionary business owners, politicians, scientists, and consumers are preparing the frontlines for the rest to follow.

5. New economy business
The title gives it away; this book zooms in on one group at the forefront of the new economy – entrepreneurs. Why? Because it is the business world that is at the heart of the new economy revolution. In a revolution for a sustainable economy, it can be no other way.

6. Seven windows of opportunity
New economy business is more entrepreneurial than ever before. The following chapters will expand on this and show how opportunities in the new economy relate to seven classic management areas. These management themes are undergoing a completely new and disruptive makeover. The seven chapters describe seven windows of opportunity that give a whole new outlook on business and the economy. It is a view to success.

7. The new economy; all assets count
The new economy is comprehensive and focuses on all our assets: ecological, social, and financial. At its core, the new economy is value driven, sustainable, and circular.

8. Interacting transformative trends shape the new economy
Current transformative trends, including digitalization and global internet use, as well as changing consumer values, harmoniously interact with the principles of the new economy.

9. Pioneers
Today's trailblazers are shaping tomorrow's economy. Visionary business owners, politicians, scientists, and consumers are preparing the frontlines for the rest to follow.

10. New economy business
The title gives it away; this book zooms in on one group at the forefront of the new economy – entrepreneurs. Why? Because it is the business world that is at the heart of the new economy revolution. In a revolution for a sustainable economy, it can be no other way.

11. Seven windows of opportunity
New economy business is more entrepreneurial than ever before. The following chapters will expand on this and show how opportunities in the new economy relate to seven classic management areas. These management themes are undergoing a completely new and disruptive makeover. The seven chapters describe seven windows of opportunity that give a whole new outlook on business and the economy. It is a view to success.

Old economy	New economy
SCARCITY DRIVES VALUE	USE DRIVES VALUE
COST-ORIENTED	REVENUE-ORIENTED
PROTECTION AND CONTROL	COLLABORATIVE AND OPEN
LARGE-SCALE	PERSONAL
PREDICTABLE	EXPERIMENTAL AND INNOVATIVE
CLEAR BORDERS	MOVING, OPEN BORDERS
LINEAR PROCESSES	COMMUNITIES
GRADUAL CHANGE	HIGHLY ADAPTABLE
FORCED PERFORMANCE	PERFORMANCE OPPORTUNITIES

Illustration 2
The old economy versus the new economy

1 The new economy revolution

You only need to flip through a few business magazines or check out some recent management books to see that the new economy is a popular theme. If you were to Google the search term “new economy” you will get more than 125 million hits and you would find more than 8,000 books on Amazon.com.[2]

Each one of these publications revolves around significant economic revolutions. Until recently, the term, ‘new economy’ was primarily connected to the technological changes and globalization since the 1980s. *Time* magazine spoke about the new economy in their May 1983 issue as the transition from the industrial age to the technological era. Kevin Kelly’s bestseller in 1998 outlined strategies suited for the new connected economy and the enormous growth of information technology (IT) and the internet. A revolution that, to this day, continues to evolve.

It is noticeable that the publications regarding the new economy all have a positive undertone. Authors appeal to the opportunities and the potential of the new economy. For example, you see titles such as: *51 Marketing Strategies to Dominate your Competition in this New Economy!* (Kasten, 2013); *Agenda for a New Economy: From Phantom Wealth to Real Wealth* (Korten, 2009); *Financial Fresh Start: Your Five-Step Plan for Adapting and Prospering in the New Economy* (Olefson, 2013).

The economic revolutions of the previous decades have dominated the conversation. They were not simply revolutions on paper, they permeated the heart and soul of society. They were visible and pervasive. Sometimes the revolutions flew quickly by, such as the internet bubble in the 1990s, while other times they were more resilient such as the continuing digitalization, mobilization, and globalization.

Sustainability is also one such resilient revolution. When we think about the relatively short history of the sustainability debate, we can see that apart from the economic revolutions, we can also pinpoint a number of 'sustainability revolutions' on our timeline. Although the following paragraphs outline the inception of the various revolutions and they were, admittedly, on a small scale, these 'wake-up calls' were the catalysts of an explicit, societal debate.

For the first wake-up call, we need to step back in time to over forty years ago. In 1972, the Club of Rome (a global think tank dealing with a variety of international political issues) spoke about "The Limits to Growth." They were concerned about economic and population growth and the effects on finite natural resources and pollution. Unfortunately, the seriousness of the situation only got through to a few scientists and experts at the time. (Club of Rome, 1972).

The Environmental Protection Agency (EPA) was founded in America around the same time (1970) in response to the budding concern about the environment, although only incremental changes were implemented. The United States and Europe did put several regulations in place to deal with these issues but they were not linked to a shift in economic strategy.

The next marking point came in 1987 when the World Commission on Environment and Development made the connection between ecology and the economy. The World Business Council for Sustainable Development (WBCSD) was born and companies started making an effort to develop a more environmentally friendly production process and recognized the business advantages of doing so. The pioneers of that time increased the support within

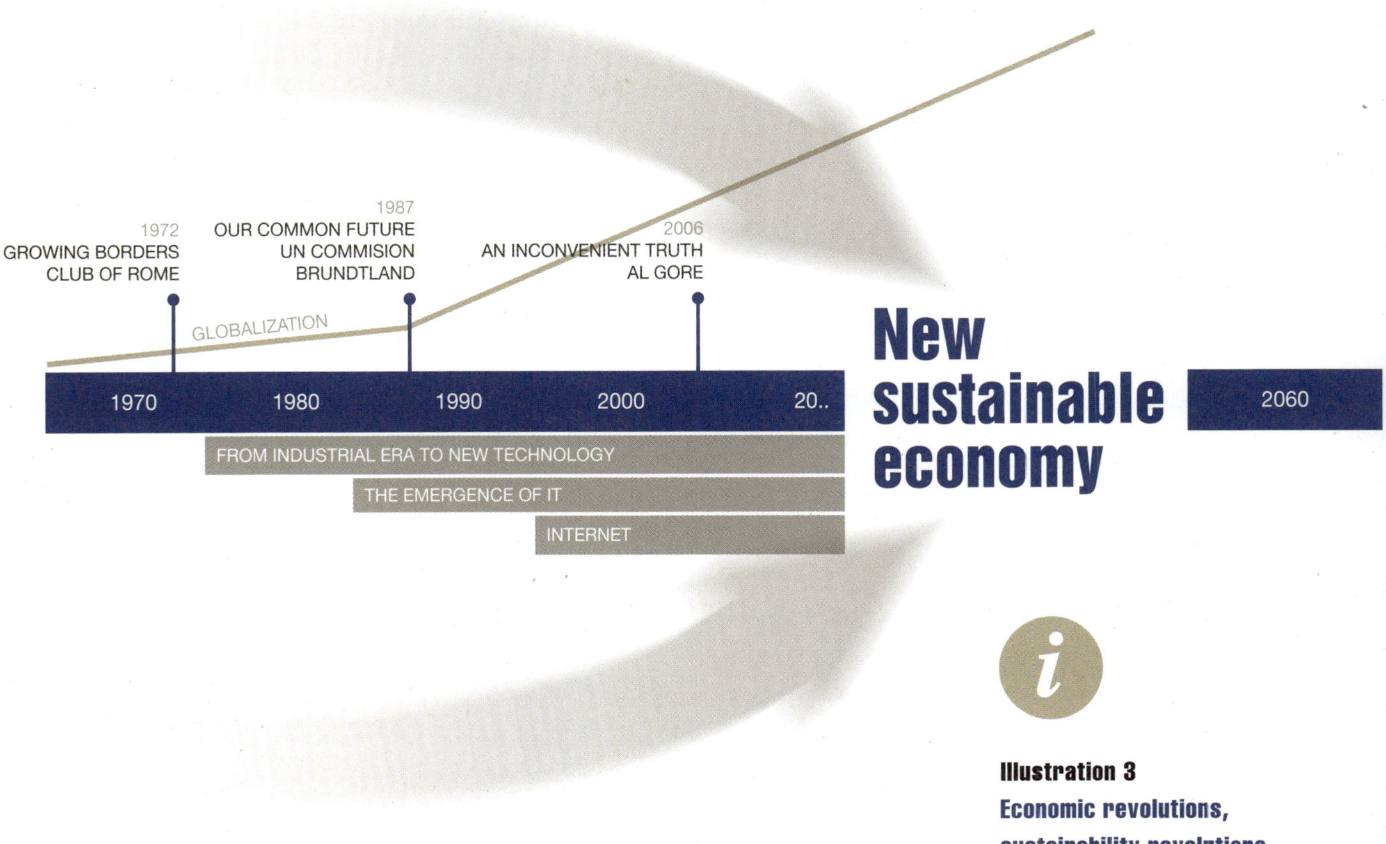

Illustration 3
Economic revolutions, sustainability revolutions

the business world by spreading the word that environment and economics can go hand in hand.

Then more recently, Al Gore presented the third marking point with his film *An Inconvenient Truth*.[3] In his film and with his speeches, he clarified a number of connections. Namely, the rapidly growing BRIC countries (Brazil, Russia, India, and China), the exploding world population, the alarming studies regarding global warming and the downturn of biodiversity. From that moment, many people began to realize that the only way to solve the question of sustainability was to construct a sustainable economy. It was also a trigger for many companies to develop their Corporate Social Responsibility, but even so, sustainability fell short of becoming a leading economic driver.

Two things stand out while considering these wake-up calls and revolutions. The first is that the economic debate had not made a real connection with the wake-up calls relating to the environment and sustainable developments. The second is that the positive undertone from the management publications had not, until recently, reached the sustainability debate. Economics and sustainability have been separate issues. Additionally, the perspective towards each has been different. The publications about the new economy have outlined the possibilities and the renewed prosperity, while threats and obstacles have dominated the sustainability debate. This is understandable, of course, and in a way it is justified as the prediction of doom of our very existence is hardly a positive message. The opportunities that this new economic order would provide in terms of sustainability had not been adopted as a driver for change. Although the connection has been made more often in recent years, the wake-up calls were not the trigger for a revolutionary way of thinking about the economy (See illustration 3).
Illustration 3 shows the historical lack of balance between economic renewal and environmental sustainability. Despite scientific breakthroughs, a variety of studies, and numerous attempts by sustainability pioneers, the wake-up calls have not heralded a new economic era in the way that technological advances, globalization, and the digital revolution have done.

I am absolutely convinced, though, that the new economy, tomorrow's economy, is a revolution in a sustainable *and* economic sense. When economic players are operating from integral sustainable principles, they open new windows of opportunity, and unimaginable possibilities emerge. Today's revolution is bringing the paths of sustainable and economic development together and paving a new road towards a *sustainable economy*. This new sustainable economy does not revolve around becoming *less bad* or reaching neutrality, but it is an economy that underpins the creation of value.

Ten times another economy

A new or differently oriented economy has been announced many times over the years. However, there has yet to be a clear *connection* between the economy, sustainability and the previously mentioned transformative trends. The authors' perspectives were based on either sustainability or current transformative trends but not on both, although sometimes it was from an overarching perspective or from a specific angle (See frame). However, as Bob Massie, CEO and President of the New Economics Institute in Boston notes,

"They all possess an awareness of the same thing: namely, the necessity of, and the movement towards, a new economy." To get an idea of how the revolution has evolved to where we are now, we should look at some economic models and observations that have influenced the economic perspective.

1 **Circular Economy (1976)**
The circular economy is an economic system focused on *maximizing the re-use of products and raw materials, and minimizing the destruction of ecological value*. Although this concept has been discussed by many people, Walter Stahel (See 5: The Performance Economy), Michael Braungart from Germany who came up with the "Cradle to Cradle" philosophy, and Gunter Pauli (See 9: The Blue Economy) were the pioneers of the circular economy. In recent years, the ideas have been further developed by the Ellen MacArthur Foundation. Great Britain, parts of Western Europe, China, and Japan have been particularly receptive to the ideas of the circular economy.[4]

2 **Information Economy (1996)**
Manuel Castells, a Spaniard, introduced the information economy in 1996. It was described as an economy in which productivity and competitiveness of companies, regions, and countries heavily depends on the degree to which they are prepared and capable of *sharing knowledge*, and generating and processing information (Castells, 1996).

3 **Network Economy (1998)**
In 1998, the American author Kevin Kelly wrote about the network economy, also known as the *connected economy* and the *internet economy* (Kelly, 1998). He was inspired by Peter Drucker who wrote the book *Post-Capitalist Society* in 1993 about a network society in which companies compete on the basis of their knowledge.

4 **Experience Economy (1999)**
The experience economy was introduced by the American authors Joseph Pine and James Gilmore in 1999. They based their work on that of Alvin Toffler (1970). In a move away from the traditional quest for possessions, Toffler had spoken about an *experience-oriented industry* in which people were prepared to spend money on amazing life experiences.

5 **Performance Economy (2006)**
The Swiss author and architect Walter Stahel came up with the concept of the performance economy in 2006. According to Stahel, a prerequisite for the circular economy is for *products to be sold as services*. The company maintains ownership and thus remains responsible for the entire production and usage cycle .

6 **Green Economy (2008)**
Sustainable use of resources is an important part of the green economy.[5] It also links prosperity and social equality with a decrease in natural resource exploitation and environmental risks.

7 **Challenge Economy (2009)**
In the book *From Experience to Challenge Economy*, Dutch authors Lier, Heiblom and Waijers introduce the challenge economy. They show that not only is experience a central theme for consumers but it also produces fertile ground for motivation and reflection which in turn leads to creating new challenges (Lier et al. 2009).The *changing socio-economic trends* offer interesting opportunities for business.

8 **Subscription Economy (2012)**
Tien Tzuo, CEO of Zuora – a leader in technical support for subscription businesses – coined the phrase 'subscription economy' in 2012. The concept is based on a business model which encourages customers to secure a subscription for a particular product or service. This *new business model* is discussed further in this book in Chapter 1: Customers.

9 **Blue Economy (2012)**
The blue economy was introduced by Gunter Pauli, a Belgian entrepreneur, in 2012 and is sometimes referred to as 'The green economy 2.0'. In his book, he describes hundreds of *technologies* based on natural systems which should lead to hundreds of innovative projects and a hundred million jobs. Whether it is growing mushrooms from coffee bean pulp or using garbage to cultivate worms, nature can teach us a lot.

10 **Sharing/Collaborative Economy (2013)**
The sharing economy, or the collaborative economy, was proclaimed by Rachel Botsman and Lisa Gansky in an economic model based on sharing, trading, or renting products and is the *counter-balance of ownership*.[6]

2 The new economy; all assets count

The three wake-up calls mentioned previously revolve around ecological sustainability in order to try to turn back the tide on the havoc mankind has perpetuated on the environment. I am convinced, however, that the new economy revolution is fundamentally driven by *comprehensive* sustainability. Although the environment demands our utmost care and attention, the new economy is not only focused on the ecological assets. It incorporates *all* of our primary assets: our environment, of course, but also people – human beings also deserve a sustainable existence. Global health, education and equal opportunity are vital to the wellbeing of our species. Financial assets cannot be ignored either, poverty and destitution are issues across all borders. Money is the common thread. It is especially the financial aspect that is often used by traditionalist as the reason why social and environmental sustainability cannot be achieved. Therefore, the new economy movement approaches all three assets at once: ecological, social, and financial and shows that if you broaden your view and incorporate all three in a sustainable approach, profits can still be made (and in many cases even more than now) while making a net positive impact. The new economy promotes *Business with a Purpose*.

In essence, the economy revolves around how we deal with resources. When we think of resources, we tend to think of our natural resources, but it also includes the people who use them to perform economic activities. Therefore, it defies logic that the benefits and burdens associated with these two assets (ecological and social) are seen as separate elements. It also makes no sense to leave these assets out of the financial equation. But this is exactly what is happening.

Our Gross National Product (GNP) is currently one of our most important and relied upon economic thermometers, and it is a perfect example of this observation. It is therefore no surprise that Harvard professor Michael Porter stated in 2014 that the current means of economic measurement is not adequate to determine a country's prosperity. Economists Joseph Stiglitz, Amartya Sen, and Jean-Paul Fitoussi presented this opinion as well in their book *Mismeasuring our Lives* (2010).[7] Even the man who came up with GNP said way back in the 1930s that GNP hardly had anything to do with the prosperity of a nation.

In fact, our standard of living is, to a large degree, determined by social aspects such as the quality of our living environment, for example. This is much broader than the measuring stick of the GNP. Porter rightly observes, "If we use the wrong starting point, then we strive towards the wrong goals."

An illustrative example of this comes from my own country, the Netherlands. In 2013, we experienced an unusually warm winter. As a result, we naturally spent less money on heat for houses and office buildings.[8] Economic commentators, with GNP numbers in hand, spoke on radio, television, and in newspapers about an economic dip. However, if you thought about it a bit more, you began to wonder why there was no talk of economic growth. After all, the CO_2 emissions had decreased by 20 percent, consumers were, on average, sixty euros better off, and no one was complaining about comfort! So, from an ecological, financial, and social viewpoint, it was a favorable winter.

Then why do economic experts talk about a dip? My answer is that real value creation, and devaluation, are currently not the predominant principles leading our economic models and perspectives. They are simple left out of the picture.

All assets

How can this situation improve? As outlined in the introduction, the new economy is focused on creating value for *all* our assets (ecological, social, and financial) and all the movements within them that contribute to true prosperity. We include these assets in our economic domain and in this way give prosperity a broader meaning.

In the new economy, all assets and asset streams are gathered together in order to create a future with a higher value for mankind and the world.

However, the new economy is not just there for the asking. We are currently faced with significant challenges in the development of a sustainable economy. Climate change and the predicted transition within the energy sector, an explosive population growth which is increasing by a rate of one billion people per decade, and the depletion of our natural resources all lead to issues we have never faced before. It requires hard questions and creative solutions in order to take charge of our future.

At the same time, there are many innovative developments currently taking place that make the time ripe for dealing with these issues. The pervasiveness of technology in our daily lives, for example, and the ensuing globalization drive our societies towards an unprecedented connectedness. Robotization, nanotechnology and other technological innovations are transforming how we live and work. These modern developments are well-suited to creating solutions to our current issues and challenges.

Illustration 4
Towards a new economy

Digitalization opens many new windows of opportunity. There are more than three billion people connected to the internet worldwide and it is increasing rapidly. Jonathon Porrit, founder of the Forum of the Future, expects 97.5% of the world population to have access to the internet by 2050. This total connectivity creates untold opportunities. Collective intelligence is one such opportunity. Information from personal devices is collected and then connected to big data in order to generate predictions, assistance and advice for internet users and supply valuable consumer behavior information to businesses.

The new economy is also gaining support from changing consumer values and greater awareness of the challenges we are facing worldwide. Information about climate change and the urgency for a sustainable economy is becoming a recurring theme, and there is increased demand and availability of affordable sustainable products.

Beyond zero impact

To create value, there must first be signs of recovery. The negative effects of our economic behavior must stop and be reversed. *From minus to zero*. Fortunately, we are seeing a lot happening around the globe in this direction. For example, optimizing energy use, and reducing waste and CO_2 emissions are becoming prevalent goals. Although these endeavors are promising, they are, by far, not enough. To achieve a resilient, sustainable economy which will endure long into the future, we need to move beyond par; *from minus to zero to plus.*

We see examples of this in the business world. There are companies that make a positive impact by extracting plastic waste out of the oceans and using it to make new, recyclable, products. Or take a company like Redes Energéticas Nacionais (REN), the Portuguese energy management company. REN has started an afforestation project with the aim to protect biodiversity and restore ecological balance. REN extracts the tree stumps that are left in deforested areas and plants new trees in their place. There are many stakeholders involved including landowners, schools, local governmental agencies, and other authorities. In this way, in addition to the ecological benefits, there is a positive social impact as well. The project also delivers economic advantages due to the increase in fertile land areas and the decreased risk of forest fires. So far, nearly a half a million trees have been planted in an area of approximately 600 hectares. [9]

This book is filled with examples which are often disruptive to the traditional economy but serve as trailblazing endeavors towards a net positive impact on our economic assets. An incredible example comes from Daan Roosegaarde, a Dutch artist who went to Beijing and built an enormous vacuum cleaner to clean smog out of the air. Filthy air went in and clean air came out. The debris that remained was then exposed to extremely high pressure which could be turned into high-end jewelry – proving that waste does not exist. The sale of the jewelry was used to support the use of the machine; one ring, for example, counted for 1,000 m^3 of clean air for the city.[10]

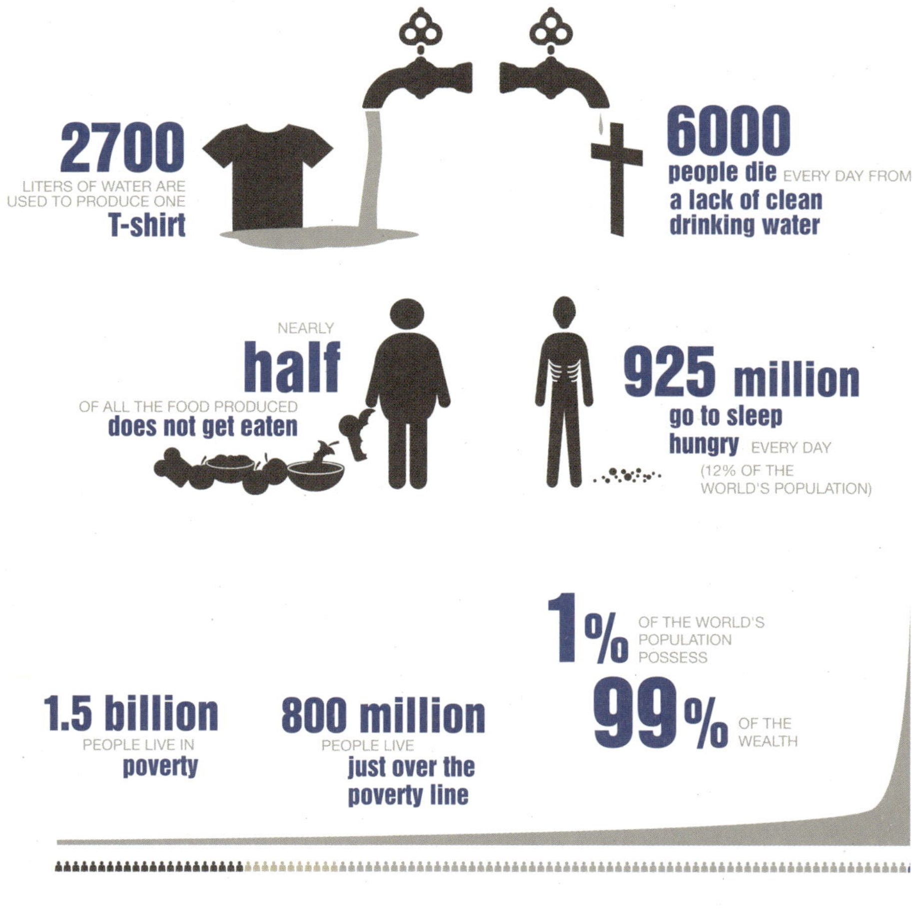

Illustration 5
Asset expoitation

3 Three assets

There have been periodic attempts to define our economic working capital and determine its value. Some attention has been given to the non-financial components of our economy. The British advisor John Elkington coined the phrase, 'The Triple Bottom Line' in 1994 when he discussed the 'Three Pillars of Sustainability', namely: People, Planet, and Profit.[11]

Some other theorists and businesses have since added their nuance. The accountancy firm Ernst and Young (EY) adopted the principle of 'The Five Capitals' from the organization Forum for the Future.[12] In this framework, the financial assets and the manufactured capital goods form the central layer. The second layer consists of the social, human, and intellectual capital. Lastly, the outer layer comprises the natural capital - the ecological assets.

Many formations have actually been made. Natural Capitalism Solutions,[13] a research institute in Colorado, distinguishes four kinds of capital: Human capital (including labor, intellectual, and culture), Financial capital (cash, investments, monetary instruments, and financial institutions), Manufactured capital (infrastructure, machines, tools, and factories), and Natural capital (resources, ecosystems, and other systems that support our lives).

In this book, we have narrowed the five, and the four capital divisions mentioned above to three prime assets: ecological, social, and financial.

The ***ecological assets*** are the natural resources such as energy, raw materials, and water. But it also covers other resources we depend on, such as material goods, infrastructure and sources within ecosystems: plants, animals, organisms, air, water and earth. [14]

Social assets are essentially people and society (with their knowledge, innovations, experience, and skills). Together with the ecological assets, they form the basis for the creation of products and services. People make products, and deliver services from tangible materials.

The ***financial assets*** have a given value but are in fact a reflection of the value of the other two assets. Because money, after all, has no inherent value of its own and is always a representation of what it can be traded for. It serves as a tool to calculate and convert the physical and social assets which are created,

distributed, and used as products and services.
The flow is essential. The capital streams that move within the three assets; that is where the real value creation takes place.

Illustration 6
Ecological facts & figures

The choice to use these three assets as the foundation for the economy leads to *a different economic system* that fundamentally differs from the old, purely financially driven economy. The social and ecological assets have, until now, been relegated to an external position or, at best, have found a place on the sidelines of our thinking when it comes to doing business. They were viewed as elements that served the old growth model; they were referred to as 'production factors'. The new economy gives these assets their rightful stature and places them firmly in the center of the new economic system.

Ecological

Definition

As mentioned above, our ecological assets are 1) natural resources and processes (energy and materials); 2) material goods and infrastructure.

The natural resources and processes have the ability to function as ecosystems: to absorb, neutralize or recycle (e.g. forests and oceans); the natural materials such as wood, grain, fish, and water are renewable while other materials are not renewable, such as fossil fuels, minerals, and metals. Climate control and the carbon cycle are natural processes that are also essential to our very existence.

The material goods and infrastructure include buildings, transportation networks, communication systems, waste management, and technological attributes – from simple tools and machinery to complex information technology, robotics, and other technological devices. [15]

Ecological assets in the new economy

It is not surprising - with everything we are experiencing today with climate change and scarce resources – that there is plenty of interest in the ecological assets of our economy. It is, and should be, our primary concern to keep our planet inhabitable for our growing population and for the many generations to come. It is predicted that by the year 2025, one billion people will be added to the world's population. This growth in numbers, together with the burgeoning prosperity in the Asian-Pacific regions, will lead to the middle classes growing considerably. Forecasts show an increase from 1.9 billion people who are considered to have a middle class standard of living in 2009 to 4.9 billion people by the year 2030. An enormous surge in consumption is the expected result with predictions that the amount of packing materials needed for goods produced will increase by 47 percent (Ellen MacArthur Foundation, 2013: 14-15).

The second driver has a more economic nature. Although prices for natural resources have, over the last 100 years, decreased by 50 percent it is inevitable that the escalating scarcity we are currently experiencing will result in a dramatic price increase in the twenty-first century.

Resource scarcity is, in this respect, of the utmost importance for both the private and public sectors. The circular economy foresees 'resource security' as an emerging concept. Walter Stahel, author of *The Performance Economy* (2006) talks about optimal management of the existing streams of materials. It is based on the idea of using the goods of today as resource banks for the products of tomorrow. This is illustrated in Chapter 1: Customers with the extraction of precious minerals from telephones. This approach is a typical new economy solution: efficient use of resources, no waste, and more profit. Chapter 2: Value Cycle goes deeper into this principle.

Despite the attention to our ecological assets, an essential step – also in the sustainability world – has been largely overlooked: the valuation of these assets. The value of the natural resources and other natural materials is not truly expressed in the market price.[16] Ecological assets are not adequately represented in the current economy. In the new economy, however, the ecological costs are put into the equation and not pushed to the side. They are taken into account in the pricing of products and in this way ecological assets are given appropriate value within the economy.

Some companies do currently bring the creation and devaluation of assets into the picture with an environmental profit and loss (EP&L) calculation. But when you look closely, it becomes clear that the emphasis is placed on the L – limiting the ecological *loss* – and that the P – the creation of ecological value (or *profit*) – is brought up less often.

This quest for value and residual value for our ecological assets characterizes the new economy, an economy founded on maintaining and creating value, an economy that is, itself, circular.

Social

Definition

Social assets are 1) the individual; 2) the added value of human relationships; 3) the intellectual value that 1 and 2 contain.

The first component of the social assets is the individual. This includes health, knowledge, skills, intelligence, motivation, emotions, and the ability to establish relationships.

The individual creates social value when relationships are present or established. Examples of this are families, communities, companies, networks, organizations, unions, schools, and volunteer organizations. It is these relationships that form an organic and organizational whole and ensure stability for society.

Intellectual value consists of intellectual products such as collective knowledge, information, experience, talents, and creative, innovative prowess. Social norms and values, trust, education systems, innovations, technological progress, and organizational phenomena such as globalization fall into this category.

Illustration 7
Social facts & figures

Social assets in the new economy

The new economy is, in my opinion, also focused on creating value for social assets. In the same way that the economic activities are designed so that they are not exhausting natural resources, they are also no longer devaluing human capital.

Recently, the book *Capital in the 21st Century* by the French economist Thomas Piketty has caused fierce political debates.[17] Piketty states that the growing income gap is no accident, but is caused by the fact that interest on capital (about 5% per year) is greater than the increase of income from labor (about 2%-3% per year). The consequence of this is that those with capital see their wealth grow much faster than those who make a living from labor. His conclusion: the gap of income and capital are built into the current economy.

What got the most attention was the moral component: are these kinds of differences in prosperity justified? Of equal importance, however, is the economic side: do differences in prosperity lead to a stronger, healthier, and more resilient economy?

The degeneration of social capital, such as public health and safety, and decreased participation in cultural and social activities leads to a downturn in civil motivation and positive participation in society. This, in turn, leads to a decrease in productivity which is detrimental to the economy as a whole.

In the new economy, we see this as social devaluation. Whereas economic activity that contributes to social cohesion, health, safety, and security as well as building societal strength, creating value, and increasing social capital, counts as growth. The primary focus is on presenting opportunities for people and communities to increase their vitality and utilize it for the creation of value. Civic engagement is stimulated. The new economy holds at its core the aim to enhance communities, promote a better quality of life, and develop wellbeing and prosperity.

Intellectual capital receives special attention within social assets. In the new economy, this collectively created asset gets a radically new interpretation. Knowledge, information, creativity, innovative technology, and experience are, in a connected economy, no longer exclusive possessions (Intellectual property), but are collectively built and shared. By sharing information, the value increases. This presents opportunities to multiply the intellectual capital and channel it towards the creation of physical ecological assets and social capital.

Financial

Definition

The financial assets make it possible to create value for the other assets. The financial assets, such as stocks, loans, bank notes or coins carry limited value in themselves. But as representations of ecological and social capital, they are very valuable.

Money originated as a commodity, a method of payment, which derived its value from a corresponding tangible object such as gold or land. These days, however, nearly all financial systems are based on fiat money – money that has no tangible base but derives its value from governmental regulation and trust in the currency exchange.

In the new economy, money gains a concrete equivalent again, namely the ecological and social assets that it represents. In this way, it is again the substantive means of exchange that makes value creation possible.

Financial assets and the new economy

Financial value creation, related to the social and ecological assets, is essentially an equivalent to reuniting money and goods. The disassociation of money from goods (such as gold) has, certainly over the last twenty years, had a significant impact on the financial sector and the rest of the economy, and has led to disastrous crises. Just look at the trillions of dollars of U.S. national debt, and the millions and trillions of debt that other nations have as well. The tremendous fall in housing prices was also due to the real value of property and its skyrocketing prices being miles away from each other.

In the new economy, the connection between money and value is restored. The saying 'money makes money' is being replaced by 'money creates value'. Over the last few decades, financial value and real value has had little to do with each other. We have seen this in the housing market, the national debt, but also in the short-term returns derived from the inflated value of companies. Financial value in the new economy, however, is a real reflection of actual value; exactly the reason it was introduced thousands of years ago. With the reunion of financial and real value as described above, the perspective

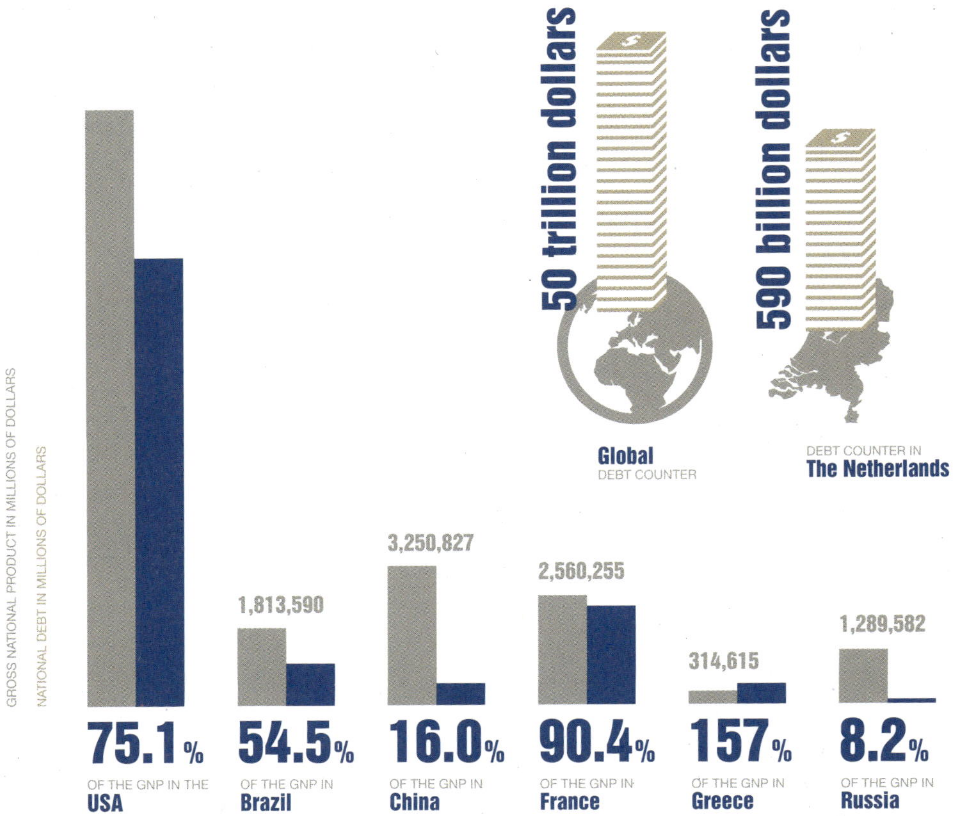

Illustration 8
Financial facts & figures

of value management is extended. The connection of financial assets to long-term ecological and social assets, and the creation of lasting partnerships offers stability and carries less risks than goods and services that quickly lose their value. Long-term perspectives also stimulate business and governments to create value over longer periods of time. Thus the reconnection of financial and real assets form an automatic driver towards sustainability.

The new approach to money also urges us to reassess the financial sector and the basis of valuing companies, products, and services as well as other assets. It also requires a structural change in the measuring instruments we currently use, such as the GNP. Ideally, these new instruments will reflect the creation of value as well as opportunities for value creation in the future. The first steps in this direction have already been made on a business level, and it deserves to be brought to the macro-economic scale.

4 Interacting transformative trends shape the new economy

The sustainably driven new economy interacts with current transformative trends. There are three developments in particular that are fundamentally transforming and shaping the economy: disruptive innovative technology, Glocalization, and changing consumer values. These powerful trends can be expanded on further to include developments in connectedness, the digital and mobile revolution, geopolitical shifts, and the growing demand for transparency as well.

The following developments and those that are described further in this chapter, and in the rest of the book, have varying origins and foundations, yet they all relate and interact with the pursuit of sustainability for our three assets. The three overarching transformative trends make sustainability visible and applicable and they reflect the face of the new economy. The comprehensive, triple sustainable endeavors of the economy are the 'what'; the interacting transformative trends provide the answer to the question of 'how'.

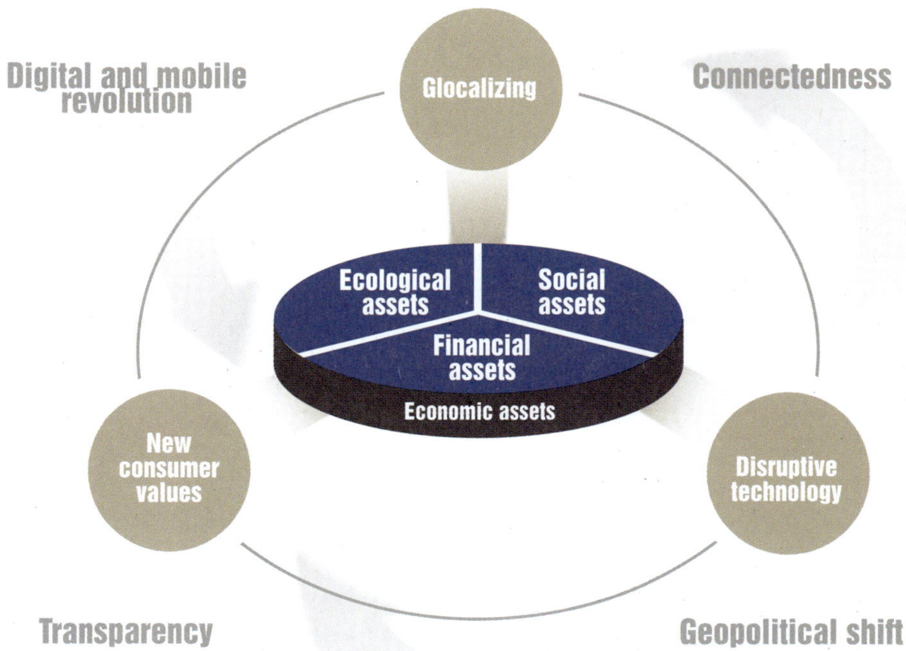

Illustration 9
Three times sustainable

Transformative developments and trends

1 Disruptive technological innovation

Disruptive technologies reshape business and in fact our global economy. Technological breakthroughs in areas such as advanced robotics, autonomous vehicles, 3d printing, next generation genomics, advanced materials and renewable energy have an enormous impact, and technology continues to advance in leaps and bounds.

The parade of new technologies and scientific breakthroughs is relentless and is unfolding on many fronts. Almost any advance is billed as a breakthrough, and the list of 'next big things' grows ever longer. Yet there are quite a few technologies which do in fact have the potential to disrupt the status quo, alter the way people live and work, rearrange value pools, and lead to entirely new products and services.

The combination of technologies makes things possible that we can hardly imagine, and even that businesses can't imagine. They disrupt existing business sectors and models. These disruptive technological advances are making their debut in rapid succession.

2 Glocalizing

The glocal economy (global and local simultaneously) has been developing for a while. Globalization started to accelerate in the 1980s with the advent of the digitalization of economies and markets on a micro and macro-economic level. Since then, economies and global markets have become increasingly intertwined. Networks interact with other networks and geographic borders are losing their relevance. In the meantime, local presence has seen a resurgence in significance for consumers. Locally established enterprises, shorter supply chains, and locally designed ecosystems which are cleverly combined with global upscaling creates value across the board. This is discussed further in Chapter 3: Scale.

3 New Consumer Values

Curiosity and broader awareness play an important role in the changing values of consumers today. Affordability of sustainable products supports these changing values as well. Consumers are moving away from the *big* and *plenty* ideal. They are looking for products and solutions that are esthetically designed, functional, efficient, and accessible.

The individualism of the 1990s has been replaced – partly because of the ramifications of the financial crisis – by a renewed longing for social interaction. This desire has been facilitated by the numerous social media outlets. Facebook alone counts well over one billion active users. Although social media is undoubtedly a hit and a thoroughly ingrained method of communication for the younger generations, it has also had the interesting effect of re-awakening our human need for physical contact and is resulting in the renewed value of our local environments and communities.

4 Connected - everywhere and always

Connections between people, organizations, and governmental agencies are expanding exponentially. Individuals are constantly connected, no matter where they go. There are already six billion people on this planet with a mobile phone, and that number is growing every day. [18]

Social technology and networks have become part of our daily lives. The young generations are growing up with this technology and it is an integral part of their everyday communication. Social networks are not only used for socializing, they have pervaded business communication as well and are transforming organizations and societies from the inside. The connectedness of individuals and organizations leads to an expanded outlook on business endeavors; maximizing the value of an individual company is being replaced with maximizing value for an entire network.

5 ICT, Digital and mobile revolutions

The transformative developments and trends we have just mentioned are each facilitated and driven by the continually evolving ICT innovations and ensure that knowledge, communication, and communities are formed and facilitated in entirely new ways.

Digital and mobile revolutions have resulted in unprecedented digital mobility of individuals and organizations. Knowledge can be shared and accessed anywhere and anytime, and the speed of communication has accelerated thanks to social media. The increasing accessibility of information and communication technology (ICT), big data and the ever booming and evolving social media has an enormous effect on innovation which is finding new avenues on the digital map. ICT, and mobile internet are influencing the broad dissemination of information which has significant implications for the opportunities for innovation in upcoming markets and developing countries. They can benefit considerably from the mobility of knowledge, information, as well as the digitalization of payments as a new digital grid. Consumers who are now transformed into 'prosumers' can seize opportunities of forming communities online quickly and easily. The impact of these ICT innovations is huge since most disruptive technologies are directly or indirectly enhanced by information technology.

6 Geopolitical shift, say 'hello' to the next eleven

The rising power of the BRIC countries (Brazil, Russia, India and China), as well as other developing countries (Goldman Sachs has identified "The Next 11"[19]) is changing global geopolitical relationships. It is often forgotten, but it can also be said that some of the more stable regions in Africa are seeing strong growth in their economies as well. Unfortunately, this economic growth is not always matched by a growth in social prosperity. Between 2001 and 2010, Angola showed even stronger growth than China. The economies in other countries such as Myanmar, Nigeria, Ethiopia, and Kazakhstan also grew during that period.

7 Transparency, global public exposure

Consumers, governments, and shareholders are demanding more transparency. The business world in particular has seen a clear push in this direction. The multiple and pervasive connections described in the previous paragraph go hand in hand with the need for transparency. Businesses are simply unable to shield information from the public eye. Just consider how quickly word spread of the oil disaster caused by the explosion of the oil platform in the Gulf of Mexico, resulting in consumers expressing on Twitter and other social media outlets their disgust at this preventable ecological catastrophe. BP suffered more than the fine imposed for causing the spill and the costs involved in the cleanup. Their public image suffered immeasurably at the time as they lost a considerable amount of good will and brand respect. In this way, the trend towards transparency leads companies to behave more responsibly and sustainably.

The following chapters will illustrate that disruptive innovation and value creation come about when economic players, such as businesses and consumers, utilize and combine multiple, transformative trends. For example, one aspect of consumers' changing values is the devaluation of ownership. It is especially evident in the younger generations. We see a growing trend towards accessing products and services, as people are now used to accessing knowledge and information. They may want to go from point A to point B but do not see a real need to own a car in order to do this. This transformative trend is not only due to changing consumer attitudes but is brought to visible fruition because of the advances in digitalization. The integration of these two developments makes initiatives such as easyCar, the British car-sharing company, or Swapstyle, the Australian clothing exchange viable and profitable business endeavors. And this combines beautifully with preserving our ecological resources. It is the combination of transformative trends and the creation of value for our primary assets that supports a sustainable economy.

5 Trailblazers on the forefront

The new economy is tomorrow's economy. But who is shaping this sustainably driven economy? Who is doing that today and who will do it tomorrow? We will go to the forefront of the revolution and examine who the players are, what they do, why they do it, and how they reach their goals. And most importantly, how their endeavors and their results can be an inspiration for others to follow.

The trailblazers on the forefront, the pioneers, can be found on different levels in various segments of our economy. They are forward-thinking entrepreneurs, scientists, artists, politicians, and people from every walk of life. They are focused on creating value and initiatives to close the loop of our ecological, social and financial assets. These pioneers are essential because they guide the way and show how the potential of the new economy can be developed and put into practice. They do this from a sense of purpose, the feeling of intrinsic motivation of a true explorer.

New economy explorers are focused, convinced and convincing, persistent, and prepared to go first even if they have to go alone. They are creative, curious, and courageous. They are not afraid to take risks. As the late American Senator Robert F. Kennedy once said: "Only those who dare to fail greatly can ever achieve greatly." Explorers have the vision, drive, and innovative urge to set the change in motion.

Explorers sometimes choose a route without having the faintest idea where it leads. They set the target even if they do not yet know how they will achieve it. An example of this behavior on the business front is how the late Ray Anderson, 'America's Greenest CEO', turned his company around. Anderson founded the carpet company Interface in the 1970s. When he read Paul Hawken's book *The Ecology of Commerce* in 1994, he initiated a radical shift in his company. He was convinced that he could no longer run a company that was exploitive and decided to do things radically different. He set a course to a point on the horizon – to 'Mission Zero'. His progressive plan was to eliminate any negative impact his company was having on the environment and be completely sustainable by 2020. He wanted Interface to be transformed into a *zero waste corporation*. At the time that he initiated this plan, he had no idea how he would achieve his goal, nevertheless, he set the course to his ideal destination. Over the last two decades, Interface has made great strides. They have implemented many innovative, sustainable business cases and produced value for all assets while doubling their revenue.

The vision is clear to the explorers and it is crucial that they gain support from the rest of the world; from other business people, scientists, politicians, artists, and individuals from all walks of life. It is imperative that the new economy is propelled forward at top speed. There is no time to waste. Once everyone is convinced that sustainability is our goal, then we can build an economy that is here for the world instead of subsisting in a world that is here for the economy.

6 New economy business

In this chapter, we have outlined what new economy business is exactly and we have seen how transformative socio-economic developments and trends interact and how they present opportunities to integrate sustainability in daily practice. As mentioned earlier, in *New Economy Business*, we zoom in on one group: entrepreneurs. It is exactly this group, as has been shown in the previous paragraphs, that has ushered in the other economic revolutions. Business pioneers are showing the courage to do things differently and blaze a new trail for others to follow.

The sustainable revolution must be bold and comprehensive. Renewing business practices is renewing the engine of our economy. An engine that has stalled on occasion, but at the same time, an engine that bursts with energy. It is this energy that leads to motivation to do things differently and take responsibility. We see it manifest in a variety of ways; it is a food sector that takes its responsibility for the problem of obesity, an energy company that reduces energy use, or an automobile manufacturer that promotes sustainable travel options. These examples show companies taking a course that may seem contradictory to its traditional interests but is in fact a course that creates new earning models.

Although the business pioneers pave the way, it often seems that those who follow take two steps forward then one step back. They are fickle or hesitant, and they shroud themselves in the motto: when in doubt, stay where you are. Some may put up a nice facade, yet keep their real endeavors firmly behind closed doors.

Why are they not choosing to set a steady course? Frankly, the answer is because it is enormously difficult to radically change course. I am the last one to claim otherwise. Additionally, there is often a lack of supportive governmental policies in many countries. Sometimes government regulation is even contrary to sustainable processes or too complicated for compliance. There are, however, plenty of companies working on a transition. Some are innovative, but then fall into the same patterns and use the innovations to continue the traditional course. This actually blocks the transition of a governmental context that would promote value driven business. It also holds true the other way around. The government is not unwilling to provide a framework for the creation of value, but is often held back by fear of losing the current security of the status quo.

The most significant bottleneck for a value driven revolution is the current fact that the business potential of the new economy is fragmentally visible. There are Best Practices available, however these sometimes read as a handbook with half of the pages missing. The cohesion and links are missing. Many entrepreneurs see the destination on the horizon, but the path to get there is often obscured and littered with pitfalls and assailants along the way. For this reason, upscaling business cases in a sustainable way can feel rather challenging, to say the least.

New Economy Business strives to create cohesion and offer workable models and instruments gleaned from a variety of current business cases. It opens a window with a view to the new economy and new opportunities. It is important to recognize, as far as I am concerned, that we should in no way diminish or negate the entrepreneurial spirit that resides in our present economy. It is the channeling of this innovative spirit into profitable, sustainable, non-exploitive enterprises that can make a powerful difference. The new economy is not soft, nor are financial frameworks irrelevant. It is an emerging approach that a great deal of pioneers are pursuing in order to alter the economic landscape for the benefit of mankind, our planet, and ultimately our economy. Because the economy is here for the world, the world is not here for the economy.

7 Seven windows to success

The seven windows of opportunity are not new in terms of management themes, but the approach to these classic themes is new, and yet also common sense. In other words, in is an approach to business that is dynamic, sustainable, innovative, and profitable. Of course, we saw business in the traditional economy that took this shape as well, but in the new economy this approach blossoms.

The **customer** is the central point for new economy businesses. Not only as the target of the service or product, but also as a source of inspiration. The customer is seen as the user, co-creator, innovator, and even financier. Customers, in their central position, also remind companies of their responsibilities and their primary position, namely: local, between users, other companies and competitors.

Businesses, like their customers, are no longer bound to a time and place. They see themselves as a part of the worldwide market, strengthening their competitive position by creating connections between players on various economic **scales**: local, regional, national, and global.

These connections, networks, and relationships offer opportunities and new possibilities for sustainable, innovative **business cases**. Business cases that push conventional boundaries and profit from breaking them open. Entrepreneurs are building their business cases with partners outside their sectors and traditional parameters. They are attracting private and public parties, consumers, and scientists.

The openness and cooperation that they are achieving provides competitive advantages and puts entrepreneurs in the position to move to the forefront of **innovation**. Traditional, closed, in-house innovation is becoming old-fashioned. Open innovation of business cases, products and services facilitates sustainable value creation for multiple parties. This kind of innovation results in a new, circular supply chain: the **value cycle**. This is a cyclical structure in which businesses work cooperatively to close the loop of natural resource use. It is a sustainable, efficient way to reduce – or erase – their environmental footprint. Additionally, the value cycle opens up new financial avenues.

Financing no longer needs to come from a bank. Businesses are financing each other, and they are also finding a multitude of other sources for financial means – including from their customer base. Bartering has also made a comeback with more companies forming deals with each other where no money changes hands and yet both parties profit. Financial institutions, meanwhile, are developing new approaches to meet the changing interests and needs of potential clients. They recognize the opportunities and potential markets in the area of sustainable development. Therefore, financial institutions are providing new services to keep pace with the rigorous transformation of business.

New economy business requires new **leadership**; an approach that does not gain its strength from hierarchy but from networks. Leaders who do not try to "get the most out of their people", but develop their people so they can contribute to the overall value. Leaders accept their leadership role of course, but they also place themselves in a supportive role when appropriate and share the leadership when it suits the situation and serves the goal. New economy leaders create an environment conducive to the co-creation of value.

8 From theory to practice

New Economy Business connects what was fragmented and exceptional in the traditional economy and brings it together into the common thread of the new economy. New or renewed theories are presented based on examples that can be seen around us and many that are illustrated in this book. *New Economy Business* strives to be a source of inspiration, to help and support further innovation and upscaling of new economy businesses. Although the book zooms in on entrepreneurs as the drivers of the new economy, entrepreneurs are not the only target group of readers. This book is also for government workers and policy makers to gain insight and understanding of the new economic approach and as a result, find the inspiration to create the right conditions for the new economy to flourish. It is also to stimulate scientists to focus their research on realizing a new economy and finding solutions to the questions that are raised by sustainable endeavors. It is for business and economics students as well. When learning about traditional economic models and how they manifest, it is important to incorporate the emerging economic models and research, discuss and contribute to the development of the new economy. And lastly, it is, of course, for consumers too, as consumers are in a stronger position than ever before. The internet has connected people in a way that an individual's voice can be heard worldwide instantaneously. By joining voices, people have power.

Through interviews with numerous CEOs and representatives of multinational companies, extensive desk research, interventions from scientist, a broad crowdsourcing process, and checks done by a number of knowledge bureaus, the content of the seven management themes has been strengthened and honed. They have enriched the explorative image that *New Economy Business* presents and stretched the perspective as far as the eye can see.

New Economy Business shows how the seven management themes develop in the new economy. It shows how promising and dynamic the new economy is and how the traditional economy no longer suffices. It is good to look back occasionally so that we know what we are leaving behind, but we must be sure to move ahead, as fast as our feet can go, towards the new world. The potential for renewal is strong yet often just bubbling under the surface. It needs to explode! And we are justified in placing high expectations on the business world. It is, by definition, the mission and ultimate goal of business to develop potential and reveal new possibilities.

The challenges we face related to the environment, society, and financial stability are pressing issues that require urgent attention. The explorers of our time are building an economy that reflects our values. We are a global community now. We know it, we feel it and we live it. Our collective consciousness is no longer ignorant of suffering due to poverty, natural disasters, scarce resources, and financial devastations. Our morality, ethics, and our survival demands solutions.

By turning the next page, you are stepping through a virtual door to the new economy. You will see how the new business approach takes shape and you will find concrete guidelines on how to organize business endeavors in the new economy. I hope that it opens your eyes, inspires, and motivates you as an entrepreneur, consumer, politician, manager, student, or scientist. The new economy, tomorrow's economy, can be today's economy. As the words at the beginning of this chapter state: To change something, build a new model that makes the existing model obsolete.

Customers in the new economy want access, not ownership.

Chapter 1

WINDOW OF OPPORTUNITY:

Customers

Product ownership has lost its luster. Service, access, and usage are now of paramount interest.

Long-term connections are replacing quick transactions, making trust essential.

Service agreements are superseding points of sale. Related services are the new accessory.

All you can listen to, all you can watch

EUROPE | **SWEDEN** NORTH AMERICA | **USA**

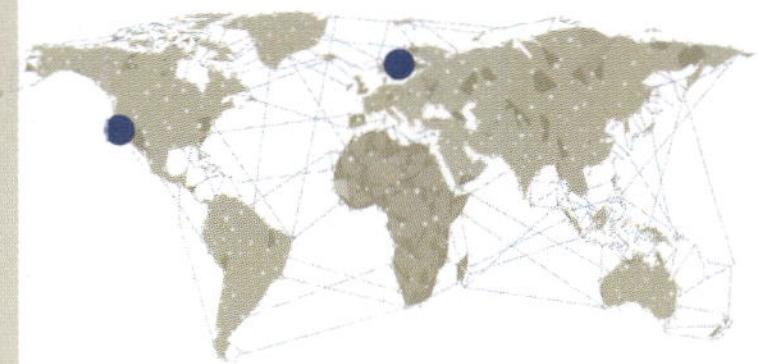

Spotify and Netflix are well-known online services. They both illustrate the effectiveness and the sustainable potential of the transition from product to service. Spotify, which currently has more than 20 million users, offers customers access to practically every kind of music, every musician and every album for just 6 - 12 dollars (€ 5-10) per month. Netflix uses the same concept. For 10 dollars (€ 8.00) a month, customers can choose from a wide range of films, television shows, and documentaries. Subscribers to these two services can get any song or any movie on their computer, tablet or smartphone at any time they want – without having to buy them. They never own the CD or DVD, and therefore do not need to store them either, yet they still have an endless collection at their fingertips. Another added bonus to this business model is that both of these companies can easily analyze the preferences of their customers and make specific suggestions for new titles that would probably be of interest. Going a step further, Spotify offers users an avenue to share their playlists with others in the 'Spotify Community' making the customers not only users but also ambassadors of the service. Consumers who use Spotify and Netflix not only save costs but they also prevent excess pollution. The production of CDs and DVDs and the associated packaging is wasteful. Moreover, physical discs, with all the wear and tear they sustain, are becoming obsolete.

Introduction

Businesses in the new economy sell *performance*, not products. This is a fundamentally new customer proposition which no longer revolves around the *ownership* of products, but rather *access* to the products. The manufacturer retains ownership and the user pays for the performance of the product and the continued service from the manufacturer even after the 'sale' is made. Manufacturers and users are in closer contact with each other in the new economy. The continuity of the client relationship is a determining factor in a company's success in the new economy. To estimate the value of this changed proposition, and its earning structure, let's first look at the traditional economy. What was the old model of consumption like? Why has it lasted so long? And most importantly, why is it no longer sensible in the new economy? The inherent system in the old consumption model was: *take-make-waste*.

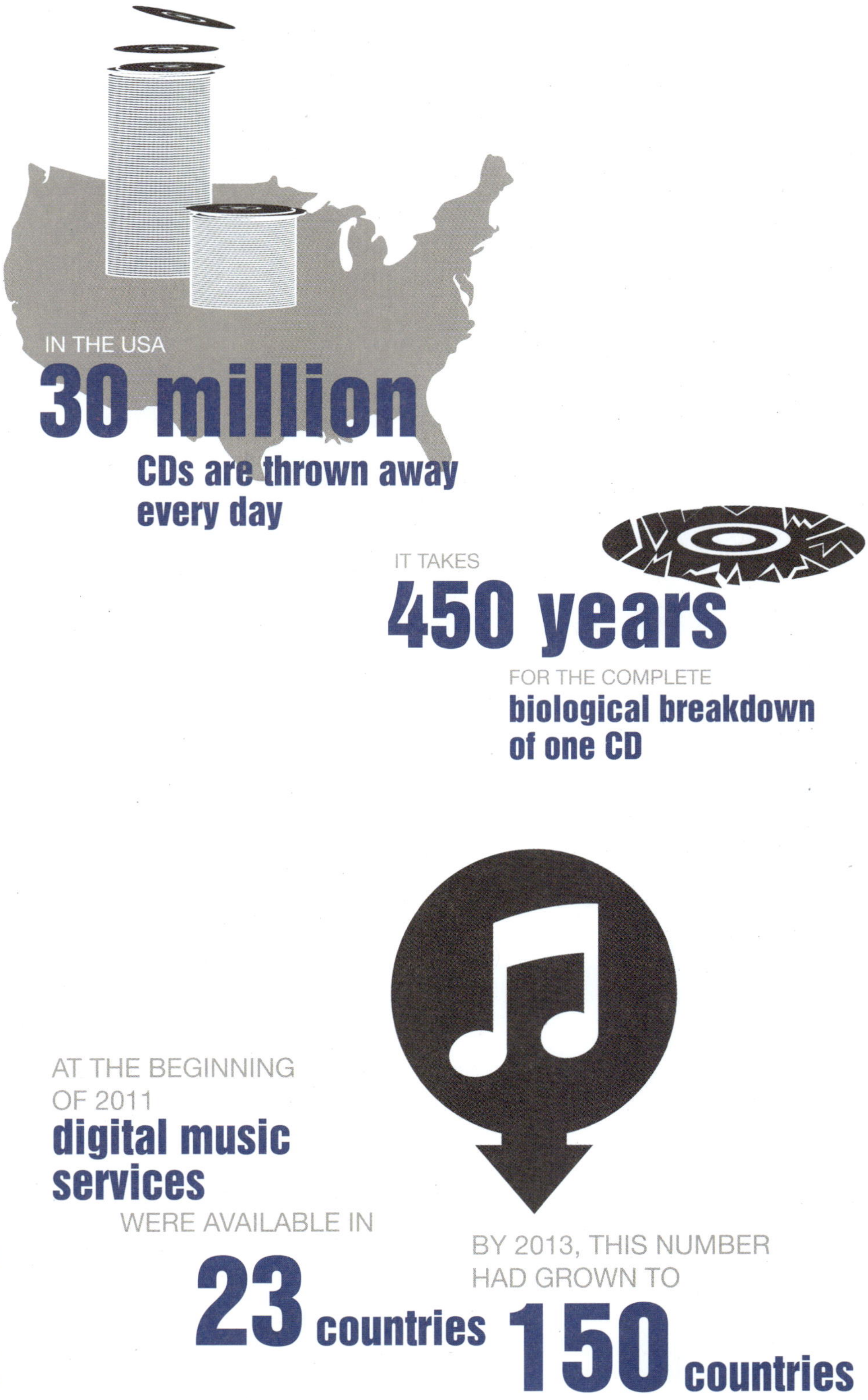

Illustration 10
Facts & figures cd's

Companies take materials and resources from the earth, then use labor and energy to make the product. The ownership of the product is transferred to the buyer after the sale. Buyers then use the product as long as they want. When customers are done with the product, it ends up on the scrap heap – or at best – in a collection box for charity. Products – and their ownership – follow a linear route.

New economy businesses have thrown that linear model overboard, due in part to its many drawbacks. The limitation of natural resources and the ever rising costs of resources and energy are the most well-known disadvantages. The *take-make-waste* approach and the associated speculation and hoarding of resources to drive up the price do not contribute to a sustainable relationship with ecological assets. On top of that, the linear model does not leave much room for an enduring customer relationship. While brand loyalty is important in the traditional economy as well, the focus is primarily on the transaction. What happens after that is of little interest to the retailer or manufacturer. In the new economy, businesses realize that this approach creates limited value because consumers are starting to consider ownership of the products to be of less importance. Research has shown that consumers in the 21st century are less focused on possessions. This used to be very different. Up until the mid-20th century, possessions were a status symbol. The steady rise of the service economy in the 20th century has, little by little, diminished the value given to possessions (Van den Bos, 2012).

This movement accounts for the success of novel companies such as Airbnb which facilitates private parties renting out their apartments or houses to travelers; Liquid, another innovative company, offers people a platform to rent bicycles from one another; then there is Uber, the successful (and disruptive) startup that turns the average driver into a potential taxi, and Fon, which lets people share their WiFi network with others and already has over seven million users. It is interesting to notice that these digital startups interact with the transformative trends as described in Chapter 0. The abovementioned services use digitalization to ensure customer satisfaction. In fact, through peer reviews (online reviews from customers) the quality of the product or service is made immediately transparent.

A very telling example of the move away from ownership and towards access is the enormous decline in the number of American youths that drive a car. For decades, American youth culture revolved around their cars. The Beach Boys even sang about it in their song, "Little Deuce Coupe" when they boasted,

"I've got the fastest set of wheels in town", but today young Americans are not as interested in owning a 'set of wheels'. In 1983, 80 percent of American 18-year-olds had their driver's license. In 2010, it was down to 61 percent.[20] Between 2001 and 2009, the number of Americans between the ages of 16 and 30 who drove a car shrank by 25 percent.

A similar trend can be seen in Japan where cars used to be a 'must-have' status symbol. But these days "young people don't think cars are cool anymore" writes the Japanese journalist, Junko Edahiro. "The younger generations, especially, are not interested in possessions" states Edahiro. "The Japanese youth wants to go from point A to point B. If a car is needed, fine. If they can get a ride with someone, that's also fine. If they can get there by public transportation or by bike, that is also perfectly fine with them. But just ten years ago, carpooling in Japan was not popular at all," says Edahiro. "The common complaint was that, 'we don't like to sit in someone else's car or use someone else's stuff when we don't know the history'. But today things are different. Along the main highway in Tokyo, you can now find plenty of car-sharing services and it is spreading across the rest of Japan as well."[21]

In Great Britain, companies offering products wrapped in service agreements are popping up everywhere, according to Tien Tzuo, CEO of Zuora, an online invoicing and payment platform for subscription businesses. "Girl Meets Dress lets women rent a designer dress for just 15 dollars (£10) a day, easyCar allows drivers to share cars, and the Larder Box delivers a recipe to your doorstep together with a box filled with all the necessary food ingredients. There is even FlexPetz that allows you to hire trained dogs, by the hour or day, whenever you feel like taking a nice walk in the park with a friendly canine."

According to Zuora, there is no turning the tide on the subscription economy. "In North America and Europe alone there are an estimated 15 million companies that could offer their products in a subscription form."[22]

Companies are finding many ways to sustain longer relationships with the customer while providing desired services and preventing waste. The Polish Telecom provider Orange lets their customers return their telephones and accessories at the end of the contract period so they can be recycled. By using their online portal, customers have the choice to offer their telephones for resale or recycling.

Rolls-Royce

EUROPE | **ENGLAND**

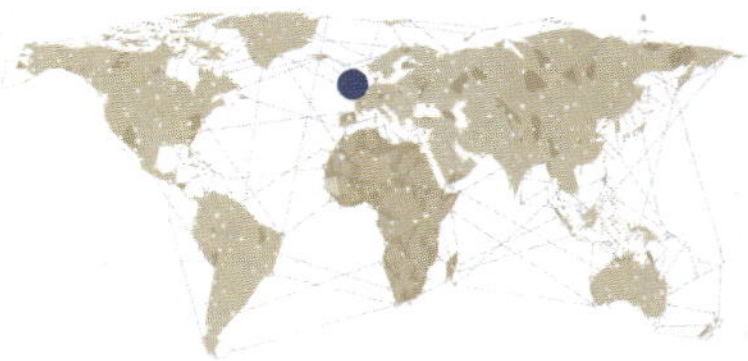

For some companies, the transition from selling a product to selling a service is easy. Rolls Royce, who not only sells luxury cars, but also airplane motors, introduced 'Power by the Hour' in the 1980s. Instead of selling the airplane motors, the company initiated selling flight hours. This way, Rolls Royce retains ownership of the motors while the airlines pay for the hours that they use. Rolls Royce naturally benefits the most when the motors work flawlessly. Therefore, they introduced a stringent track-and-trace system to ensure that the motors are well maintained. The manufacturer can also proactively replace any parts that may be wearing out. The result is a significant decrease in the number of malfunctions and a happy customer whose airplanes seldom stand still waiting for repairs. As a consequence of this business model, Rolls Royce has seen the value of their service contracts soar to nearly 50 percent of their overall revenue.[23]

This type of development sees its culmination in the new economy. Businesses are no longer focusing on the transfer of ownership, but on service and performance. They realize that approaching a client as a 'user' rather than a 'buyer' is a more dynamic and profitable venture. It calls for an innovative perspective. For instance, instead of trying to figure out the best way to sell their cars, they concentrate on answering the client's need for mobility. 'Service-orientation' takes on real meaning in the new economy.

Another change we see is that the performance economy is making high end products accessible to people with less disposable income. In the traditional economy, a potential buyer's only choice was to either (reluctantly) pay the high purchase price or not. In the new economy, however, the buyer only needs to pay for the use of the product and no longer for all the resources that went into making it. Consequently, the net price is lower for the customer which in turn leads to less resistance and less initial investment. While this is advantageous for the consumer, it also benefits the manufacturer who gains access to a broader market.

Does this fundamental change lead to better and more sustainable results for both the consumers and the manufacturers? What does it take to make the transition from product to service? And how exactly do companies make this vision a reality? To address these and other questions about the new consumer proposition, it is helpful to break it down into four parts.

1. **The transition from ownership to use**
   Why are merchants now selling access to a product instead of the product itself? Why is there a demand for that? And how does this new consumer proposition not only provide users with improved performance but also decrease costs and increase profits for companies?

2. **Segments and product types**
   How does the transformation from product to service take shape for various types of products? Which sectors are most suitable for this new proposition and why? How does the length of use play a role?

3. **The ownership model**
   The relationship with the customer is being extended from a short, one-time transaction to a long-term connection for the entire time the customer uses the product. But what arrangements do businesses need to make in order to make this transition from ownership to usage?

4. **Capacity and financing**
   As the point of sale has lost its value in the new economy, what adjustments are required in the production, planning and financing? Who carries the costs now that the consumers are freed from the purchase investment?

Products and services

What is a product?
According to Lynn Shostack, former Vice-President of Citibank, products are tangible objects that take up time as well as space. The time and place of the production are often not the same as the time and place of consumption.

What is a service?
Services consist of trade and processes. They do not take up space, only time. You cannot own a service. You can only experience, create or participate in

one. A service requires interaction between the supplier and the client. The production and the consumption of the service happen at the same time. (Shostack, 1982).

1.1 Farewell to the ownership model

The shift from prizing ownership to prioritizing performance has much to do with the rapid development of technological innovations over the last few decades. The market is being overrun with new products, each one better than the last. Technology is moving so quickly that manufacturers can offer more functions or more energy efficiency each time they introduce a new item.

The ownership model of the traditional economy and the ever accelerating technological innovations conflict with each other. A good example is the smartphone. For instance, someone invests in model X, then, just a few weeks or months later, model Y comes out - the new and improved version with more functions, better resolution, a better camera, and even some new features like being able to connect the phone automatically to your car's audio and navigation systems. But the buyer is stuck with the phone he/she just spent so much money on and continues using this outdated model rather than investing in a brand new phone. In this case, ownership of the product actually stands in the way of using the latest technology to communicate. This conflicting relationship between ownership and the optimal use of a product affects users across the board. Businesses in the new economy are responding by ditching the ownership model and allowing customers to pay for performance, not the product. No telephone but communication; no TV but access to programs; no CDs and DVDs but music and movies on demand; and no car but mobility.

This kind of complete, integrated approach fits new economy business like a glove. It is better oriented towards the customer than the fragmented proposition that characterizes the traditional economy. Customers are no longer interested in the old complex combination of products, services, and guarantees. They want long term total solutions that are innovative and broadly applicable with good service and repair options (Michael, Brown & Gallan, 2008).

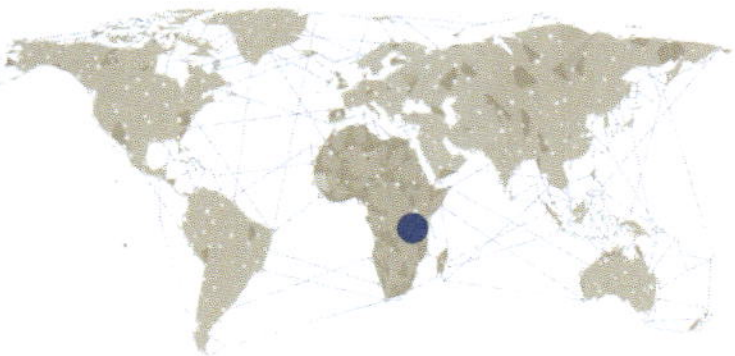

Off Grid Electric

AFRICA | **TANZANIA**

A good example of this can be found in Tanzania where the company Off Grid Electric provides light to people living in rural areas for only twenty cents a day. By utilizing highly efficient, hyper-productive solar panels, Off Grid Electric is able to increase the light production by a factor of fifty compared to the traditional, unhealthy and dangerous kerosene lamps. The company also employs thousands of local workers for their distribution and installation.[24]

Ownership on the wane

In the traditional economy, the producer transfers ownership of the product, complete with all its components, to the buyer at the time of sale. The company is only responsible for defects or poor performance through means of a guarantee. In the new economy, the company retains ownership and is thus responsible for the performance of the product for the duration of its use and for fixing any problems or defects. This not only applies to the quality of the product but also to the services related to it. Therefore, it is to be expected that a customer who brings a television in to be fixed does not walk away with a meager second rate model while waiting for the repairs to be done.

The Dutch architect Thomas Rau is a fervent advocate of performance based consumption. Rau has determined that consumer behavior has changed significantly in the 21st century compared to decades before. "An old analog telephone of the last century easily lasted 20 to 30 years. If it started to malfunction then grandpa would get his tool kit out and replace a wire and that was it, he would be able to use the phone for another ten years."

However, the continuous hype of new products these days invokes a whole different kind of consumer behavior. "One or two years after the launch of product X, product Y is launched with even more fanfare. Everyone wants it! Is model X broken? No. But model Y adds new features and that excites potential customers. The functional lifespan of the product has become irrelevant."

Duration of customer relationship

Because the ownership of the product remains in the hands of the merchant and the end user keeps the product for an agreed period of time, there is a radical shift in the relationship between the buyer and seller. While in the traditional economy there is a short, one-time transaction, in the new economy, the buyer and seller are bound by a long-term agreement for the entire length of use.

Therefore, the goal is no longer to close the deal and make the sale. The goal is to build a relationship and increase loyalty, thus turning the client into a profit-making instrument. Consequently, the sale is no longer the connection between the producer (supply) and the client (demand), but the beginning of the connection *process*. Extending the relationship with the customer is an integral part of the earnings potential in the new economy. Businesses therefore do not pursue short-term goals anymore as this actually damages the relationship with the client in the long run. (Michael, 2012).

In order to build and maintain these long-term relationships in the best possible way, product manufacturers are looking to long-standing service providers who know the art of cultivating a trusting relationship with their clients. Take, for example, the doctor-patient or accountant-client relationships in which integrity plays an important role. The supplier of the service depends heavily on a trusting relationship.

The American company Zappos is inspirational in their approach to their clients. Since Zappos is an online store for shoes and clothes, their sales are automated making the contact with the client entirely digital, with one exception - the telephone helpdesk.

Zappos therefore decided to center its business strategy around the helpdesk. Contrary to some helpdesks, the staff at Zappos were not instructed to note the complaint and quickly get off the phone, but rather to listen patiently to the caller, ask questions and attempt to solve the issue. What is important here is that Zappos employs intrinsically motivated workers. In order to achieve that, Zappos has an unusual approach. After the month-long training program, Zappos gives the potential employees an interesting choice: either sign an employment contract and come to work for Zappos, or decide not to work for the company and get 4,000 dollars deposited into your bank account. The people who do not go for the quick money are clearly motivated to work for the company. This unusual strategy has proven successful. Zappos has won numerous awards for being the best service center and has transformed its customer service department into a powerful marketing instrument without a big budget investment. 75 percent of their sales is to returning customers.[25]

Small business owners such as Chris Zane also see the value in developing long-term connections with customers. Zane wondered how much could be earned from providing life-long service to his clients. "If we imagine the customer buys his first bike from us at age four and we provide all the repair service and subsequent bike sales until that person retires, we can estimate a profit of 15,000 dollars (€ 12,500). But to achieve that we would need to find a way to build a life-long relationship."

No matter what type of business you are in, you should develop your skills in 'experience selling' and 'relationship building'.[26]

1.2 Product types: The difference between property and food

There is no template for the transition from product to service. In fact, different products have different lifespans and vary in length and intensity of use. Therefore, according to the categorization specified by the Ellen MacArthur Foundation (2013), new economy businesses are divided into three product groups.

1. *Products with a long lifespan*, such as property, roads, and other industrial infrastructures.
2. *Products with an average lifespan*, such as appliances, computers, tools, vehicles, furniture, and other factory goods.
3. *Products with a short lifespan*, like clothing, food, paper and other goods that are used within a few days to a few months.

1 Products with a long lifespan

The transition from product to service for goods with a long lifespan, such as buildings and roads, is particularly attractive to businesses because the period of use is easily 10 to 20 years. The deals that are arranged for these products usually relate to long-term performance, especially regarding energy saving or durability of the materials. As a result of these performance agreements, suppliers will more readily choose high-quality materials.

Paul de Ruiter is the architectural firm responsible for designing the head office for TNT in the Netherlands which was named the best sustainable design for an office building in Europe. For this special project, a Green Lease Contract was set up with the tenant, TNT. This is a performance contract which specifies the contractual agreements related to the energy-saving and environmental targets of the building. The project developer, OVG, founded their own energy company which supplies the energy to TNT for a fixed price per square meter.

In order to achieve the ambitious performance standard, a lot of thought went into creating an energy efficient design based on climate principles such as sunlight, warmth, wind and water. The use of recyclable materials and the limited use of fossil fuels was also a consideration. Because using a large amount of materials naturally leads to more CO_2 emissions, the developers put a great deal of attention into the reduction of the total amount of materials. The result was a building that was 25 percent lighter than average. By positioning the building north/south and applying innovative sun screens, there is plenty of sunlight which gives the building a pleasant work environment. The centrally located atrium allows daylight to reach the inner work places and provides a place to meet and interact with colleagues in an energy efficient and open environment.

2 Products with an average lifespan.

This product group encompasses more than half of the production from EU member states and accounts for approximately 15 trillion euros in revenue, representing a large part of the economy and at least as much waste. Products such as appliances, office equipment, vehicles, furniture, and other factory goods are in this category. Because many of these products are made up of individual components they are relatively easy to disassemble, thus giving these types of products the highest potential to transition from a product to a service model.

A good example is Ricoh, a Fortune 500 company in the field of printing, office solutions, and IT services. Ricoh developed the GreenLine program which focuses on minimizing the environmental impact of their products. Ricoh supplies clients with printers and copy machines on the basis of usage and allows the machines to be returned after the agreed term. After inspection, the machine is dismantled. Any defective or worn-out parts are replaced and the machine is reassembled and given a software update. Subsequently, Ricoh puts the same machines back on the market under the GreenLine label. New clients receive the same quality guarantee and warranty as buyers of new machines.[27]

The thirteen minute drill

One of the characteristics of the traditional economy is the enormously inefficient use of products. Consumers purchase mass amounts of goods which they hardly use. Then, on the rare occasions when they need the item, they are outdated. This means that if a small part needs to be fixed, it can be next to impossible to get it repaired. For example, in the United States, approximately 70 percent of the households owns a drill. But on average, a drill is really only used once in a while and then for only a minute or so. In the United States alone, there are 80 million drills which, on average, are used for only thirteen minutes during the entire time of ownership.[28] When you look at it this way, it can seem absurd. Therefore, in the new economy innovative entrepreneurs are building platforms where consumers can rent products or even rent out their own products to other people in their neighborhood. NeighborGoods is an example of one such platform where friends and neighbors can lend various goods to each other. The website also shows how much money you save and how much money you have saved someone else. In addition to being economical, the platform has a social element.[29] As one woman posted on Twitter, "NeighborGoods not only helped me save money but gave me the opportunity to meet neighbors I wouldn't have met otherwise."

3 Products with a short lifespan

Food, paper, T-shirts, and other products with a short lifespan are more difficult to fit into the new customer proposition. These products are only used for a short time and certainly in the case of food, the products are not reusable. To apply the new consumer proposition to products with a short lifespan, manufacturers and suppliers are exploring new opportunities of combining their traditional product sales with service offers.

While some items may be more challenging, significant steps are being taken when it comes to clothing. For example, the Dutch fashion label, aWEARness produces its clothing according to the principles of a circular economy. Clients do not buy the clothing, but get to use the clothes for a prearranged amount of time and pay in installments depending on the length of use. The client then returns the clothing to the store and the material is subsequently used to make new items of clothing. This is made possible partly due to their use of "Returnity", a cradle-to-cradle material that can be entirely reused at the same level in the chain. The chains of production also work closely together and share the costs and the benefits. "We relieve the wearer by making arrangements for the care of the garment. For example, as part of the contract for a suit, the client gets to bring it in twice for dry cleaning and once for repairs for free. For that purpose, we have made arrangements with local services where the client receives a pass allowing him to drop off the garment for cleaning or repair and pick it up a couple of days later," says Rien Otto from the clothing label. In order to give transparency into the production line, aWEARness works together with Royal HaskoningDHV. They have created a track-and-trace system to give insight into what their partners are doing, supplying, and what costs are being made. "By working this way, we ensure that the product ownership remains in the hands of the chain. We are all responsible for the use of the resources which we rework and reuse for the production of new products."

Different products have differing lifespans. While a washing machine can easily last 10 years, a rug may need replacement after 5 years. Moreover, the life of a particular item will vary. It may be able to be sold again after a few minor repairs and updates, or it may have seen its best days and be ready for dismantling and its parts used for the production of another product. While some products, such as clothing, lend themselves easily to renewal during the period of use by simply being taken to the dry cleaners, other items like appliances are more difficult to update while they are in use.

Such differences present new challenges and dilemmas in the new economy. Therefore, the capacity to adapt and the ability to be flexible are crucial competencies for new economy businesses.

1.3 Four stages of de-ownership

The transition from product to service in the new economy requires different arrangements and contracts. As stated in the previous section, the 'sale' is just the beginning of the client-seller relationship. In the following section, you will read about the 'De-ownership Model' and the Four Stages of De-Ownership.

Varying the approach

1. **Financial lease:** Consumers lease products rather than buying them outright. This is something we also see in the traditional economy.
2. **Circular use:** At the end of its lifespan, the product and the valuable resources used to make it are returned to the beginning of the chain.
3. **Full operational use:** Producers not only provide access to the product but deliver services needed for its use, such as energy or water.
4. **Diversified use:** The producers deliver the products as described above but also seek opportunities to horizontally diversify. For example, a television manufacturer may also supply a network subscription.

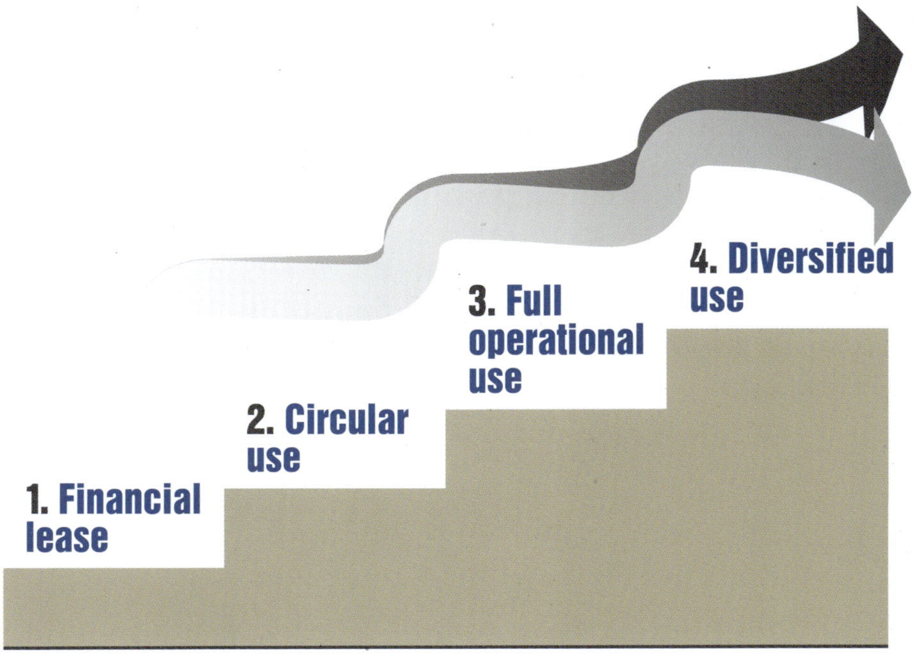

Illustration 11
Four stages of de-ownership

You can see these four stages as a ladder with four steps. Businesses on the first step are at the beginning of the transition process. To reach the second step, considerable innovation is needed in production design and chain management. The third and fourth steps require far-reaching cooperation among all links in the chain.

Stage 1 Financial lease

Consumers in the traditional economy buy a new television set every so often. However, in the new economy, they no longer need to purchase a TV but have the option to subscribe to the viewing hours instead. The manufacturer guarantees good quality audio visual reception and provides any necessary repairs for free. The result is that buyers and sellers stay bound to each other for the entire time the product is being used. Replacement, repairs and the disposal of the TV are paid for by the manufacturer. To keep the costs down, the TV should be low maintenance and provide the best quality for as long as possible. Manufacturers that produce poor quality televisions do not stand a chance in the new economy. In fact, manufacturers in the new economy benefit the most by making products that are durable. Although leasing is common practice in the traditional economy too, it is not innovative enough for entrepreneurs in the new economy. The existing financial lease arrangements only cream off the top of the de-ownership approach by relieving customers of the initial investment and some of the responsibility.

Stage 2 Circular use

Circular use goes a step further than financial lease. The television set that the customer buys circulates back to the beginning of the chain. Products then become resource carriers in which valuable resources are temporarily stored. Consumers are thus spared the expense of paying for the resources that are used to make them. They only pay for the performance of the product and any associated costs.

Telephones are goldmines

According to a US Geological Survey, there is about 0.001 ounces (0.034 grams) of gold in the average cell phone. The value is approximately 1.80 dollars (€ 1.50). There is also about 0.56 ounces (16 grams) of copper worth 0.11 cents (€ 0.09), 0.01 ounces (0.35 grams) of silver at 0.34 cents (€0.28), and there are traces of platinum as well. For comparison, there is less gold in a pound of ore than in a pound of electronics. Moreover, extracting gold from ore is far more labor intensive than retrieving it from a telephone.[30] The American company, ReCelullar, collects enough gold in one year's time from old telephones to make 1,500 wedding rings and enough copper to recreate 2 Statues of Liberty.[31] The yield from products produced in the new economy is even higher because electronics are no longer glued together but, in keeping with the circular model, are built with modular components. Appliances can be cheaply and easily dismantled so that the resources can quickly be reused.

Stage 3 Full operational use

New economy businesses deliver full operational use by not only supplying the primary service but also supplying the services around it as well. All the costs that are incurred during use are worked into the user agreement. For example, a renter does not receive separate bills for the rent, gas, water and electricity, but instead gets one bill based on performance agreements in which all the costs are included. So, using this example, with *full operational use*, the customer gets the security of knowing what his monthly expenses are for the whole length of the contract and that the expenses will not rise but could only lower.

The supplier, on the other hand, ensures a long-term relationship with the customer and has an economic incentive to make the premises as sustainable as possible. To further encourage both the energy supplier and the customer to use the resources responsibly, an agreement is arranged where both parties benefit from any cost saving that is achieved. In this way, the customer and the supplier remain stimulated to explore sustainable innovations and ideas. An added advantage for the supplier is that he can influence the extent of the sustainability. He no longer needs to convince tenant after tenant to make the change to renewable energy. He offers a complete package and is therefore free to pursue the sustainable use of energy and resources.

ESCo

A good example of this approach on the business-to-business side is an Energy Service Company (ESCo), which is specially created to ensure energy saving measures. It develops, finances, realizes and guarantees the sustainability of one or more buildings. The company performs this service by arranging long-term contracts based on energy performance. They may also arrange a contract that includes a long-term maintenance agreement. All of the initial investments that are made are earned back by the maintenance and energy savings they deliver. With this arrangement, the owner or manager of the property does not need to take any financial risks because the amount of energy savings is specifically stated in the contract. If the savings is more than expected then both parties profit. If the savings is lower than expected, then that is the risk that the Energy Service Company takes. A penalty clause may also be included in the contract. This way, the company is motivated to monitor the effectiveness of their measures and continue to search for innovative solutions. [32]

Stage 4 Diversified use

The last step on the ladder to transition from product to service is offering a complete arrangement. In addition to supplying their customers with the product and the accompanying services, new economy businesses are also exploring opportunities to expand their offerings horizontally. Entrepreneurs are asking themselves questions such as: On which other products or services are my products and services dependent? And which products or services fit in well with the use of my products? For example, an office supply shop may also want to offer an air hockey table for relaxation during a work break. Or a bathtub supplier could also offer relaxing music and waterproof loudspeakers. Because of the relationships the suppliers have built with their customers, they are in a perfect position to offer new merchandise and capitalize on the specific needs of their clientele.

Sustainable fashion

EUROPE I NORTH AMERICA I **AUSTRALIA, ENGLAND, SWEDEN, THE NETHERLANDS, USA**

The fashion industry has a waste problem. In England, for example, over 1 million tons of clothing are consumed and disposed of every year. Approximately half ends up being used again, 14 percent is recycled, but the rest winds up on a garbage heap and is ultimately burned.

New business models in various countries in Europe are providing alternatives that not only illustrate the potential transformation from product ownership to product usage, they reduce waste. A good example is the British clothing chain Primark which offers a 'Primark subscription'. With this arrangement, the subscriber leases the clothing. Subscribers may return the clothes and lease new items as often as they like. When the customers no longer want a particular item, they simply return it to Primark and the item either gets repaired, upcycled[33] or reworked into a new item.

The Dutch company Mud Jeans doesn't sell jeans. Instead, it has created a system in which the clients pay a fee of 7 dollars (5.95 euros) per month to lease jeans for one year. The company uses easy to recycle organic denim and buys the material from nearby suppliers in Turkey and Italy. During the one-year period, the clients may bring the jeans to the store for free repairs if needed. When the year is up, the clients have three choices: they may keep the jeans, in which case they just pay four more months at the same rate; they may switch them and pay just 12 dollars (10 euros) for a new pair of jeans; or they may send the jeans back to the store where they will be used for the repair of other jeans or reworked into a new item. Inspired by the success of the lease-jeans, Mud Jeans has begun Lease a Fleece.

Other alternative types of business models that invest in sustainable client relationships or clothing exchanges are popping up elsewhere as well. Nudie Jeans, for example, is a Swedish store that offers free repairs and collects worn out jeans for the manufacturing of new clothing items.[34] And SwapStyle is a very successful example from Australia where they have created a forum for women to exchange clothing.

The last step on the ladder to transition from product to service is offering a complete arrangement. In addition to supplying their customers with the product and the accompanying services, new economy businesses are also exploring opportunities to expand their offerings horizontally. Entrepreneurs are asking themselves questions such as: On which other products or services are my products and services dependent? And which products or services fit in well with the use of my products? For example, an office supply shop may also want to offer an air hockey table for relaxation during a work break. Or a bathtub supplier could also offer relaxing music and waterproof loudspeakers. Because of the relationships the suppliers have built with their customers, they are in a perfect position to offer new merchandise and capitalize on the specific needs of their clientele.

Through horizontal diversification, businesses are also in a better position to offer services instead of products. For instance, a supplier of electric cars that also develops the appropriate infrastructure and offers the associated maintenance sells 'mobility'. In contrast, a car dealership that only sells cars, sells only cars. The complete arrangement leads to the expansion of the supply for the business and a better proposition for the customer.

Let's take education as another example. Many schools face several issues in the current economy. They have too little money, low enrollment, and too much property. Moreover, the property they have is not designed with sustainability and environmental factors in mind. In order to actually provide education to students, schools must first invest in the acquisition of desks, lesson materials, playground and gym equipment, computers and other IT provisions. Limited budget and the burden of owning the property and the goods are often bottlenecks for many schools that would like to invest in high-quality, innovative education.

New economy businesses are no longer offering separate products and services but have come with one all-encompassing service: educational supplies. They are creating consortiums consisting of all the parties involved in supplying what schools need. This complete package is provided to schools based on a contract for an agreed price and period of time. In this way, the consortium is guaranteed sales and the schools are assured of a high-quality educational environment.[35]

New services

The service sector is undergoing its own transformation. Service providers in the new economy are differentiating themselves by offering clever combinations of adjoining services. The possibilities to combine varying content are endless, bearing in mind that consumers in the new economy are more interested in performance than in the product itself. As we saw in the example of the car, in which customers buy mobility, service arrangements are an attractive alternative to owning the vehicle outright. This means that there are now many more opportunities for the service sector to become involved in conventionally product-oriented industries and expand on this new approach.

A good example is XXImo, a Dutch company that transformed the 'fuel card' into a 'mobility card'. This card ensures practical and cost efficient mobility. While the fuel card offers a discount at the pump and a collective bill at the end of the month, the mobility card from XXImo is a payment card for all transportation costs. The card holder can use it to pay for gas and also for public transportation and even to rent a bicycle. The company even offers a route management app which can be connected to a digital calendar. This gives cardholders the extra service of being able to avoid traffic jams by using alternative routes. "XXImo also presents a personalized feature", says CEO, Ruud Koornstra. "If the card holder wants to exercise for a half an hour a day, the planner can be programmed to opt for a 20 minute walk and a ten minute bicycle ride – unless the weather is bad of course."

1.4 New starting point: usage, financing, and cost price

Usage

In the new economy, maximum usage is crucial. An idle product is a money-losing proposition. Since the producer of the product retains ownership, a product that is not being used does not earn any money. Consequently, companies are applying logistics, servicing, IT, and efficiency management to ensure the maximum use of their products and thus optimize profits and margins.

Some products in particular, such as electric cars, present interesting possibilities to optimize usage. Most cars are, in fact, not being used 90 percent of the time, meaning that electric cars are parked next to a loading station having their batteries charged most of the time. This amount of stored energy can add an extra dimension to the electricity network. Conceivably, the fully charged batteries could be used to offset the high demands on electricity during peak hours, says Koornstra "If you were to give a hundred thousand electric car owners a power station in exchange for permission to use the energy they have stored in their car batteries once in a while, then you could probably shut down an entire power plant."

Local Motion
NORTH AMERICA | USA, CALIFORNIA

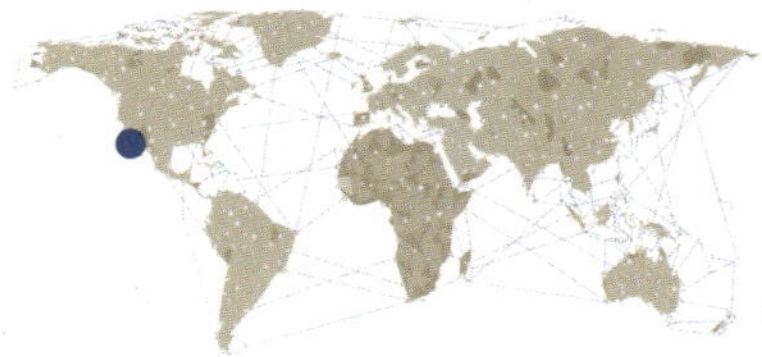

The American start-up Local Motion thinks it is a shame that the average car stands still 90 percent of the time. So, Local Motion, which is situated in Silicon Valley, developed a piece of hardware which makes it easier for companies, governmental agencies, and universities to share their vehicles within their organizations. "Tens of millions of vehicles owned by governmental and business organizations are used extremely inefficiently," explains Clément Gires, Co-Founder of Local Motion.[36] With Local Motion's hardware, an organization can make its fleet available to all its employees. The associated software keeps track of which vehicles are being used and which are available. A green light indicates that it is available and employees can access the car by using their employee pass or smartphone. The built-in GPS gives the management insight into the operational data and provides an overview of how many vehicles are in use or available. Google is already one of Local Motion's clients.

Financing

The transition from ownership to access brings with it the need to approach financing differently. Since customers gain access to the products by means of a service contract, they become bound to the seller for a period of time. Therefore, the customer's ability to pay for the services for the duration of the contract is crucial. In order to keep the financial wheels turning smoothly, a number of conditions are essential.

1. **Know the client**
   What is already the case for the banking industry, also applies to new

economy businesses: know your client. After all, the client is using a product that is still owned by the manufacturer.

2. **Who bears the risk?**
   In the traditional economy, once the product was purchased, the risk mainly belonged to the customer. If the TV set was defective and suddenly burst into flames causing a fire in the house, insurance policies and guarantees would most likely cover the damage. In the new economy, much of the risk is shouldered by the manufacturer or retailer, who is still the owner of the product. So in a way, the manufacturer or retailer not only provides access to the product but also a form of insurance. For each type of product, they need to evaluate the best way to deal with the risks and especially how it should be arranged financially, for example by integrating potential costs into the service premiums.

3. **Financing the product**
   In the traditional economy, the buyer of the TV was more or less the financial backer, paying in full for the television upon purchase. In the new economy, suppliers finance the product themselves and only at the end of the contract period has the product been paid for in full. Because other costs, such as interest, are incurred with this kind of arrangement, the company must work these costs into the user agreement. A retroactive cash value calculation could be used, for example, by estimating the value of the total amount paid by the end of the contract period.

Cost price

The cost price of a product is accrued in a whole new way in the new economy. In the traditional economy, the resources and distribution costs are the biggest expenses for the manufacturer. However, in the new economy, a variety of other factors comes into play. For example, the costs involved in building the product in modules, dismantling, updating, cleaning, and the costs of creating a viable plan for the collection and re-distribution, reuse and recycling of the natural resources.

Given the fact that the price of scarce natural resources is on the rise, and as a result so are energy costs, new economy businesses are able to save considerably on their costs through reuse and recycling. In fact, recovering, processing, and circulating resources can also be done with renewable energy. The technology related to this is getting cheaper and thanks to the fast paced technological developments, the trend continues.

The conclusion is that the transition from product to service as described in this chapter is inherently connected to a long-term relationship with the client and the creation of a new way of selling. There is a relatively high investment needed at the beginning, but that does not detrimentally affect the client since the costs are spread over a longer period of time.

Wrap up

The desire for ownership is on the wane in the new economy. Consumers are focused on access and performance. Manufacturers and retailers are capitalizing on this new perspective by adjusting their customer proposition. They are looking past the point of sale and using service contracts and product diversification to establish long-term relationships with their customers. This opens many windows of opportunity in the new economy and naturally leads to sustainable business endeavors. Since suppliers retain ownership of their products, they also retain ownership of the components and the raw materials that go into making the product. Therefore, once the customer is finished using it, rather than the item getting thrown out, it is returned to the supplier and can be dismantled or resold. Scarce raw materials stay within the chain and do not end up on a waste heap. The efficient use, and reuse, of these resources and the supply chains that handle them are the subjects of the next chapter.

The Value Cycle creates maximum value for all assets: Financial, Ecological, and Social.

Chapter 2

WINDOW OF OPPORTUNITY:

Value Cycle

The linear supply chain is obsolete. The circular economy requires a circular production process.

Pioneering entrepreneurs are forging cross-sector relationships; new avenues are being explored to create valuable solutions.

Shared responsibility is the key to success. A mutual bottom line encourages risk-sharing and creates greater profits.

Introduction

The supply chain as we know it is obsolete. That may sound a bit extreme, but you just can't see it any other way. A fixed linear supply chain fits into the new economy like a carrier pigeon competing with email. Slow, no longer of this day and age, and certainly not compatible. There are three primary reasons for this shift. The first one is the changing nature of global business. The progressive globalization on all fronts has had a huge impact on the way businesses develop and deliver their products and services. The traditional linear, country specific, proprietor-led supply chain has simply passed its expiration date. Secondly, dwindling natural resources and the global rise in prosperity prompts governments, scientists, businesses and consumers to look at supply chains in an entirely different manner. And last but not least, we have recognized that the *take-make-waste* system that characterized the traditional economy takes a heavy toll on our natural resources.

Problems with the System

Although much progress has been made in improving the yield of natural resources and finding new energy sources, governments and the business community have not put enough attention to waste management nor to energy and labor efficiency. The consumption system of the traditional economy has a serious flaw, namely that the raw materials used for many products meet their untimely death in a waste heap or end up at some other point of no return. However, businesses in the new economy realize that a system based on the use, rather than reuse of non-renewable resources leads to a considerable loss of value for the entire material chain. This loss of value damages the environment just as it damages the business itself. New economy businesses therefore develop, distribute, and supply their goods using an entirely different approach. They transform the traditional, linear *take-make-waste* system into a circular *no-waste* system that is focused on value creation. Simply put: they develop products that double as resource banks. The old products are returned to the suppliers and the materials are reused rather than discarded.

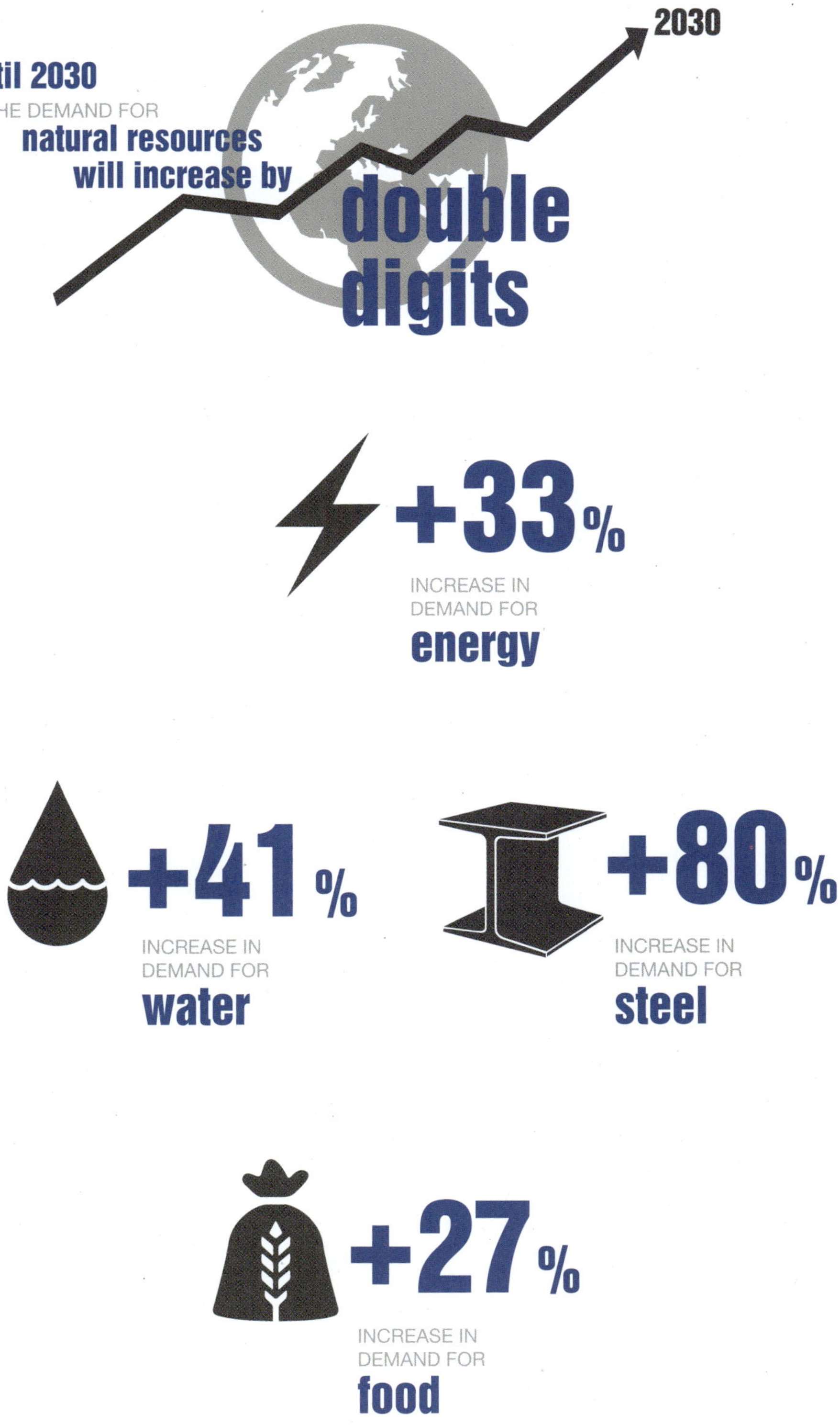

Illustration 12
Facts & figures
natural resurces

The screw that loses its threads when heated

EUROPE I **ENGLAND**

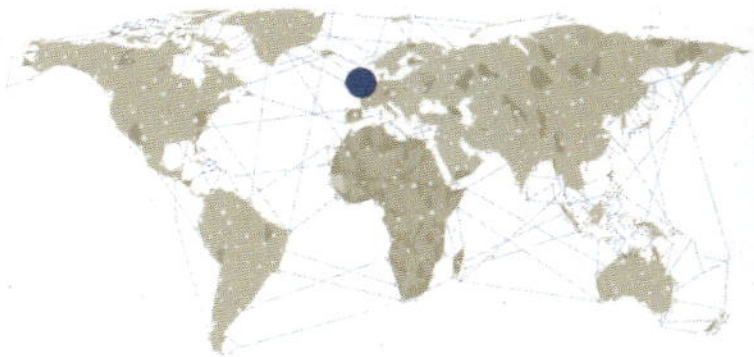

To develop products that are made to be 're-made', there are certainly hurdles to overcome. It is time and labor intensive to repair and remanufacture products. And there are costs involved in creating a radically new design and in securing quality resources.

Joseph Chiodo of Active Disassembly Research in London has been working with this goal in mind since the 90s. His Active Disassembly design concept uses materials and processes in such a way that the product can be systematically disassembled without causing any damage to the existing materials. An impressive example of his efforts is the screw that loses its thread when it is heated. This invention is extremely valuable in the disassembly process allowing products to be easily dismantled.[37]

Another comparable example is the British company Wear2. The clothes that they produce are high quality and durable. However, after a few minutes in the microwave, the stitching falls apart and it becomes easy to dislodge the components. Labels, company emblems, zippers, and buttons are all easily removed so that the materials can be directly reused for new products.[38]

To be clear, closing the loop is not easy. It is a highly complicated operation that demands a whole new approach and management of the production process. It also requires extensive collaboration among all the parties in the cycle. This is naturally more achievable for simple products such as carpets than it is for more complex products such as consumer appliances.

That said, the shift from a supply cycle system to a value cycle system can be enormously profitable. The Ellen MacArthur Foundation calculated in 2013 that European producers could save up to 700 billion dollars by adopting the circular economy. Additionally, as the demand for natural resources continues to skyrocket, we can expect even higher prices for those resources. This will also lead to Resource Security becoming a big issue not only for companies, but for countries as well.

Several countries in Asia have already caught on to this. Japan is a prime example of how to address this issue. Since they do not have much in the way of natural resources themselves, they have passed a law that requires the great majority of electrical appliances and devices to be reused. As a result, they actually dispose of a mere 5 percent of all waste. And if that isn't impressive enough, they can also boast the reuse of 98 percent of all metal components. Most importantly, a large proportion of the materials that becomes available after dismantling is reused for the production of the same type of product as the item it came from. In this way, Japan closes the circle, which is the requisite of the circular economy. The Japanese approach, which we will expand upon later, is not only a verifiable success, it accounts for 650,000 jobs in Japan. The recycle-and-reuse business represents 234 billion dollars, or 7.6 percent of the gross national product.[39]

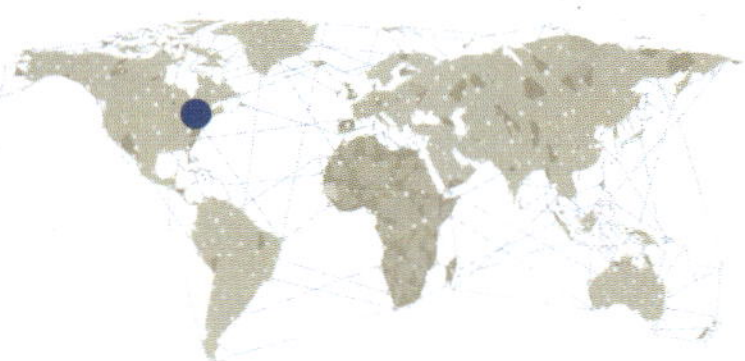

Packaging made of mold

NORTH AMERICA | **USA, NEW YORK**

Closing the circle is easier when manufacturers limit the waste products from the beginning of the production process. To help meet this goal, the American company, Ecovative came up with an alternative to traditional plastic packaging. A completely biodegradable solution made from mycelium: the "roots" of a mushroom, together with agricultural waste which can be made into any shape needed. The founders, Eben Bayer and Gravin McIntyre hit upon the idea when they saw mushrooms growing on logs and ascertained that the mycelium, a network of threads from the mold essentially glues the mushroom to the wood.

Based on this observation, the team at Ecovative developed a material using mycelium which actually has similar characteristics to plastic. But with the important difference that at the end of its use, it is completely biodegradable.[40]

Sustainable business is not a stand-alone activity. It is truly functional when suppliers as well as consumers choose sustainable solutions. According to Jacques Reijniers, professor of Purchasing Management at Nyenrode Business University in the Netherlands, "Entrepreneurs that choose to create sustainable business practices can only realize their strategic goals when their suppliers are on board as well. That means that purchasers should not create price pressure. Unfortunately, too many purchasers are still being rewarded for doing this."

In the new economy, entrepreneurs feel connected and partly responsible for what happens in the rest of the supply chain. This approach and the resulting insight has led them to develop their supply chains in an entirely new manner. They are getting away from the classic model of links in a chain and are moving towards a model that lends itself better to collaboration: the value cycle.

In this chapter, we will address the question of how a supply chain becomes a value cycle and how businesses can create and utilize this cycle. We will explore:

1. Why the transactional character of the supply chain leads to an unnatural economic pressure and the unsustainable use of natural resources.
2. How to create maximum value by designing and producing products according to the principles of a circular economy.
3. How long-term collaboration creates more value than short-term transactions.
4. How the application of new financial models can help yield maximum results from the value cycle.
5. Why redefining the business-to-customer relationship has far reaching effects on how businesses organize themselves.

2.1 Why the supply chain is obsolete

The traditional supply chain has a transactional nature. Businesses buy and sell to each other and the consumer is the last link in the chain. This may sound fine, except for the fact that this model encourages each link in the chain to try to get the lowest price possible from the previous link. This results in enormous price pressures within the chain which in turn leads to non-sustainable effects. Natural resources, labor, and capital are not priced at their actual value but kept artificially low by shifting the expense. Resources are seen as one-time additions to the chain and disposed of after they are used. Supply chains are dependent on the fluctuating prices of the raw materials. Ultimately, the chain is supply-oriented which leads to the production of non-sustainable goods. (Source: Pallas Achterberg, Alliander)

Therefore, you could conclude that price competition within the chain encourages unsustainable business. But it goes even further than that. This method also has an effect on the company's viability. The continuing price pressure can lead businesses to price themselves right out of the market. In the food sector, for example, companies are sometimes forced to work below cost. A number of trends in the last decade have made this more of an issue. Because of the growing globalization, chains have become longer and more complex. The 'over-individualizing' of products (more varieties, more distribution channels) and shorter lifecycles has also placed higher demands on the links within the chain. The result: more risks and higher logistical costs in the chain. It is no wonder that during the financial crises, many parties within supply chains folded, while only the more powerful enterprises profited and sustained.

Businesses in the new economy are making a conscious choice to organize things differently. They are striving towards creating maximum value, not one-dimensional profit at the expense of the others in their supply chain. They are not pressuring suppliers to lower their prices, but working together to reach an end result that is not only profitable for all parties involved, but is also ecologically, socially and financially responsible. In other words, they aim to produce a TV, for example, that can be profitable but does not drain our natural resources, pollute, or exploit workers. Only then is there true value creation.

2.2 Maximum value creation in the value cycle

From TV to TV

ASIA I **JAPAN**

In the Panasonic Eco Technology Center (PETEC) in Japan, televisions, refrigerators, air conditioners and washing machines are being dismantled. The materials that are extracted from these easily disassembled appliances are then reused to make new items. [41] "From product to product", say the Japanese.

But in order to provide these sustainable solutions, companies in the new economy need to organize the supply chain in an entirely different way. A TV that is designed to be easily disassembled can only be created if all the parties involved work together, innovate together, and share the costs. This is known as The Sharing Economy.

In Japan, this kind of collaboration has more or less been forced by legal regulations. But with success, as presented earlier. Japanese recycling facilities are controlled, under law, by a consortium of manufacturers. Because these parties directly profit from the reuse of resources, they are financially motivated to create a good functioning recycling, remanufacturing, and reuse process. Because reusing materials is legally required, Japanese businesses invest heavily in the infrastructure to support long-term solutions. Inherent to this process is for manufacturers to visit recycling facilities. They see for themselves how frustrating and time-consuming it can be to disassemble the average product. So in order to make products that are 'dismantle friendly', some manufacturers send a sample of their product to the recycling facility before they initiate the production phase. [42]

In the new economy, we are seeing a similar development as we have seen in the Japanese market, namely the move away from rigid linear chains and towards a circular design. Circles of collaborative 'satellites' are set up. Each one makes an indispensable contribution to a sustainable end result: the value cycle. In order to do this well, each 'satellite' also needs to create a circle. This will ultimately lead to an extensive network model that will replace the current linear model.

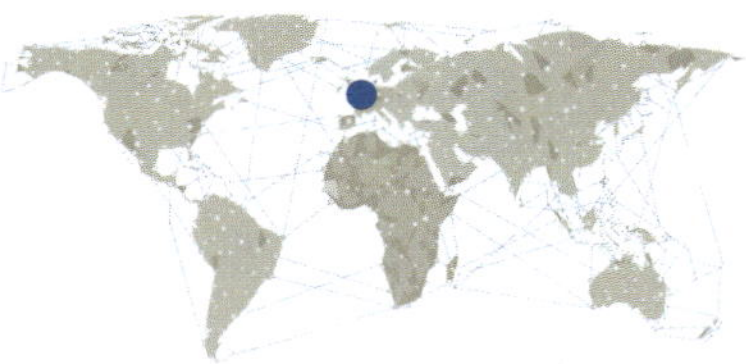

Recover E Program

EUROPE. | **THE NETHERLANDS**

Many organizations either give away their old computers or sell them off for next to nothing. The Dutch companies, Royal HaskoningDHV and Siso have looked into that loose end in the chain to see if a circular model could be applied to get these computers back into the business market. According to Sustainability Consultant Jan Paul Kimmel, "The value of the raw materials in IT equipment is considerable, especially given the foreseeable shortage of natural resources. Additionally, the computers that companies no longer want are often in good enough shape to give them a second life." Under the name Recover E Program, a non-profit foundation has been set up where computers may be donated. "We maintain ownership of the equipment and place them on the market by way of a user's contract. We then invest the money into further innovation to come up with product designs, in the beginning phase of production, that make them more adaptable to a circular existence. We also work with a track and trace system to clearly define where the resources can be found, how much there is, what the value is, when they would become available and when they can be reused. Although recycling is an issue, the more essential question is how to develop a product group in such a way that recycling is hardly needed." The Recover E Program has already garnered the interest of large companies, and may partner with the Salvation Army and a company called Fairphone to enter the consumer market as well. According to Kimmel, "Eventually, we hope that this program will provide the insight needed to make the circular model commercially attractive. Then companies and individuals won't buy computers anymore but will rent them instead." (See also Chapter 1: Customers)

The most important driver in a transactional supply chain is profit for the individual company. Whereas the most important driver of the value cycle is added value for the cycle as a whole. This value is then shared among the participants according to previously arranged agreements.

The premise is simple. Working together to create a bigger pie to share actually delivers more profit than working on your own to get a big piece of a smaller pie. Moreover, the intensive collaboration in the value cycle results in higher efficiency because all parties benefit from reducing unnecessary costs. This was put into practice when IKEA invested 1.8 billion dollars (1.5 billion euros) into clean energy in China. They put solar panels on every IKEA roof,

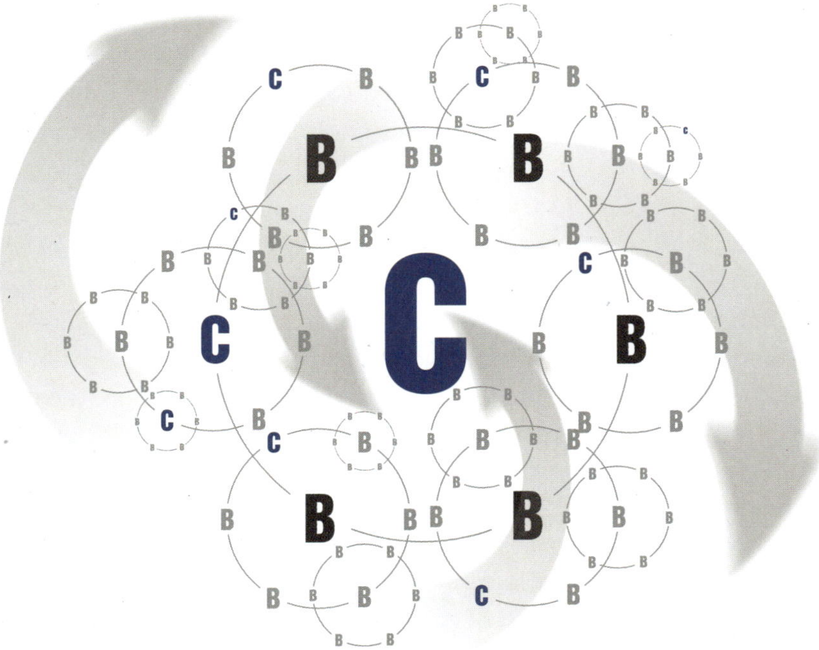

Illustration 13
From chain to cycle

but also on every Chinese IKEA supplier's roof. The Swedish company involved all of its local Chinese suppliers in its search for solar panels which would give the quickest return on investment. From this collaborative effort, IKEA made its entire chain sustainable and they all saved money.

Another example is the Dutch NGO Cordaid who set up the Sanitation Value Chain in Kisumu, the third largest city in Kenya, together with the drinking water organization Vitens Evides, and other local companies and NGOs. The Sanitation Services Company leases safe, hygienic and comfortable toilets to the public. The company also offers a disposal service, collecting the waste two or three times a week. They in turn use the waste to produce biogas, clean energy, and organic fertilizer. The fertilizer is sold to farmers in the surrounding area. The company is meant to be fully viable within five years and the project is being rolled out in twenty other cities.[43]

An umbrella platform for information exchange

Within the value cycle, associated manufacturers, logistic and financial service providers all work according to one clear protocol which is focused on maximum transparency and as little waste as possible. However, there needs to be some oversight for such a protocol to succeed. Therefore, partners in the value cycle set up an umbrella information and exchange platform (IEP). This supervisory party has insight into the flow of goods as well as the associated information and financial streams. With this overview, the return and reuse of products and resources can be well managed.

Timberland,

NORTH AMERICA | **USA, NEW HAMPSHIRE**

The American outdoor clothing and shoe manufacturer Timberland is bringing a new product to their American market, namely car tires. In the true sense of a value cycle, Timberland is using the recycling of the tires as a source of rubber for the soles of their shoes. OmniUnited, a tire factory in Singapore is helping Timberland with this new endeavor. This joint venture is not a coincidence, after all the tire and shoe industries are the biggest users of rubber. The two companies therefore joined forces to look for opportunities to use and reuse the rubber more efficiently. Now that the tires will be used as a resource for the production of shoes, Timberland is surpassing standard industry recycling efforts and they are even adding value by upscaling. Timberland has secured agreements with a number of recycling collection points to guarantee that all Timberland tires collected are returned to them. The first shoes to be made from recycled Timberland tires is expected in 2017.[44, 45]

2.3 Three rules of thumb

The value creation previously described is made possible because businesses in the new economy have embraced the following rules of thumb:

1. Collaborative efforts generate higher value than forced performance levels.
2. Long-term partnerships are more valuable than isolated transactions.
3. Value has a broader definition than financial gain.

1 Collaborative efforts generate higher value than forced performance levels

In the new economy, the initiative to close the value circle has come from market leaders who have direct or indirect access to a large customer base. They have shown the leadership necessary for this organizational transition and recognize that collaboration creates more value than forced performance.

Dutch Train Service

EUROPE | **THE NETHERLANDS, GERMANY, FRANCE**

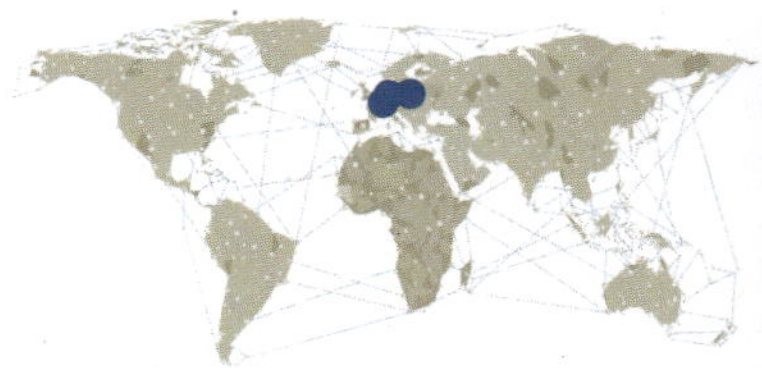

The Dutch Train Service is largely dependent on its suppliers in order to meet its sustainability targets. Therefore, they use a special assessment tool to keep track of their performance. Because the French and German train systems use many of the same suppliers as the Dutch, the three parties have started using the same tool and sharing information as of March 4, 2015.

According to Bas van Kempen, Procurement Manager, "There are 21 aspects of Corporate Social Responsibility which we are interested in examining. However, that is too many for one company to handle alone. That is why we developed a tool that can also be used in other countries." Each supplier receives a score between 0 and 100 per commodity based on the assessments of each criteria.

The tool is a big success for the Dutch Train Service. Last year the first milestone was reached with the first 100 suppliers. There was still room for improvement though explains Kempen, "We often have contact with our French and German counterparts, so it makes sense to make agreements about how to use this tool and to share the results."

The collaboration was born under the name 'Railsponsible'. In addition to the Dutch, French and German train services collaborating, industry partners Alstom and Bombardier have joined as well. "It is not only a question of efficiency, you also develop a collective norm within the rail industry."

In the traditional economy, it was still open to discussion whether contracted manufacturers and logistic services were subcontractors and what their actual added value was. In the new economy, by contrast, the added value is irrefutable and the question of subcontractor is no longer relevant. Businesses are not thinking in terms of over and under, but in terms of essential contributions to a collective endeavor which is cooperatively managed. This manifestation is already in practice at leading companies such as ASML, Philips, Intel and Apple. ASML, the Dutch producer of advanced technology systems for the computer chip industry, controls a network of companies. Each company makes a crucial contribution to the production of the end product. Furthermore, ASML's customers also play a role in the collective success.

ASML and Intel

NORTH AMERICA I **USA** EUROPE **THE NETHERLANDS**

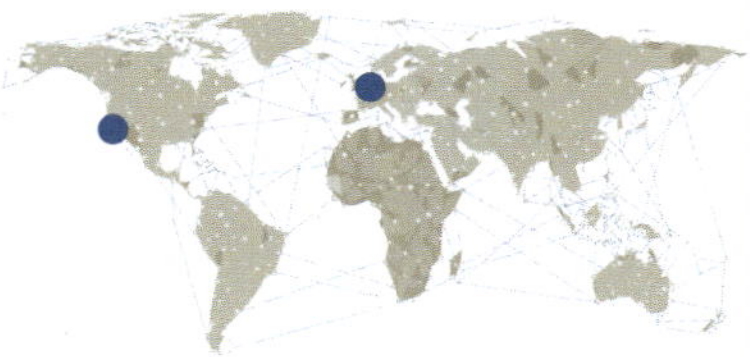

In 2012, ASML closed a unique deal with Intel, an American chip manufacturer and one of their customers. Over the next several years, Intel agreed to invest 4 billion dollars (3.3 billion euros) in ASML. From that total, nearly 1 billion dollars (830 million euros) will be added over a 5-year period to ASML's own 730 million dollar (600 million euro) budget for research and development. Moreover, Intel has already committed to buying the machines that will be developed. According to ASML, this deal will accelerate the creation of machines capable of fabricating chips for the new Extreme Ultraviolet technology (EUV).

Developing this kind of cutting edge technology requires huge investments and brings with it many risks. Although ASML is the global market leader, they are no longer satisfied with simply keeping their position and sharing costs with their clients. They realize that sharing the risks is a worthwhile model as the complexity of the chips is growing and it can be difficult to find financing for innovations. For ASML, this weighs more heavily than the idea that this model may have a slightly damaging effect on its authority in the market and on its future pricing power. Entrepreneurs understand that good business is no longer about power but about cooperation, staying innovative, and creating permanent value.[46]

2 Long-term partnerships are more valuable than isolated transactions

Creating overall value is the determining factor in the value cycle. This means that companies continue to challenge each other to come up with new solutions that add real value. For this, long-term partnerships are crucial: daring to invest in sustainable innovations should also be accompanied by the assurance of a return on that investment. That is why large and small companies are more inclined to invest in each other's innovations when they share the returns as well as the risks. This approach also makes it easier to finance innovations, and the risks become smaller for each invested party.

3 Value is not only defined as financial gain

If we talk about value creation in a broader sense, then we do not confine ourselves to only a financial definition and there is room for other kinds of contributions towards this goal. In the new economy, we often see exchanges between parties where a high level of value is created without money changing hands. Smaller entities who do not have access to a lot of capital, but do possess special expertise or other assets, especially benefit from this way of building their business.

2.4 Creative financing in the value cycle

Businesses in the new economy are approaching financing in a whole new way. In Chapter 6: Financing, the Trias Pecunia model will be explained. This model is based on three steps. The first is that businesses limit their financial needs. The second is generating long-term assurances and lowering risks by engaging in long lasting partnerships. And the third is that banks and other standard financial channels only need to be approached for the remainder of the financing. In other words, financing is not a one dimensional track that controls and colors the entire financial picture, it is a process of creating value and bringing each business case to a higher level. This approach gains its distinct shape from the way in which entrepreneurs design their value cycles. As mentioned in the introduction of this chapter, the current economic model is vulnerable to price pressures in the supply chain. This not only causes adverse consequences, it also results in a great deal of working capital being tied up in the chain - capital that should have been earning interest. This system makes it attractive for businesses to pay their bills as late as possible which in turn drives up the costs as well as the risks. And higher interest fees ensue. The unfortunate consequence of this process is that at a time when it is needed the most, it becomes even more difficult to get financing for a supply chain driven business.

The old chain is, to put it bluntly, rooted in power and control. But businesses in the new economy think differently. Their approach is cooperative, win-win, utilizing each party's strength to achieve a common goal. This also involves seeing the financing as a joint interest. After all, if one party has financial problems, everyone is affected. Businesses in the new economy apply new financial concepts which collectively contribute to lowering the working capital. Thus preventing too much money being trapped unnecessarily, building up costs instead of profits. This ultimately lowers the financing costs of the cycle as a whole.

New financial models

In a financial sense, the essence of the value cycle is for entrepreneurs to determine what they can contribute and bring that to the table. For some, it may be innovative ideas or new applications, for others it is the capability to attract financing for these innovations.

The transformation of supply chains to value cycles leads to applications of new financial models. An example is reversed invoicing which has regained popularity in recent years. To put it in a nutshell, it basically comes down to the parties in the cycle financing their working capital based on the credit worthiness of the biggest party. The party with the most capital leverage solves a 'problem' for the other parties who are bringing other valuable assets to the cycle. Reversed invoicing offers advantages for everyone and strengthens long-term relationships in the cycle.

Reversed invoicing

In contrast to traditional invoicing procedures where suppliers enlist banks or collection agencies to collect payments, reversed invoicing gives the initiative to the buyer. They send the invoices from their suppliers through to a web-based value cycle platform. This platform functions as a credit provider and quickly evaluates and approves the invoices. Based on the acceptance of the invoices, the credit provider allows the supplier to quickly collect payment. [47]

Banks also benefit from reversed invoicing. It means more turnover as they offer more loans at a lower risk. The parties they are dealing with are essentially making each other more financially sound as the cash flow improves. Lower risks for the banks translates into lower interest rates for the participants in the cycle. Thus, a positive financial spiral ensues for all parties including the financiers.

Another example of an innovative financial model is 'buyer driven payables'. This method provides the opportunity for the buyer to pay the bills early with the possibility to earn discounts. This diminishes the supplier's problems related to payment terms and ultimately eliminates the need for financing. This arrangement does not cost buyers anything extra, on the contrary, they generally get a discount. Consequently, both supplier and buyer benefit. Win-Win. [48]

Companies finance each other

Using a value cycle model, it is common practice that the participating companies play a role in financing each other. They may also expand this role by financing the suppliers of their suppliers. By including secondary suppliers, they are able to lower the financing costs for the entire production circle and increase transparency. We will examine this approach further in Section 6.1: The first two steps of the Trias Pecunia.

Value cycles are all about creating value through innovation. The innovative ideas are generated from a network of connected individuals, groups and activities. Therefore, it is necessary that the organizational structure of the participating companies is focused on knowledge exchange and utilizing the existing expertise within the network (we'll call it the 'supply cloud').

Companies recognize that although the best and most sustainable solutions are often available within the value cycle, it is still a matter of connecting the key people or groups. This connection, called the 'Social Supply Network' is facilitated on many levels. It is based on the idea that combining the expertise of many individuals creates more knowledge and leads to better decisions than depending on one expert. According to the Australian scientist Len Fisher (2009), there is what he calls 'swarm intelligence'. This form of intelligence is based on collective behavior of a decentralized, self-organized system. There is no central control structure; the collective interactions ensure the generally intelligent behavior. A swarm can quickly gain insight into new information and consequently change direction if desired. This produces more knowledge, insights and ideas than ever before. Within a large network, ideas can be validated and enriched at an early stage with insights from other angles.

Communication in the value cycle

Sharing knowledge and solutions to problems requires a different form of communication. Businesses that lack certain knowledge often do not know exactly what they are missing. There is a desire or a goal – "this is what we want" – but how to go about it is sometimes unknown. Fortunately, there is a new set of tools to work with. Social media has made networking, information exchange, and management much simpler. Regardless of time zone or location, any organization within the value cycle can post problems and utilize the collective intelligence 24/7. This leads to higher productivity in the value cycle as well as better problem-solving capabilities.

Additionally, numerous innovative platforms (based on the Facebook concept), have been gaining ground. Companies that are interested in innovative collaboration present their top talents or ideas. Personal contact is also of growing importance. For that reason, associations such as 'green business clubs' are flourishing as they allow for the kind of cross-pollinating that makes innovation so fruitful. In fact, most innovations stem from inspiration from others and from recognizing opportunities; taking a specific idea, shedding new light upon it and subsequently using it to achieve one's own goals.

2.5 Adapting the organization

When the client-supplier relationship is redefined, there are far reaching ramifications for the way companies organize themselves. To really maximize value and achieve ultimate sustainability, companies need to not only purchase and produce efficiently, they need to contribute to the cross-cycle and cross-sector expertise as well. As a result, a number of classic business disciplines acquire a whole new look and feel in the new economy.

From purchasing to value cycle management

In the traditional economy, purchasing revolves around four main tasks: ensuring continuity in the organizational processes; reducing purchasing costs; diminishing strategic vulnerability in the marketplace; and to a certain extent, contributing to product and process renewal.

In practice, this approach results in purchasers trying to secure discounts based on bulk purchases or trying to adjust the suppliers' conditions (e.g. with 'just-in-time' deliveries) in order to minimize the costs associated with too much inventory and risk. The natural consequence of this approach is to limit the dependence on specific suppliers and spread the demand for goods over several suppliers. Also, when developing new products, the purchasing department plays a role in obtaining the least expensive raw materials and semi-finished goods that meet the set requirements. As already outlined in this chapter, this 'rational and legitimate' approach throughout the chain leads to a strong focus on the lowest price and has negative consequences on sustainability.

In the new economy, purchasing is no longer primarily focused on reducing costs, but on bringing parties together who can collaborate to create maximum value. The traditional Purchaser is being promoted to Value Cycle Manager who functions as a coordinator, assessing the needs and connecting appropriate parties. This requires a different way of thinking and other broad organizational competencies. More about this in Chapter 7: Leadership.

Interface

NORTH AMERICA I **USA, GEORGIA**

Cross-sector collaborations are crucial in the new economy. An example of this is the threads that are used in Biosfera carpet tiles from Interface. For these hundred percent recycled threads, not only can old carpets be used, but Interface discovered that old fishing nets can be used as well. This is significant because old fishing nets are a burden on the environment as they are often thrown out at the end of their lifespan. Sometimes they end up in waste areas on land but often they are dumped at sea. By using these discarded nets to make new products, Interface is not only solving a problem but creating value by turning something that would otherwise be judged as waste into a resource to be used for the production of new products. They are now working together with the Zoological Society in London to overcome this pollution issue. The partnership was founded in the Philippines where not only the environmental problem is being dealt with, but also the local people are given the opportunity to create another income stream. By retrieving and collecting the discarded nets, the local fishermen become a supplier of recyclable material to a carpet manufacturer. A good example of how a clever approach can aid environmental sustainability as well as social sustainability.[49]

From product design to Lifecycle Design Strategy

In the new economy, a core principle is to use recycled, upcycled, or reusable materials and components as much as possible. This philosophy is also the basis for the value cycle which means that maximum value is created at the aggregate level if the end product is:

- Mostly made of recyclable materials;
- Able to be inexpensively disassembled and made into new products.

Therefore, the classic Product Design is currently transforming into a Lifecycle Design Strategy. Designers are not only focusing on the sustainable functions of the product, material choice, material use, product technique, and distribution, but they are now also concentrating on the environmental burden during the user phase, the lifespan of the product and the opportunities to eventually reuse, recycle, or upcycle.

A small-scale but rapidly growing company in Ghana came up with the

Bamboo Bikes Initiative. Bamboo grows naturally in Ghana and is extremely prolific. However, there are not many applications for this natural material. But building products from bamboo is actually good for the water and air quality and a bicycle made from bamboo is better equipped to cope with the bumpy African roads than its steel counterpart. Kemi Fadojutimi, Director of Bamboo Bikes explains, "whatever is thrown on the ground in Africa grows. That is certainly the case for bamboo. It grows everywhere! But we weren't doing anything with it. Our company is changing that."[50]

Nike

NORTH AMERICA | **USA, OREGON**

In order to get a handle on the sustainability of the materials they use, Nike came up with the Nike Materials Index (NMI).[51] This index shows the environmental impact of all the materials that the Product Creation Teams use. They test for water and energy use as well as chemical waste and other waste materials. Nike is one of the first manufacturers to analyze their ecological footprint for a broad range of products. And what makes their approach even more special is that Nike has made their Nike Materials Index available to their competitors. Nike has also taken further steps in this area, such as their choice to make all their sports clothes from organic cotton, making them the second largest buyer of organic cotton. Inspired by the cradle-to-cradle philosophy, the company is producing more clothes and shoes from reused materials and even making products that are one hundred percent recyclable.

Businesses in the new economy are focused on circular product design and development. In contrast to the traditional economy, they assume that their product will be reworked at the end of its lifespan. That is why materials and production methods that only lead to making cheap products are being replaced by sustainable production methods and materials that can be disassembled, recycled and reused.

Driven by competition, alliances are being forged among entrepreneurs at the beginning and the end of the product's life. Waste management facilities and manufacturers are working together to develop new techniques to improve the separation of raw materials.

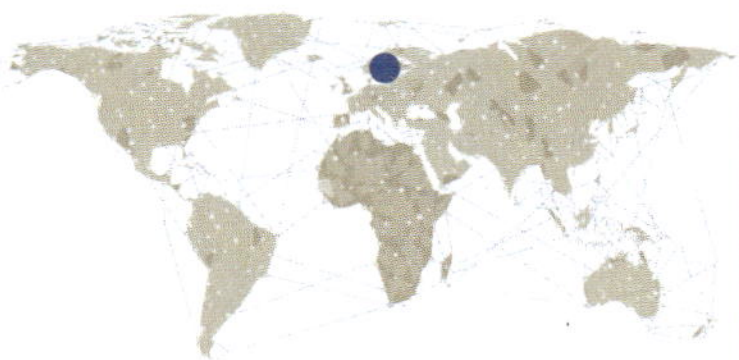

Skanska,

EUROPE | **SWEDEN**

An example of this kind of collaboration is provided by Skanska, a Swedish project development and construction group operating worldwide. They have developed an e-learning program together with their competitors to teach suppliers about building a more sustainable and efficient value cycle. Because urban areas have a gigantic impact on our worldwide carbon footprint, there is enormous profit to be made.

Skanska developed this school together with their competitors, Kier, Morgan-Stindall, Willmott-Dixon, Sir Robert McAlpine, Lend Lease, and Aggregate Industries as they were all convinced of its importance for their industry. More than 9,200 unique users from 95 different countries utilize this e-learning program. Thanks to this virtual school, Skanska has also been able to significantly reduce its carbon footprint. Incredibly, now 97 percent of its waste never sees a landfill. [52]

Additionally, businesses in the new economy are able to keep the waste that is generated during the production process to a minimum and achieve full economic value. The days when producing one five pound (2.3 kg) laptop would result in 20,000 pounds (9000 kg) of waste are definitely over. An integral part of the new value cycle is a designated entity that is in charge of collecting and re-streaming the waste generated in the production process and by the consumer. The core business of this entity is sorting, reworking, and returning the secondary resources to the various parties in the value cycle.

Collect marketing

In a linear production system, the end user is the end point of the supply chain. After the product is sold to the customer, it begins losing its value. At the end of its usefulness, the product is usually discarded or destroyed.

In the circular production system, however, the end user is, in fact, a part of the value cycle. The customer then turns into the 'supplier' of unwanted products which have raw material value.

In the new economy, companies are well aware of the new role of the consumer.

Partly because of this, they tend to set up their business model so that they retain ownership of the product, as we have seen in Chapter 1: Customers. But when this approach is not feasible, companies are coming up with other clever ways to get the products back from their customers at the end of their use so they can reintroduce them into the value cycle. As a result, we are currently seeing an ambitious marketing approach: global collect marketing. This form of marketing is not focused on stimulating sales but instead it uses the existing marketing tools to advance the concept of returning products to the producers.

For this new approach, entrepreneurs are looking at what Japan is doing. The system that they have set up for consumers to return the goods at the end of their lifespan is made so easy and accessible that it is almost more difficult not to recycle a given product. For example, old computers and accessories are picked up at the client's residence or can be sent back free of charge from any post office.

An important part of collect marketing is the convenient combination of *points of sale* with *points of collection*. A good example is the collection system that Nespresso has set up. Clients may order collection bags free of charge and give their used aluminum capsules to the delivery person when they receive their new order.[53] Another example is Philips who has opened hundreds of repair centers that serve as collection points for used electronics (e-waste). Their collection points have been responsible for the collection of half a million tons of used electronics.[54] In the new economy, we see many examples of retailers initiating brilliant concepts to keep the circular economy rolling.

Wrap up

New economy businesses have bid farewell to the supply chain. Value cycles are providing abundant opportunities to create value whereas the old supply chain offered little fertile ground. New economy businesses are activating all the parties in the value cycle, including the end user, and finding that the best and most innovative results come from collaboration. Additionally, the value cycle and the circular approach offer solutions for the emerging worldwide middle class on the one hand, and the threatening shortage of fossil fuels and natural resources on the other hand.

As we have shown, closing the loop isn't to be taken for granted. From the examples above, especially from Asia, we see that product-to-product production is not necessarily easy. It requires concerted efforts and attention from all parties involved: business, science, and government in order to yield the desired results.

New economy businesses are not outsourcing or insourcing, they are rightsourcing.

Chapter 3

WINDOW OF OPPORTUNITY:

Scale

Businesses are operating from a global perspective with overlapping geographical layers. They are global and local at the same time.

Pioneering entrepreneurs are redefining the conventional approach to globalization.

Radically innovative and inclusive approaches are being used to break open and connect markets and industries.

Introduction

In the traditional economy, a company's competitive strength is determined, to a large degree, by scale, price, and location. The scale? As big and as much volume as possible. The price? Minimize costs with large scale production. The location? Wherever capital goods, labor, and materials are the cheapest and the environmental costs the lowest. Why? That's simple. Because of tight margins, large volumes are crucial to being able to compete, grow, and increase profits. This assumption has shaped a model that has endured a long time and has gone hand in hand with the advancement of economic globalization.

To give an example of this kind of thinking, we can look at what Ronald van Zetten, CEO of the Dutch retail chain HEMA said in 2013 when he spoke about the chain's expansion to Asia. "Of course we are going after the last couple of euros that are still in the Dutch marketplace!" He shouted to a room full of HEMA employees. "But that is just not enough!" The margins that HEMA makes on its products as buyer and seller are so low that expanding to new, bigger markets is required in order to grow and make more profit. Besides the Netherlands, the retailer already has stores in Belgium, France, and Germany. And now China will be added as well.[55]

You might wonder why companies want to do business on a large scale. The answer is easy to surmise: the bigger the market, the cheaper the production costs. You can see scale expansion as an equivalent to cost leadership. Price, price, price. For that reason, in the industrial markets (such as the chemicals industry, electronics, or oil), doing business on a global scale has been a requirement for many years.

Competing primarily on cost, efficiency, and volume has had its impact on how a company functions as a whole. It means that all other facets of the business are either secondary or an extension of this model. Conducting business based on the cheapest price is inherently not sustainable. In the traditional economy, that is made very clear. Just consider the mass outsourcing of production facilities to cheap labor countries. This has led to environmental pollution, social problems, and an overflow of environmentally taxing transportation (Mitchell, 2004). The concentration of financial means and market control has caused unfair competition and the demise of independent local companies. The focus on quantity has been at the expense of quality, both in the production process and the disposal of inferior products.

The result: more waste. To illustrate, the average North American consumer buys approximately two thousand pounds (one thousand kilos) of materials per year. After six months, a mere one percent of the raw materials that were taken from the earth are still being used. (Hawken, Lovins & Lovins, 1999: 81). The amount of food waste is just as telling. The 2013 Global Food Report from the institute IMECHE, stated that 30 to 50 percent of the total food production never actually ends up being eaten.[56]

Globalization

Scale expansion has, as mentioned above, gone hand in hand with advancing economic globalization since the 1970s. *Globalization* is a much talked about phenomenon. The late Harvard professor, Theodore Levitt used this term in 1983 in one of the first publications about the topic, called "The Globalization of Markets" (Levitt, 1983). The consulting firm, SustainAbility has found, now 25 years later, at least five thousand definitions of the term.[57] A popular one is from two journalists associated with *The Economist*. They state that "Globalization is the free movement of goods, services, ideas, and people around the world."[58]

But how should we do it? Businesses in the new economy compete with a holistic perspective of scale. They do not see the burgeoning global connectedness merely as a means to maximize expansion, volumes, efficiency and price competition. Instead they search for opportunities, through cooperation, to encourage the interaction of the different markets, and the levels of scale, to create broad value for their own organization and the environments where they operate.

Whole Foods

NORTH AMERICA | **USA, NEW YORK, NEW JERSEY**

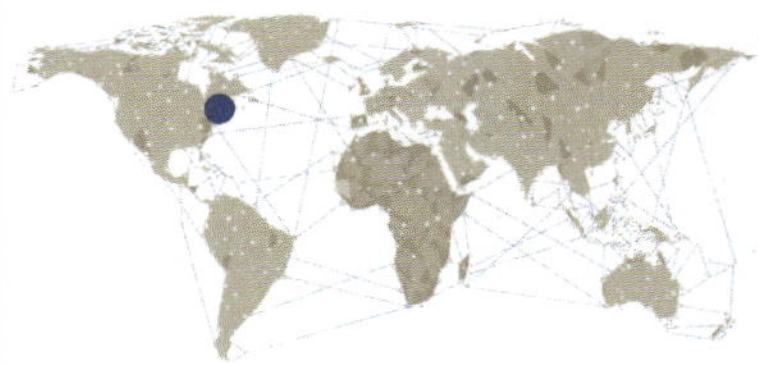

Whole Foods Market is a large supermarket chain in the United States, Canada and the United Kingdom that specializes in organic foods and local products. Last year, they opened another store in Brooklyn, New York and showed how a large, international organization can establish itself in the local community. For the construction of their new, energy efficient building, Whole Foods used wood from scaffolding in Coney Island that was destroyed by hurricane Sandy. They also used 250,000 bricks from an old building in Newark, New Jersey. In this way, they were able to reuse materials which would have otherwise gone to waste. Whole Foods also grows their own fruit and vegetables on the roof-tops of their locations. They have greenhouses full of organic produce which they sell along with hundreds of other locally produced products. With this approach, a large multinational such as Whole Foods is able to establish close ties with the local community and quickly become a mainstay in the neighborhood.[59] [60]

Their approach is also based on a circular model. The new economy and the circular model rely on strength, not power. The strength of the organization no longer depends on the ability to find a location where its products can be produced cheaply, but rather in the ability to build long-term relationships with their customers. Harvard Business School professor, Rosabeth Moss Kanter speaks of three essential, yet intangible assets that every organization should cultivate: *Concepts*, *Competence*, and *Connections*.

Concepts are cutting-edge ideas, designs, or systems for products or services that create value for customers. *Competence* is the ability to translate these ideas into high-value solutions for customers. *Connections* are the alliances built between companies to mutually strengthen their core competencies, create more value for the customers, open doors, and broaden their horizons (Moss Kanter, 2003).

In contrast to physical materials and concrete assets, these intangible qualities are not bound to a time or place, and they can quickly lose their value if they are not continually maintained, suggests Moss Kanter. Leading companies ensure adequate inventory management for these assets and keep them up-to-date by being entrepreneurial, curious and cooperative. They keep searching for better concepts and ideas and continually invest in innovation. As a result, they enrich their employees' knowledge and abilities and build alliances with others in order to broaden their competencies and achieve mutual goals.

In the new economy, competition that is based on these intangible assets results in decreasing the importance of a specific location, whereas in the traditional economy, location is a crucial part of an organization's overall strategy. The location has been important in order to control production (capital, labor, and materials) and transportation - the costs for which were kept to a minimum. In the new global, information oriented economy, the location holds strategic value if it stimulates the *concepts*, *competencies*, and *connections* and is fertile ground for them to flourish. The commercial availability of one or more of these factors determines where a particular organization will develop these activities (Moss Kanter, 2003).

Although organizations operate from a global perspective, they see the world economy as consisting of overlapping geographical layers. Therefore, they are not concentrating on only one of them but on many at the same time. They are global and local simultaneously - as long as the geographical range creates comprehensive value. Companies are organizing themselves on a variety of scale levels so they are better able to implement innovative ideas and turn them into concrete products or services for a specific market. They are cost-efficient, but not because of economy of scales.

The motto of the traditional economy is, "Big is beautiful." However, the new economy does not embrace this maxim because it blocks value creation for all assets. Therefore, the motto that is heralded by the new economy is "Small meets big" or conversely, "Big meets small." This approach is essential to the competition within the new economy. Big and small players active in different market scales achieve synergy by contributing their own specific strengths and expertise. Local, national, regional and global markets each have their unique functions that businesses can utilize in order to create maximum value.

Fuji film

EUROPE | **THE NETHERLANDS**

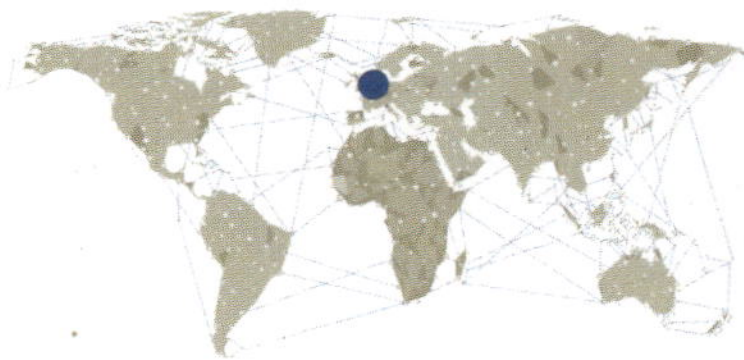

Fuji is an example of a company that has combined their worldwide clout with local knowledge and expertise. In the year 2000, film rolls still accounted for 60 percent of their profit. But by 2006, with the rapid rise of digital photography, the Dutch branch of Fuji Film had stopped making film rolls altogether.[61] They then started looking into how they could use their expertise and production techniques to develop new products. They stumbled upon a project called Blue Energy. Fuji Film went on to develop a membrane that can facilitate the generation of sustainable energy from a mixture of salt water and fresh water. "We could have waited for an assignment from the head office in Japan or we could come up with something ourselves," explained Peter Struik, Managing Director of the Dutch branch. "We opted for the latter, and began to work on this a bit 'under the radar'. By now we have become a recognized R&D facility of Fuji Film, who has consequently supplied us with extra manpower and financial backing. Our project has grown into a global initiative under Dutch leadership."

In this chapter, I will explain:

1. How entrepreneurs are creating maximum value by seeking the maximum stretch between local and global entrepreneurship.
2. How businesses in the new economy are creating symbioses through collaboration.
3. How entrepreneurs are using their market savvy in a range of scale levels to search for new opportunities and create new markets.

3.1 Glocalization: maximum global, maximum local

As described in the introduction of this chapter, enterprises compete on the basis of their global orientation and their local presence. They use the three intangible assets (*concepts, competence, connections*) to maximize value for their customers, thus securing their loyalty.

In the traditional economy, the globalization of an organization proceeded in steps. First, the local entrepreneur would become a player in the export market. He or she would operate from the home base and begin to exploit markets further away. Following this path, the business would grow to become a *multi-domestic player* – a player with many home markets. The next step would be to adopt a multinational model by establishing the organization in several countries and dividing the business activities. Lastly, the enterprise could become a real global player: a multinational with a worldwide concept without strong ties to specific countries (O'Rourke & Williamson, 1999).

This can be viewed in terms of four scale levels: local, national, regional, and global. But organizations in the new economy are not approaching these levels as a ladder to be climbed as quickly as possible. Instead, they are identifying the four different market levels and determining how their specific strengths can be applied, to their organization and to their business cases, in order to create value for a specific market.

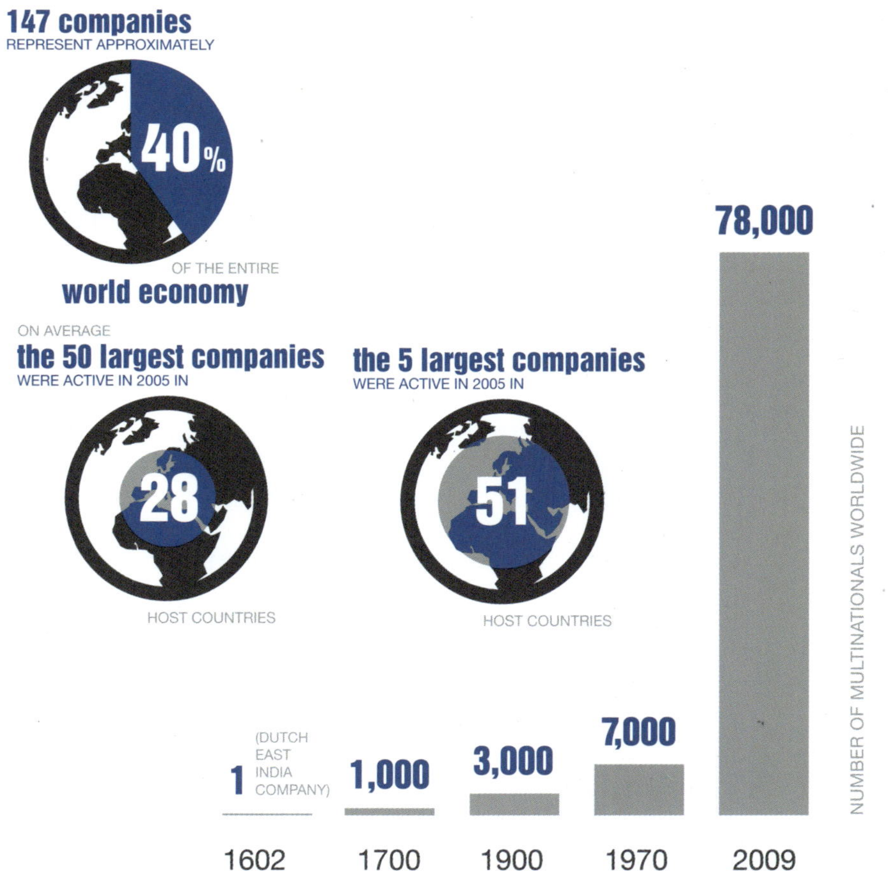

Illustration 14
Multinationals

Some sustainability pioneers of the traditional economy have brought such considerations forward in their plea for decentralization and localization: "Small is beautiful," claims Ernst Friedrich Schumacher, who in 1973 wrote about the dark shadow of globalization. Why should you get your things from China if they can also make it around the corner? We should make more products right here in our home country where there is control of the labor conditions, where there are some regulations of the sustainable use of natural resources and where you don't need to arrange transportation to carry the goods thousands of miles in order to get the products into our supermarkets or clothing stores. The advocates of a predominantly local economy argue that local production appeals to the modern consumer. Customers want to know where the products are made, how they are made and what materials are used. It also fits in well with an economy that is based on actual demand instead of building on the myth of insatiability. Other entrepreneurs bring up the economic necessity of a primary local economy. They see that energy and resource prices are soaring and foresee the demise of their business model if they remain dependent on them.

New economy businesses therefore are choosing not to *outsource* or *insource*, but to '*rightsource*'. In other words, they are creating the structures and connections that create maximum value. In this way, neither rigid localization nor strict decentralization is the answer. Organizations in the new economy are applying *both* globalization and localization principles to create maximum value and sustainability. Globalization in the new economy is not only seen in the international flow of raw materials and products, but globalization can also be of a digital nature. Localization is incorporated and does not necessarily preclude taking advantage of worldwide developments and opportunities. Localization focuses on implementation and interaction at a local level.

SCOPEinsight,

AFRICA | **KENYA** SOUTH AMERICA | **GUATEMALA**

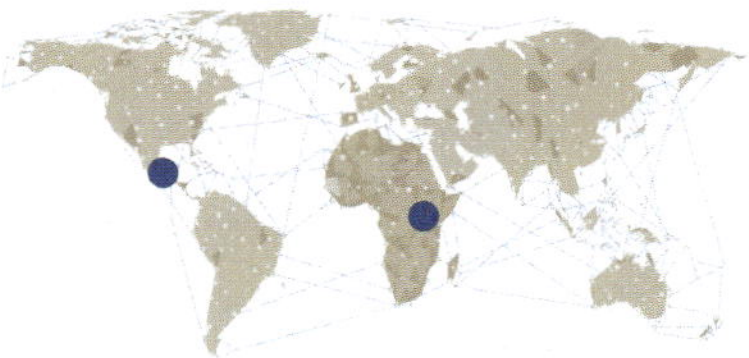

The Dutch company, SCOPEinsight, is an example of how this works. SCOPEinsight is an agricultural business. This sector is seen as one of the worst offenders in the traditional economy. According to SCOPEinsight's CEO, Lucas Simons, "The agricultural industry is the highest contributor of CO_2 emissions, is responsible for the most deforestation, destroys biodiversity like no others, is guilty of child exploitation, and the list goes on." Meanwhile, the agricultural industry is being confronted with food shortages and the gap between supply and demand is predicted to grow more pronounced in the decades to come.

Because the world population needs to use every bit of land available to deal with the growing demand for food, SCOPEinsight has set out to help farmers in Africa and South America expand their businesses in a cost effective and sustainable way. How can they do that? By providing financing. Many of the farms there are actually too big to qualify for microcredit although they are not in need of large, million dollar loans. They might need a loan in the tens of thousands of dollars. However, a bank in Nairobi, for example, would not be motivated to visit a rural farm located 1200 miles (2000 kilometers) away for that kind of loan. The problem is that without this assessment, a bank will not extend a loan. "We have therefore created a rating system and an associated online tool for this purpose." Simons explains. "We evaluate the farmer based on all the relevant points, place the report and the rating online for banks to easily access it, which allows them to obtain the required information at a fraction of the regular due diligence expense. "As a result, Simons has created a new market by closing the gap between the small, local farmers and the large, national or regional banks. "We have chosen to not simply give money to the poorest people in the country, nor to subsidize the governments. We have decided instead to aim at empowering a specific group who can create value for the poorer populations as well as for the economy as a whole."

As Thomas Friedman described in his bestseller, *The World is Flat*, and as the above example shows, the combination of technology and globalization opens new doors for companies. This is also discussed in Chapter 0: The New Economy, when we refer to the digital and mobile revolutions. Businesses have gained access to target groups that were unreachable for them a decade ago.

Entrepreneurs are using digital and mobile technology to share knowledge and create connections with other parties on every market level. These connections add value because of their local dimension as well as utilizing the benefits of a larger scale. This can be seen with our example of SCOPEinsight who has connected farmers and banks by implementing an online tool.

New economy businesses are looking for the maximum geographical range for their business, not because they want to become big (or small) for the sake of it, but to create value for the organization. They continually ask themselves the following questions: What is the most local scale and the most global scale where I can play a role in creating value? How can localization strengthen my business? (e.g. by aiding strong customer relationships through local presence and visibility). And how do my global scale opportunities, capital strength, network connections and available knowledge add value to my business?

Illustration 15
Maximum geographical range

In order to determine their maximum localization and globalization, I am convinced that businesses in the new economy base their strategy on five principles. Then they determine whether this creates value for the three primary assets of our economy, namely the ecological, social and financial assets (See Chapter 0: The New Economy).

1. **Global strength, local establishment**
   Local communities are not adverse to international companies and brands, but they do value local businesses and pay attention to the connections that international parties have with the local business establishments. Organizations in the new economy offer their customers value within the context of their local environments. After all, this is what is really important to the customer, not what is happening at the head office.
2. **Ideal infrastructure for global exchange of information and knowledge**
   Seamless knowledge and information exchange is crucial for a sustainable market to function. The developments in information technology and the internet are pivotal factors in facilitating this infrastructure. Companies that can navigate this well have a competitive edge. In this respect, it is vital that businesses in underdeveloped countries can find connections and also profit from the advantages of the global economy. According to Bastiaan Zoeteman, a professor at Tilburg University, "At the moment, however, what we find in poor countries is that this is reserved for the elite. Consequently, it is imperative that the governments there ensure that people in their country are connected and therefore able to take advantage of what the global economy has to offer while also applying and maintaining international regulations to prevent the negative influences of globalization, such as high levels of local pollution or poor labor conditions. Unfortunately, it is often the case that governments in these countries do not make these provisions a priority. Consequently, the responsibility is laid at the foot of the international companies to do business in a socially responsible manner."
3. **Minimal transport of raw materials, goods, products and people**
   As energy neutral transport on a large scale is not yet possible, new economy businesses are looking to limit the transport of raw materials, goods, products and people by setting up production facilities near their consumer markets. Furthermore, fewer business

trips are being planned in the new economy. Instead, IT solutions such as video conferences are being used more often.

4. **Focus on creating value**
   New economy businesses are based on achieving a sustainable triple play: creating *ecological*, *social*, and *financial* value. Given this premise, an organization would only become active in a given market if it is useful and creates value – not only for the company but also for the community. This is vital to establishing long-term value.
5. **Cooperation with governments**
   Businesses in the new economy are open to working together with governments and civic parties.

It is well understood in the new economy that the best, or most sustainable ideas do not always stem from the R&D department at the international head office. They often come from the local level. This is where the contact with the customers is most intense and where it is best known what the customers actually want. Sometimes knowledge centers or 'talent towns' are set up at the regional level which can also prove to be fertile ground for innovation and technological creativity.

Companies also realize that in order to cultivate a good concept, an international and intercultural 'one-size-fits-all' strategy does not lead to success. So, in order to succeed, they take intangible factors into consideration, such as local fashion trends, language and cultural norms and values. (Ekekwe, 2012).

At the same time, they may use their global networks if this helps to form a complete business case. In short: depending on the size of the company, a CEO in the new economy ensures cooperation on a global level, finds partners on the regional level or makes connections with innovative companies on a local level. In this way, large parties utilize the expertise from smaller businesses and small businesses are also in a better position to find partners for their innovations and market them on a large scale. There is a fruitful exchange, on different market levels, between innovators, creators, traders and financiers. "The globalization of the supply chain generates a reaction from the consumer as well as the business owner," adds Ernst Worrell, professor of Energy, Material and Environment at the University of Utrecht. "While the average consumer is interested in local good quality products as well as protecting his or her local environment, businesses are more interested in choosing the right place to locate their production facility. Therefore, the search for synergy – with their customers, other businesses in the chain, and at location by forming clusters– is needed in order to go beyond the old business model.”

Co-ops

A development that has grown from this search for synergy is the emergence of co-ops. These local initiatives for communal consumption, such as collective energy arrangements, sharing of transportation, or local crops are examples of initiatives that interact or have the potential to interact with larger players.

In the new economy, companies are recognizing the value and strength of local initiatives. The division of roles between local, national and global therefore becomes even more interesting. The productive relationship between the different levels also leads to a better competitive position.

The growth of co-ops in the area of energy consumption is spreading internationally, says Anne Marieke Schwencke who conducted research into ‘new utilities’. “You can see it as an international trend. Some are calling it ‘Glocalization’: a renewed appreciation for the local without throwing the fruits of globalization overboard. Everything at just the right scale. It can also be seen as a partial turnaround: ‘globalization reversing’. Taking a couple of steps back even, then looking around and seeing what we risk losing, then cheerfully moving forward. No nostalgic longing for the good old days, but a clear reversal of two decades of globalization, scale expansion, and increased complexity (with all the chaos and confusion that goes with it), to focusing on a more humane approach. A good example is the ‘transition town’ movement which came from England and inspired people to pursue sustainable energy. Comparable cross-fertilization can also be seen in food (Urban Farming) and the economy (‘Great transition’ from England; ‘Degrowth movement’ from France)” (Schwencke, 2012).

3.2 Symbiosis through cooperation

Innovative entrepreneurs realize that they increase their competitive edge when they stop seeing globalization merely as a means to decrease production costs. Instead, they are looking at globalization as a way to set up and connect markets in order to create holistic value for their business case and for the environments where they directly or indirectly operate.

An example of how businesses are exploring ways to use the strength of their local environments to build connections with global networks is given by the Dutch start-up FlexSol Solutions. They have developed solar panels that are twice as efficient as the current 'thin film' technology. These new solar panels can be used on street lanterns and as roof tiles, but can also be used for car roofs without needing to make any esthetic concessions. The founder, Lennert van den Berg, has even bigger ambitions. He wants to create fully automated production lines in movable facilities. "Think of a kind of sea freight container which can be moved to allow us to produce in the Middle East or in America, near where the raw materials come from."[62]

FlexSol Solutions wants to serve the global market but looks for advantages that can be gained by thinking local as well. Other businesses in the new economy have the same approach. They not only exploit their close proximity to productive resources, but also the proximity to their industrial partners as well. This leads to industrial ecosystems where companies can exchange their byproducts such as waste water, warmth, biogas, electricity and refuse within their closed circle. By achieving 'localization', companies enjoy economic and ecological benefits: less raw materials, less transport, less waste, less space needed, and better opportunities for recycling and reuse. Moreover, they are better able to meet the different local consumer needs.

To summarize: the concentration of companies on a local level, in business centers and industrial parks, presents the opportunity to take advantage of lower costs that would have been beyond the reach of each individual company. By grouping their local production systems, they are more flexible and are in a better position to meet the demands of their clients. Clustering also facilitates the exchange of personnel and knowledge. Furthermore, the spread of technology is creating opportunities to profit from improved efficiency.

Ecosystems

We can find a number of successful local ecosystems in a variety of places in Europe. An internationally known example is the Eco-Industrial Park in Kalundborg, Denmark where industrial organizations and networks are set up within close proximity to one another. By doing so, they are in a position to use each other's byproducts and share resources in order to create collaborative cost reduction. At the center is the Asnæs electricity plant. Asnæs not only supplies energy to the surrounding businesses and community, they also provide byproducts that are used by other industries, such as elements that can be used for cement and drywall production as well as road construction. Another example is the steam from the electricity plant that is taken and used by Novo Nordisk, a pharmaceutical company. By using the steam that is emitted by Asnæs, Novo Nordisk can reduce the amount of thermally contaminated water, which of course benefits the surrounding fjords. This is also cost effective for Asnæs because it allows them to provide more energy and warmth to the surrounding 3,500 houses as well as to the local fishery. This fishery, in turn, sells its refuse to be used as fertilizer. The industrial symbioses saves Kalundborg approximately 15 million dollars a year, reduces the use of ground water (1.9 million cubic meters) and surface water (1 million cubic meters) and dramatically decreases the use of oil (20,000 tons) and plaster (20,000 tons).[63]

Urban ecosystems

Cities such as Hamburg, Copenhagen, and Stockholm are on the forefront of interconnecting eco-relevant processes, introducing cycles, and focusing on sustainable technology. They differentiate themselves by having a holistic approach to sustainability which goes hand in hand with renewable energy, sustainable construction and living, recycling and waste management, and sustainable mobility.

The fact that every local ecosystem has a different starting point and situational factors makes it difficult to have one umbrella concept. The Dutch company Suiker Unie shows how organizations look to create maximum multiple value by joining their own local value cycles with other local value cycles.

Suiker Unie

EUROPE | **THE NETHERLANDS**

Suiker Unie, a division of the Royal Cosun group, is an example of a company who thinks globally but also exploits its local leverage at several of its production locations. According to Erik van Hellemond, a project leader in the biobased technology department of Suiker Unie, in addition to optimizing your own value cycle, connecting value cycles to create new opportunities is vital. Suiker Unie wants to connect their own sugar production with others on a large scale.

Additionally, the company is especially looking into acquiring its products from higher up in the value cycle. Van Hellemond explains, "Our goal is to not create any waste anywhere within our entire production line – from beets to sugar. The idea is to use whatever byproducts are generated to make other products. From beets we make sugar, but the leftover molasses is a resource that can be used in the fermentation industry to make yeast. The filtrate from the purification process is reworked into betacal, a valuable calcium rich fertilizer that contains minerals from the beets. The beet pulp can be used as cattle feed and is also a valuable source of energy and minerals that is useful in a variety of compounds. At the moment, we are making 'green' gas from it and will probably make chemicals from it in the future. We are focusing now on figuring out how we can connect our value circles with others in order to build a real bio-based economy. In addition to proteins, we are talking about the organic building blocks for chemistry, and the natural resources needed to make polymer. There is much research and many initiatives within Cosun to see how we can work together with other parties to use the pulp or the sugar to make biopolymer for plastics or fibers. There are concrete plans to build pilot plants for this purpose."

At the Suiker Unie location in Dinteloord, the Netherlands, a water factory has been built where processed purified water from the sugar factory is turned into fresh water that can be used for the green-houses in the nearby area of Nieuw Prinsenland. In May, 2013 the factory became operational. Paul Hagens, the manager of terrain development, responsible for the Nieuw Prinsenland business terrain said, "The filtered and processed water is usually dumped in the river. In the new water factory, the salts are removed using a specialized membrane filter so that the water is suitable for the plants growing in the greenhouses. By using our byproduct, they no longer have to extract ground water or take water from the river for their needs."

We also see businesses in the new economy exploiting the concept of symbiotic cooperation on the national level by clustering industrial ecosystems. On a national level, it can sometimes be easier to make a circular sustainable business case. This is because multiple partners, located in broad geographical locations can all participate. The specific advantages of each of their locations can be utilized on a large scale – for example, a given location may serve as a point of entry for a large region.

Industrial symbiosis sometimes also requires a large scale for it to be feasible or efficient. For instance, the river area of a European region such as the European Benelux triangle: Eindhoven (high-tech), Delft (engineering) Leuven and Aachen (ELAt – high tech region). This transnational, but geographically compact, area has the ambition to grow into one of the top European technological regions. But this is only possible if companies work together and the value cycles and networks that they participate in become integrated into one industrial ecosystem.

Thanks to the availability of specific natural resources and byproducts, we are also seeing regional production networks in the new economy that rework these base materials to make a wide range of new products.

Graz,

EUROPE | **AUSTRIA**

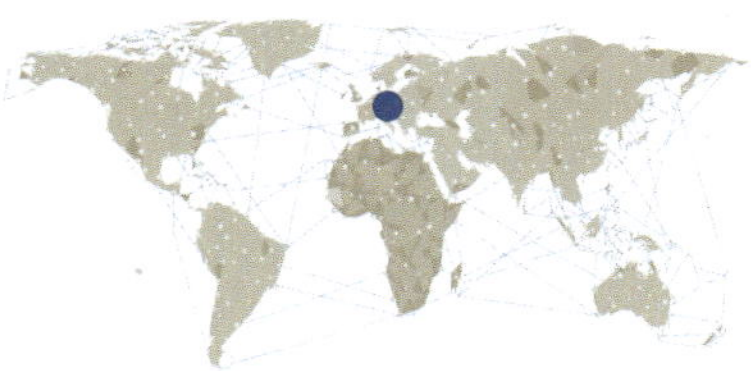

In the region of Graz in Austria, there are already networks within sectors such as the agricultural industry which connect companies who produce waste and byproducts to companies who rework and use those waste products. This connection allows businesses to save on the costs for resources by using the byproducts from other companies. Sometimes the 'waste' products are even of a higher quality than the original raw material. In addition to the economic advantages for the individual companies, the entire region profits economically and ecologically because of the recycling system. Excess warmth or ash, used oil or solvents, and plastics can all be distributed throughout the system (Konz & Van den Thillart, 2002).

3D-printing

An important driver for the explosive increase in local and regional production is the arrival of 3D printing. Otherwise known as 'additive manufacturing'. This new technique creates a whole new playing field for the distribution of products and the use of new materials. Worldwide product distribution is, in fact, an old fashioned business model that may soon become obsolete: any desired part, whether it is made of plastic, metal, ceramic, or other materials can now be printed on the spot anytime, anywhere. And this is also without (or hardly) producing any waste as this technique uses only the materials that are needed instead of taking away the materials that are superfluous, which is often the case for metal or woodworking.

In the new economy, additive manufacturing will become a full-fledged part of an industrial production system. Companies will be in a position to locally produce whatever is needed right then and there. Whether it is high volumes of parts for electronic devices, or consumer products such as shoes or telephone cases, or unique products such as tailor-made prostheses and other specialized prosthetics.

The new economy will consequently be known for its client-specific, tailor made solutions for the masses. This will result in lower costs and a new range of possibilities which will lead to the development of new products. By also integrating IT software, new materials, new production processes and web applications, a large part of the industrial production will, by definition, become local. The home market will provide ample opportunities for experimentation. For the mass market, borders must be crossed and international partners will also be sought so that products can be rolled out locally in the most cost and energy efficient way possible.

In some situations a different scale is necessary. It could be because the development costs are too high or because products cannot be produced profitably in the home country. With this in mind, it is important to note that *local* is not sacred and *global* is not evil. On the contrary, international business in the new economy is all about oversight. Businesses that recognize the three layers and employ a total concept that uses the unique selling propositions (USPs) of local, regional, and global business are in a better position to make connections. This is not only desirable for the long term but absolutely necessary. The economy is simply becoming less bound to geographical borders.

3.3 Markets: Breaking open and creating new markets

Businesses in the new economy are using their knowledge of the various scale levels to look for opportunities to break open markets, transform existing markets or create brand new markets.

They recognize that societal needs (not only the conventional economic needs) can also denote markets and generate market opportunities (Porter & Kramer, 2011). It has also been determined that damage to the social assets of an economy results in internal costs, such as wasted energy, exhaustion of natural resources, accidents caused by unsafe work situations, and extra training as a result of poor education. In the new economy, business are therefore purposefully incorporating such societal needs and limitations into their strategy. This way they can focus their innovation and adopt the appropriate new technology, methods, and management structures (Porter & Kramer, 2011). Ultimately, they are strengthening their competitive position, expanding their productivity, and renewing, enlarging, and creating markets.

However, as mentioned earlier, not everyone is in a position to profit from the advantages of globalization. This means that large groups of potential consumers and businesses are still being ignored. Additionally, the strong growth of a number of developing countries has increased the competition on western markets which has resulted in lower profit margins and saturated markets.

As a result, multinational organizations in the new economy are expanding their focus to the emerging economies. This offers new opportunities for sustainable developments due to the rapid growth of the middle classes. In addition to the traditional markets (i.e. the developed countries and the global or transnational market segments), they are focusing on the rapidly developing BRIC countries (Brazil, Russia, India, and China) and other countries on the rise with comparable economies (The Next 11) as well as the poorer populations who live in some of these countries.[64]

The strategic challenge facing multinationals in the new economy is not defining a global strategy, but choosing a 'semi-global' strategy. For this they need a separate strategy for each region.

In order to create these strategies, multinationals can define their sales markets in three different ways: as a Consumer Economy; as a Rising Economy; or as a Survival Economy (Hart & Milstein, 1999).

1 **Consumer economy**
These are worldwide economies driven by consumer spending and high consumption. This market consists of the richest billion people in the world.

2 **Rising economies**
The emphasis for this market is on finding energy efficient sources that can accommodate the rising incomes, and consumption, of the demographic shift from rural areas to urban centers.

3 **Survival economies**
For this market, it is important to develop innovative solutions. These economies represent a large part of the world population who has very little money to spend. An example can be seen in Chapter 4: Innovation, where the innovative Pureit, produced by Unilever, is described. Pureit is a home water purification installation which provides clean drinking water to poverty stricken people in India for only two cents per liter.

AN AMERICAN CONSUMER CONSUMES **17X as much** AS THE AVERAGE MEXICAN CONSUMER AND **100X as much** AS THE AVERAGE ETHIOPIAN

Market renewal or market creation in the Consumer Economy is often linked to technological innovation. Information Technology (i.e. the interactive digital revolution that is described in Chapter 0: The New Economy) plays a large role in this. This makes sense, of course, because IT is already an established component in the Consumer Economy and there have been many spectacular and revolutionary market innovations by IT parties. Take, for example, the pervading revolution in the music market by Apple's iTunes.

While IT is integral in the Consumer Economy and has brought about a great deal of innovation and renewal, it is not enough to transform the markets. These markets have often become, in the course of time, colossal, unwieldy oil tankers. In this respect, technology is too interwoven with existing business models to effect a real paradigm shift.

Better Place

NORTH AMERICA I **USA, CALIFORNIA**

Better Place is a company located in Silicon Valley. It is an excellent example of an enterprise that has combined technological innovation with a radically new business model in order to break open an industry. Although the company had to file for bankruptcy in 2013 due to a lack of financing, the story of their innovative business model is too powerful to overlook. The issue that Better Place addressed was in the electric car arena. The problems faced in the electric car market are: the batteries are expensive which substantially increases the cost of the car; the batteries have a limited life; and current infrastructures are based on cars that run on gasoline. So instead of focusing on the question of how to fit the use of electric cars into the existing system, the founder of Better Place asked himself what system would be needed to make electric cars as comfortable, effective and affordable as gas driven cars (Johnson & Suskewicz, 2009).

Better Place figured that it made sense to separate the ownership of the car from the ownership of the battery. Therefore, the battery is no longer built into the car but is designed to be replaceable. So users no longer buy the expensive battery together with the car but instead pay per mile for the use of the battery. An extensive network of battery exchange stations and a tracking system that directs the user to the nearest station ensures convenience and comfort. As the costs per mile, including battery, service, and electricity are less than the cost of gasoline, Better Place can use its margins to subsidize the purchase of electric cars. (Boons & Lüdeke-Freund, 2013).

Illustration 16
Facts & figures world population, economies

In the new economy entrepreneurs are looking for radically innovative, inclusive methods to find opportunities to break open markets or industries. There are numerous opportunities to create or maintain value ecologically, socially and financially in the fields of energy, transport, industry and agriculture without asking customers to make concessions in their comfort, convenience, or expense.

Businesses in the new economy are not much different in their approach to markets and industries in developing countries. However, where they differentiate themselves is the acute awareness of the vulnerability of these markets. Therefore, they ask themselves the following hard questions to determine if they are truly adding value:

- Is it ecologically desirable to double or triple the size of the industry?
- Which factors would prevent the growth of the industry?
- Is it feasible to fulfill consumer demand without exhausting the natural resources?
- Is it viable to make the leap to clean production methods?
- How can we satisfy the growing consumer demand without catalyzing problems caused by the associated urbanization?

One of the most important innovations for developing markets is renewable energy. This makes sense because the demand for energy will grow exponentially in the coming years. Entrepreneurs are aware of this market demand and are already investing in sustainable solutions. They are also looking at the growing demand for wood which forebodes increased deforestation and scarcity.

Developing countries (defined by Hart and Milstein in 1999 as 'Survival Economies') are the most vulnerable economies. Consumers in these markets often live in dilapidated neighborhoods on the outskirts of cities or in remote rural areas. They try to provide for themselves by growing crops or foraging. Further growth in the world population will have a big impact on Survival Economies.

Entrepreneurs in the new economy see tremendous opportunities to create value in these markets. From a commercial standpoint, this would be in the area of improving and implementing energy efficiency and sustainable applications, and the improvement of living conditions for the local communities. This large group of potential customers can be a substantial source of income for companies, provided that they first put some concerted effort into the improvement of the local environment and the standard of living for the people in these areas. To do this, unconventional business models are required.

Organizations that are active in Survival Economies should ask themselves the following questions:

- How can our products and services be a commercial success while also having a positive influence on the quality of life for the people living in the market area?
- Are we blinded by our current business model?
- Are we overlooking any market opportunities?
- How can we build a client base that will flourish and create new market demands - thus creating more business opportunities in the future?
- How can modern technology be adapted to satisfy the consumer needs of this target group?

Zain

AFRICA | **MADAGASCAR** ASIA | **KUWAIT**

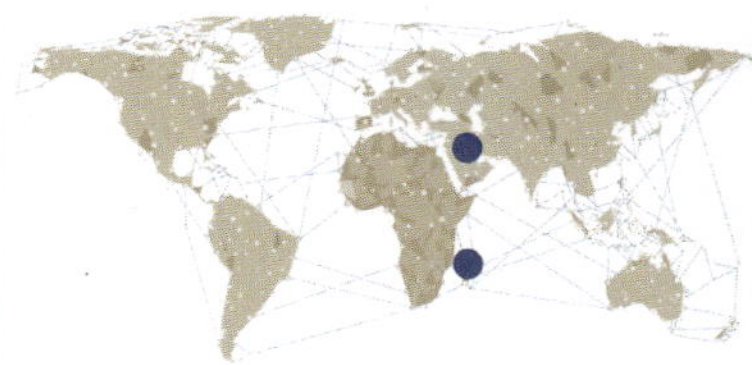

To further expand their market share in Madagascar, the telecom company Zain chose a new, innovative market strategy. The company not only established hundreds of new base stations to considerably expand the coverage in the country (in 2007, a mere 5 percent of the population had access to telecommunication), they also launched the Village Phone Program (VPP). This program was initiated so that the base of the consumer pyramid could be reached despite the fact that they do not have the money to buy a cell phone. The business model of the VPP assumes one telephone will be shared by several users. The telephone is owned by a micro-business, namely the Village Phone Operator (VPO) who gets 25 percent of the proceeds for each telephone. Every village telephone is able to connect to the established telephone networks. This is significant as often sparsely populated areas are not deemed profitable enough to justify the investment of putting conventional networks into their areas.

In order to develop the VPP model, Zain opted for a long-term agreement with the financier IFC. They lent Zain 25 million dollars, secured 21 million more from borrowed capital and provided Zain with the knowledge and expertise to develop this model. With the help of six microfinance institutions (MFI), Zain founded more than six thousand micro-businesses, created financial structures for business investments, and arranged training for the VPOs.

Thanks to the Village Phone Program, Zain became the frontrunner in providing broad geographical telecommunications coverage in Madagascar. The result of which is a commercial success story. Between 2008 and 2009, Zain saw the number of users grow by 60 percent to 1,425,000 customers, taking the market share up by 2 percent and providing the 6,600 VPOs an average monthly income of 16 dollars which is a substantial amount for the average wage earner in Madagascar. The VPOs facilitate approximately 1,130,000 telephone calls per month totaling 565,000 minutes (Jenkins et al 2010: 42).

Wrap up

New economy businesses are strategically positioning themselves in the global economy while embedding themselves locally. Local ventures create strong bonds with the community and allow them to become rooted in the home market. Global expansion presents the opportunity to capitalize on worldwide knowledge and expertise. In order to profit from the many new opportunities, entrepreneurs are exploring the maximum range between local and global business endeavors.

They are focusing on building connections (See Chapter 0: The New Economy) as this is viewed as the accelerator of business opportunities, market position and client expansion. These connections are also being utilized to form business ecosystems which are both profitable and sustainable. Scarce resources are being used efficiently and value is being created and maintained for ecological, social and financial assets while consumers are not being asked to make any concessions regarding comfort, convenience or expense.

Technology is also changing the landscape of business and production. Remote areas are becoming connected and accessible, and with 3D printing, transport of parts will become unnecessary in the near future. By continually innovating and challenging conventional market approaches and structures, entrepreneurs in the new economy are breaking open and creating new markets.

Survival of the most adaptable is the new economy credo.

Chapter 4

WINDOW OF OPPORTUNITY:

Innovation

Open innovative processes create competitive advantages.

Networks and innovative ecosystems facilitate the exchange of knowledge and expertise.

Intellectual property (IP) takes on an active role in the new economy.

Home water purification device

EUROPE | **ENGLAND** ASIA | **INDIA**

Unsafe drinking water is a major public health issue, particularly in developing countries where around 80% of diseases are water borne. As a result, in 2010, the United Nations declared that access to 'safe and clean drinking water and sanitation is a human right essential to the full enjoyment of life'. However years of efforts by NGOs and governments has been unable to produce a sustainably scalable solution.

Given this context, as part of the Unilever Sustainable Living Plan, Unilever established a team of experts headed by Vice President Yuri Jain to address this global problem. Within a few years, with the support of over a hundred experts from all over the world, the team developed 'Pureit' – a domestic water purification system. 'Pureit' represents a very significant technological breakthrough, simultaneously addressing a number of existing challenges in the quest for a scalable safe water solution. Pureit meets stringent international germ-kill standards for effective removal of viruses, bacteria and parasites from torturous water conditions - without using electricity, or pressurised tap-water - making it suitable for any kind of settings - urban or far-flung rural areas. And this has been achieved at a price that is affordable to low-income people in the developing world. What's more, Pureit's carbon footprint is at least 80% lower than the other available alternatives of boiling water or using bottled water.

In addition to Pureit, in 2014, Unilever acquired Qinyuan, one of China's pilot national enterprises in innovation and the market leader in water purifiers in China, adding significantly to Unilever's global technical capability, especially with respect to tackling the rapidly growing problem of excessive dissolved salts in drinking water and providing additional features that include in-built hot and cold water options.

With a geographic footprint spanning key D&E markets, and a much wider and stronger assortment of products and technologies, Unilever aims to provide 150 bn liters of safe drinking water by 2020.

Introduction

Chief Executive Officers (CEOs) in the traditional economy often speak about a devil's dilemma when it comes to sustainable innovation. They need to choose, they say, between the social and the ecological advantages of sustainable innovations and developments on the one hand, and the complexity of a comprehensive change and substantial investment on the other hand. While this may sound plausible, it is not.

Of course, their arguments are plentiful: 1) Developing sustainable products puts us at a disadvantage compared to the cheap, throw-away items being mass produced in developing countries. 2) Suppliers can't become sustainable. 3) Consumers don't want to pay for sustainability – especially in times of a financial crisis. And the list goes on. These arguments may sound reasonable at first, but the facts simply do not support them. For example, an American survey (Nimumolu, Prahalad & Rangaswami, 2009) of thirty large companies showed that sustainable innovations resulted in cost reductions and increased revenues. Savings are achieved because resources are used more efficiently and revenues are increased because the innovations lead to better products and new business models.

For innovation to be profitable, entrepreneurs need to transform their line of thinking when it comes to products, processes, and technology. They need to set the bar higher if they are going to contribute to the ecological, social and financial assets of our economy instead of depleting them. Entrepreneurs in the new economy are very aware of this need for a different approach and therefore integrate all three primary assets. That is exactly what led to Unilever's invention of the Pureit (See Case Study: Home Water Purification Device). Unilever's sustainable ambitions even stretched further than the current technological possibilities. However, by focusing their innovative process on creating something of value – in the deeper context of the word – they were able to achieve their goal and then some.

Sustainable innovation is a regular part of new economy business. Actually, when you think about it, sustainability, business, and innovation are becoming intertwined. After all, if you produce a bicycle made of one hundred percent renewable materials (innovation related to sustainable goals) or you develop clean fuel in an attempt to improve the performance of an engine (sustainability as a result of innovation), the ultimate result is the same: higher revenues for your organization; stronger customer appeal; and ecological, social and financial value.[65]

Innovation, based on creating comprehensive value inherently differs from innovation in the traditional economy which is centered around the concept of ownership, control and "being the first." In the traditional economy, companies would have their own R&D departments, innovate within linear chains, and avidly protect their intellectual property. This approach is economically sensible and functional in the traditional economy. In fact, for situations where scale plays a crucial role in the earnings model, maintaining control is a necessity. If you do not retain oversight of your intellectual property, you run the risk of losing your costly investments.

However, this kind of closed innovation is losing out to the open, collective, and sustainably driven innovation of the new economy. The new trend is innovation that goes beyond the borders of one's own organization and supply channels. Shared ideas result in shared success. Traditional innovation principles no longer produce adequate solutions in our current fast-paced, complex economy. Functioning on its own, an internal R&D department cannot keep up with the advances in ICT (Information and Communications Technology), new market connections, new materials, and other complex technology. Innovators in the new economy therefore concentrate on building collaborative networks which lead to highly profitable, value creating innovation.

SimGas,

AFRICA | **TANZANIA, KENYA**

SimGasTanzania is a Dutch company that established a cooperation with the local company Silafrica Tanzania.[66] The product of this cooperative effort is the Gesi550, a bio-container that uses a fermentation process to turn waste materials into a usable form of gas. The gas that is produced is suitable to use for cooking. Using this process, the average household can save up to 80 percent on its energy expenses and the demand for wood as fuel is reduced by up to 60 percent. While this is impressive, the benefits go even further, the residue that is left over after the waste is turned into gas can be used as fertilizer for agricultural land. Making this innovation not only sustainable but truly valuable across many sectors.[67]

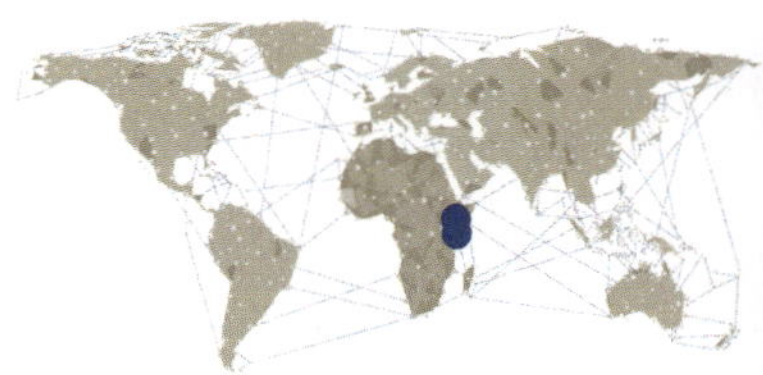

Innovation in the new economy also provides better solutions for the modern consumer who is well-educated, more informed, critical and outspoken. Consumers want to know where a product is made, where the resources come from, how it is produced, and how many miles it has travelled to get to their local stores or home delivery. In other words, consumers in the new economy want insight into the production process and are not prepared to accept non-sustainable, or exploitive production practices.

Due to the increased interest in their business practices and the demand for transparency, organizations are being forced to have a closer relationship with their partners. They need to ensure that their entire production process is pure by investigating their suppliers throughout the whole line. After all, it only takes someone 140 characters to let the world know about any unsavory or dissatisfying practices of a particular company. “I’d rather walk than go to BP to fill up my car with gasoline”, read one of the hundred thousand angry tweets in the aftermath of the enormous oil spill caused by an explosion at one of BP’s oil rigs in the Gulf of Mexico. Also the Arab Spring that began at the end of 2010 showed the world how social media can play a powerful role in the downfall of seemingly unshakable systems (Abbink, 2012).

However, this is not to say that sustainable innovation is driven by fear of the outspoken customer and the acceleration of new developments in social networking. On the contrary, businesses in the new economy see the innovation arena expanding and opening new market opportunities. With the increased interactions across sectors and among suppliers and producers, closer ties are being formed and previously unheard of cross-sector combinations are being forged. This is not only proving to be hugely productive, but is also stimulating innovation to flourish like never before.

Starbucks online

NORTH AMERICA I **USA, WASHINGTON**

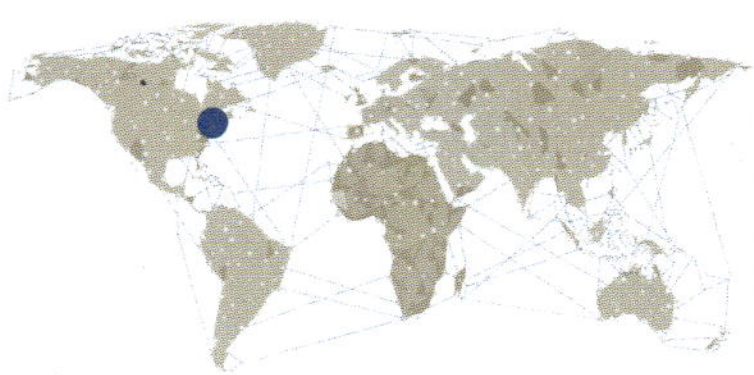

The American coffee giant Starbucks targeted its online community using *mystarbucksidea.com* to improve communication between the company and its clientele.
‘My Starbucks Idea’ was one of the first crowdsourcing initiatives to garner widespread attention. Using this specially designed website, customers and fans can express their ideas for new flavors and new experiences (such as the style and location for a coffee shop), as well as ideas related to marketing activities and policy matters. Other visitors to the website could share their opinions regarding the posted ideas and vote for or against them. The most popular and viable ideas are put into practice.
‘My Starbucks Idea’ has helped the company incorporate client feedback, promote new products and strengthen their client relationships. Additionally, the website has become an integral part of Starbuck’s sustainability strategy. Clients have come up with ideas to make the company better and help them to be more sustainable. For example, based on suggestions from their clients, Starbucks has been inspired to use a new type of paper cup that is easier to

recycle than the kind they were using before. Over three million visitors to the site have contributed more than 150,000 new ideas. This has led to 227 innovations, making the coffee community a great success.[68]

New role

Some aspects of innovation that are typical in the traditional economy have not lost their value, but have taken on a new role. A good example is Intellectual Property (IP). Even in the new open innovation systems, IP retains its value, but in a different way. Research and Development departments fixated on protecting their patents are losing out, while companies who employ an active, rather than defensive, approach to their intellectual property are gaining greater competitive advantages. The new approach to IP involves using it as a means of exchange and collective value creation.

This chapter shows how entrepreneurs in the new economy:

1. Innovate from a totally new perspective rather than improving existing innovations;
2. Create new markets with enterprising innovations;
3. Use networks and ecosystems to expand the playing field;
4. Approach intellectual property differently and consequently create new value.

A common thread throughout this chapter is the entrepreneurial heartbeat of innovation in the new economy. Companies create business cases from their innovations and look into how they can work together with other innovative partners, suppliers, customers and even competitors. In short, they make innovation an open endeavor.

Illustration 17
Four innovative eras

Four innovative eras

Scott D. Anthony, Managing Director at Innosight Asia Pacific and author of *The little black book of innovation*, discerns four distinct innovative eras (Anthony, 2012).

The **first era** was the time of the individual inventor which lasted until approximately 1915. Examples are the cotton gin by Eli Whitney (1973), the light bulb from Edison (1879) and the assembly line created by Henry Ford (1913).

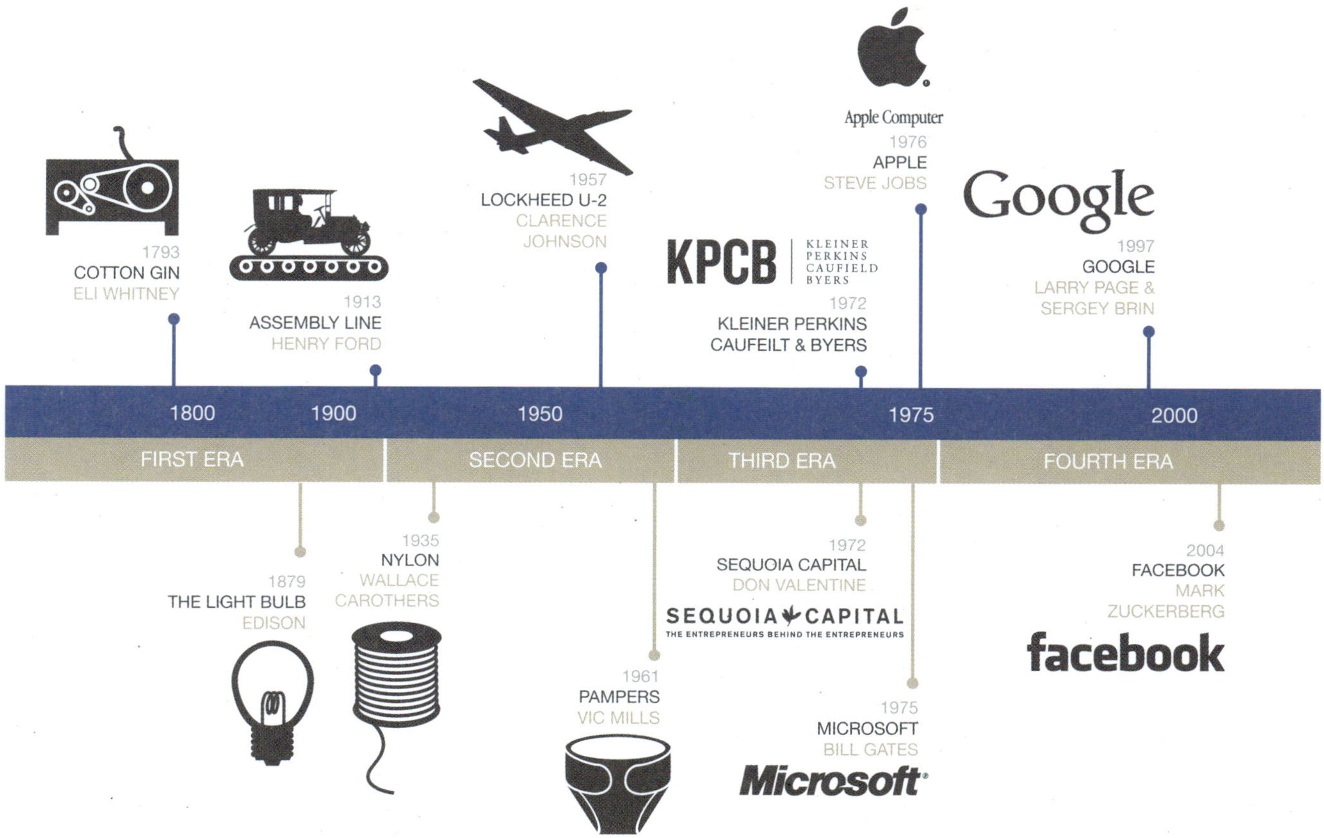

By perfecting the assembly line and the associated production costs and complexities, innovation was incorporated into the business world which led to companies becoming the innovators in the **second era.** These industrial laboratories went on to create some of the most innovative products of the next 60 years, such as nylons, disposable diapers, and the U2 spy plane by Lockheed.

In the 1950s and 1960s, the **third era** emerged because many companies by that time had become so large and bureaucratic that the innovative spirit had disappeared. The restless individualism that characterized this decade led to innovators pulling away from these large organizations and setting up their own companies.

Due to the demand for financing of these new companies, the number of venture capitalists grew. The **third era** reached its high point in the 1970s with the rise of keen venture capitalists such as Kleiner Perkins Caufield & Byers and Sequoia Capital. They, as well as others like them, financed rising companies like Apple, Microsoft, Cisco Systems, Amazon, Facebook, and Google. The amazing speed of success that these companies enjoyed made it even more difficult for large industrial companies to compete on the innovation front. According to Anthony, venture capitalists started expecting faster results. Anthony wrote in the *Harvard Business Review* that in the year 2000, when Facebook founder Mark Zuckerberg was still a student, Microsoft still had an unshakable monopoly and Google was still busy establishing their business model.

The breathtaking speed and the associated tools and conditions have given way to the **fourth era** in which innovation can come from anyone. While the third era was primarily characterized by technological breakthroughs, according to a study done by *Forbes* magazine, the success of the groundbreaking innovations in the fourth era is predicated on the business model that is used. In the years between 1997 and 2007, more than half of the companies that made it to the Fortune-500 list before their 25th anniversary gained their place on this list thanks to their business model being based on innovation.

Today, innovation is simpler and more accessible than ever before. The wealth of cheap (or free) online tools combined with markets that are nearly seamlessly connected has placed innovation in the hands of the masses.

4.1 From improvements to collective creation

Innovation in the new economy is centered around creating maximum value. In order to achieve this, businesses are renewing their innovation systems. To differentiate real system change in the new economy from what is referred to as 'sustainable innovation' in the traditional economy, it makes sense to divide the transition to system renewal into three steps or three stages of innovation:[69]

1. Operational improvements
2. Organizational transformation
3. System renewal

Illustration 18
From improvements to system renewal, three stages of innovation

1 Operational improvements

In the **first stage**, organizations incorporate ecological and social criteria into the existing quality and earnings criteria. The aim of this type of innovation is to improve efficiency and reduce damage to their assets caused by daily business activities. You could call it, *doing the same things better*. Although eco-efficiency does limit the negative impact of an organization, we are only talking about incremental change. An innovator at this stage is focused on answering one particular question and is not looking at the big picture. Innovation is dependent on internal sources and the results are typically company-oriented such as reducing costs and increasing profits.

Innovation at the operational improvement level:

At organizational level
- Teleworking (e.g. teleconferences to cut down on travel)
- Pollution control
- Waste separation
- Merging of facilities or locations
- Use of sustainable energy
- Reduced use of paper

At product level
- Reduced use of packaging materials
- Reduced use of natural resources
- Reduced use of environmentally damaging materials
- Efficient product size and weight for transport

At service level
- Hybrid electric vehicles
- Waste collection

2 Organizational transformation

Organizations in the **second stage** recognize that sustainable innovation creates value for the organization *and* the primary assets of the economy. They see opportunities to build business models which lead to products and services that create value for the world around them. In other words, *doing good by doing new things*.

'Organizational transformers' are less focused on creating products and more focused on providing services which may have a lower environmental impact. They develop innovations that are both technologically and socially oriented to improve the quality of life for their own people within their organization and outside of it.

Although Transformers are mostly focused internally, they see themselves as an independently operating part of the economy. They intensify the contact and collaboration among partners at the beginning and end of the chain in order to create a better, and less damaging production process.

Innovation at the organizational transformation level

- Radically new products that change the consumer pattern. An example is a cooking appliance that can turn every type of biomass into a super-efficient heat source. The sales and distribution of the cheaper models can be subsidized in developing countries.[70]
- Radically new and beneficial products. For example, portable and affordable CT scanners with a long lifespan that can be used by relief organizations in developing countries.
- Leasing arrangements replacing product sales (See Chapter 1: Customers). For example, the leasing and maintenance of carpets instead of the one-time sale. Or leasing initiatives related to car or bicycle parts.
- Electronic services replacing physical services such as invoicing by email instead of by post.

3 System renewal

The **third stage** represents the actual *new economy innovation*. Businesses reach this stage by realizing that innovation within the four walls of their organization can never deliver as much value as collective innovation. Entrepreneurs see themselves as part of the connected industrial ecosystem that finds its reason for existence in creating value for society on the whole. *Doing good, by doing new things with others* is the motto for the third stage. These system changes require a radical paradigm switch that is largely based on trust.

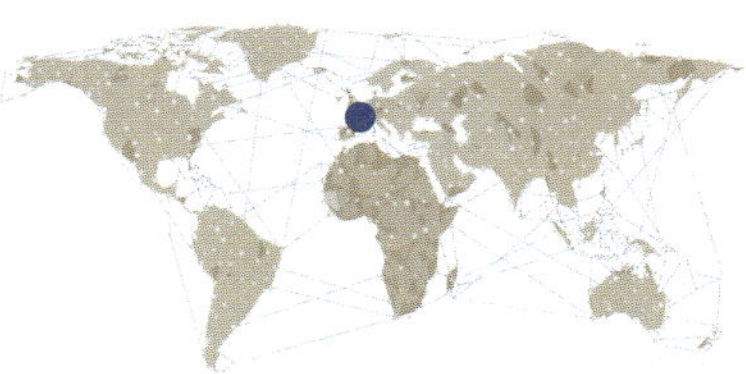

Veolia

EUROPE | **FRANCE**

Veolia is a global player in the field of resource management. They discovered that there was not much being done with biomass ash which is the waste product when making whiskey. This seemed a shame since this ash is rich in phosphate which is an important, non-renewable resource for artificial fertilizer. Therefore, they collaborated with Diageo's Cameronbridge Distillery and started a pilot program to see whether it was possible to extract the phosphate from the biomass ash. Once it is collected and processed, it can be sold for use in the agricultural sector. If the pilot is successful, it will open new opportunities to utilize and commercialize waste products that are rich in nutrients. This is also beneficial in the development of circular resource management.[71]

Organizations who build new systems see their economic activities as an integral part of society. They recognize that individually, nearly every business fails to be truly sustainable. It is through collaboration that real sustainability can be achieved. Therefore, system builders are thinking cross-border and looking for partners in the broadest sense.

The following paragraphs and other chapters in this book give further explanation and examples of innovation at the system renewal level. This kind of innovation is oriented towards a circular production cycle (See Chapter 2: Value Cycle) and in this respect, is also predicated on the transition from product ownership to product access and usage (See Chapter 1: Customers). The collaboration that facilitates such changes often meets resistance in the way businesses build their business cases and attract financing (See Chapter 5: Business Case and Chapter 6: Financing). Needless to say, innovation that is based on trust, collaboration, and value creation for ecological, social and financial assets requires leadership that makes this comprehensive approach possible (See Chapter 7: Leadership).

4.2 Creating markets through innovation

LEGO

EUROPE | **DENMARK**

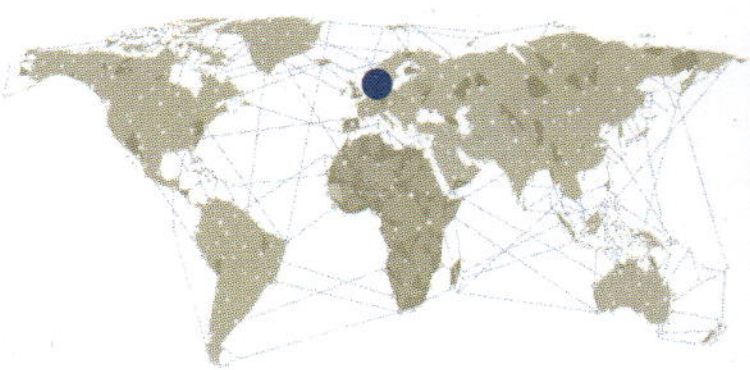

A prerequisite for sustainable innovation is openness. LEGO is a trailblazer in this regard as they continually explore collaborations with large and small partners ranging from other businesses to individual LEGO enthusiasts. One of LEGO's more popular products is LEGO Mindstorms. In addition to the well-known blocks, Mindstorms has a programmable motor. This gives buyers the possibility to let their self-made constructions move. After a while, however, the software was hacked to allow the motor to perform other tasks as well. LEGO considered discontinuing the product line but instead of viewing this consumer hack as an affront to their design, they saw it as an innovative contribution and consequently adjusted the software to allow people to program the motor any way they would like. This innovative and open approach brought LEGO into the school system in the United States. Schools are using LEGO Mindstorms to teach kids about robotics, design, and programming language. The result is not only a success story for the company but also a social contribution of value to the educational system.[72] Moreover, LEGO Mindstorms and other open projects from LEGO have resulted in an active internet users' community. Customers show their constructions on YouTube and also give input about the kinds of innovations they would like to see. Additionally, there is a crowdsourcing platform where people can post their ideas for new LEGO products. The community judges the constructions which gives LEGO ideas about new designs and it also functions as a source of market research.

Enterprising innovators have found a way to deal with the fast-paced developments in the IT arena, the nearly seamlessly interlocking markets, new materials, and technological advances. They have come to realize that innovation can come from many different parties by using inexpensive online tools. They are also taking into account that consumers want to be better informed and that non-sustainable production chains are vulnerable to public disfavor.

The collective approach has a positive effect on the viability of sustainable innovations. Innovators are able to make their business case attractive by guaranteeing a market.

1. Entrepreneurs put their innovation request out to the market. They choose the most suitable party and buy shares in that company.
2. If an innovation already exists but the company behind it is too small to successfully bring it onto the market, the entrepreneur will take an interest in the company and guarantee sales.
3. If it is more advantageous, a company may take over a smaller innovative party but without making it lose its identity, which would only lead to killing the innovative power of that small enterprise.
4. By co-creating together with their market, companies give their customers the opportunity to think along with them during the innovation process.

The last method lends itself well to software development as can be seen with the social network Facebook. This platform has an API (Application Programming Interface) that allows enthusiastic users and companies to create games and applications. The games and apps are accessible to everyone with a Facebook account. Incredibly popular games such as Farmville and Mafia Wars attract tens of millions of players worldwide and bring more notoriety to the platform as well. Because users and players get to participate in the design of the new product, it is perfectly aligned with what the customers want.

The process from market research to development to sale is taking a 180 degree turn in the new economy. Companies are already creating a demand during the development stage and they are guaranteeing sales by allowing the customers to participate in the innovative process. They absorb a much larger range of visions, possibilities, and suggestions that can be put into a business proposition; not at the end of the process, not halfway either, but from the very beginning of the innovation.

The beginning is crucial for the success of any innovation. As Albert Einstein said, "If I had an hour to solve a problem, I would spend 55 minutes defining the problem and 5 minutes on the solution." Innovation begins by asking the right questions, not by offering a solution. Therefore, entrepreneurs in the new economy are working together with innovative partners from the beginning and not after the problem has already been defined. In this way, open collaboration results in an innovation that offers a solution in the broadest sense even if the result is uncertain. An innovation process may start off as an initiative to create a new product, but could ultimately lead to the development of a new service or organization.

Kraft Foods, Collaboration Kitchen

NORTH AMERICA | **USA, CHICAGO**

Kraft Foods is one of the largest producers of food products in the world. It is also known for its brands, Milka and Côte d'Or. Recently, Kraft Foods launched the Collaboration Kitchen, an open innovation platform where Kraft Foods can combine its iconic brand with external innovations. With this platform, Kraft Foods endeavors to explore innovations related to packaging, technology, ingredients, products and processes. Anyone participating in the platform is welcome to submit their ideas and if a particular innovation is viable, Kraft Foods will, if possible, create a partnership with the innovator. An example is the partnership with TerraCycle, a company that uses waste materials – such as the juice packs from Capri Sun – to make new products.[73]

4.3 Expanding the innovation playing field

Businesses in the new economy use a bigger innovation playing field. Collective, open innovation is split into three areas in that field:

1. Within their own chain
2. Outside the chain and the sector
3. Together with competitors

1 Within the chain

Collective innovation is simple within one's own chain. Innovations benefit the innovators and their products or services. Sharing the innovation within the chain also takes nothing away from the parties.

In the traditional economy, the chain is linear. A company would give meaning to its position in the chain by adding value to the input they receive and subsequently moving it along the chain. Each link in the chain has its own solitary position. In the new economy, the chain has been replaced by a network (See Chapter 2: Value Cycle). In other words, this network is an innovative ecosystem in which there is a holistic perspective for all the parties within it. Businesses are dependent on each other and choose their roles in relation to the other players. In the network structure, they are not adding value step by step but rather gaining and retaining overall value as a whole and together improving their competitive position.

Start-ups

This new approach leads to other kinds of innovative exploitation. Established companies are investing in start-ups that are in a better position to develop targeted products and solutions. The start-ups gain the opportunity to accelerate and expand their market reach by using the larger company's global infrastructure, name recognition, partnerships, knowledge and expertise. This kind of collaboration also appears to a certain extent in the traditional economy, for example, with the Dutch food wholesaler Sligro Food Group. The company was looking for a way to separate its waste so that it could be divided into four recycling streams. This way, the recycled materials could be used more easily within the production chain to make new products. Sligro was perfectly able to organize this process internally, however the retrieval service was not feasible. Therefore, Sligro contacted a relatively small company that had an innovative retrieval service to ask them to develop a special truck that would separate the waste at pick up, and deliver it to Sligro already separated into its four types of waste and ready to go into the recycling process. “This small company had the know-how to develop such a truck and wanted to do so, only they did not have the funds for it. Therefore, Sligro guaranteed a long-term sales agreement with 25 of its facilities,” explains Koen Slippens, CEO of Sligro Food Group. “With this financial leverage, they were able to develop the system and break even from their investment within one year.”

Out of the box

When companies openly collaborate on an innovation, it offers advantages for all the players in the network. Producers, intermediaries, suppliers, and customers each benefit from a better product, less waste, more efficient energy use and faster production. “The collaboration can also help those parties that are not directly involved by presenting an opportunity for them to view their own business model from another perspective,” explains Marko Hekkert a professor of Dynamic and Innovative Systems at Utrecht University. “In the *business-to-business-to-consumer* chain you often see that the party that is closest to the consumer is so focused on the customer experience that they have difficulty thinking out of the box and, as a consequence, there is little innovation. They are used to their own business model and are not likely to question it. However, the parties that are not directly involved with the customer are less likely to fall into this cognitive block. They can take more distance from their customer-related business model and are in a better position to look at things from an innovative perspective.” Therefore, businesses in the new economy know that it is most advantageous to share their knowledge and resources for innovative purposes within their entire network in order to reach a higher plateau.

2 Outside the chain and the sector

In the new economy, business networks extend past the direct chains and industry sectors. Companies recognize that in-house research and development cannot compete with open innovation models that are utilizing a wide range of knowledge sources including customers, scholars, innovators, competitors, suppliers, and enterprises in other industries.

Most products do not add value all by themselves, but gain a valuable position when combined with other products or services. Simply put: a computer, a word processing program, and a mouse are three separate products; yet to write a book or create a presentation, you would need all three of these products together.

This inter-dependence of products is additional motivation for companies in the new economy to bundle their knowledge of the products, customers, and markets in order to come up with valuable innovations aimed at the entire experience.

Businesses are utilizing three instruments to maximize revenues from their innovations:

1 Pooled R&D
2 Spin-offs
3 Complementary sales

1 Pooled R&D

Companies are setting up their R&D departments together with other parties in, or through, collective platforms. This is cost-efficient and has the added benefit of being able to use each other's 'spill-overs'. Additional knowledge does not go unused but is mutually beneficial to the collaborating parties. This is discussed further in Section 4.4.

2 Spin-offs

Sometimes the knowledge that has been acquired is no longer useful for a particular company. Consequently, companies make this knowledge available to others and in exchange take an interest in the other company or become involved in the business in some other way. This leads to the transformation of excess IP being used for external open source projects, and adds value to the company because this kind of open innovation process often generates new products for the company to sell.

3 Complementary sales

The sale of complementary products and services is the third innovative instrument. For example, a company might develop a free software program and sell the specialized products and services that go along with it.

Zelfo
EUROPE | **GERMANY**

Materials such as old paper and soft board that contain cellulose are an excellent basis for the production of sustainable alternatives for wood and plastics in both the construction and production industries. The small German enterprise Zelfo is the technological frontrunner in this area. Zelfo can transform any form of cellulose-based 'waste' into high quality 2D and 3D materials that are biodegradable and have a very low impact on the environment. The global flooring manufacturer InterfaceFLOR decided to establish a joint venture with Zelfo to not only exploit the potential of their innovation in the flooring industry, but also to commercialize it as broadly as possible (Hoek & Jonker, 2012: 60).

Trust
Collective, open innovation can only function if all the parties in the innovative ecosystem (which was described earlier) trust each other. But trust, as the saying goes, is hard won but easily lost. In the traditional economy, there are plenty of examples of large parties buying out, swallowing up, or competing unfairly with smaller parties (Hekkert, 2011).

In an open innovation system, it is becoming more difficult to get rid of smaller parties in this way. A crucial reason for this was stated in the introduction of this chapter: consumers are better informed, more outspoken and are able to reach a million people with one tweet or Facebook post. According to Wouter Kersten from the organization Enviu, "A large company with an army of lawyers can probably still overpower a small innovative start-up, but if word gets out that you treat your partners that way, you'd better believe that the Zuckerbergs and Pages of tomorrow won't be knocking at your door."

Silicon Valley

Silicon Valley in California is the poster child of the innovative ecosystem. What prompted high-tech organizations who are direct competitors to establish themselves within such close proximity? The answer can be found in the small neighborhood around Sand Hill Road in Menlo Park where a large number of venture capitalists have their offices, or on the campus of Stanford University in Palo Alto where talented students from all over the world can be found and where scientists and high-tech companies work closely together. The secret of Silicon Valley is no secret at all: the businesses there compete for market share and for the top technicians, but at the same time the concentration of all those high-tech companies in close proximity attracts unlimited venture capital, entrepreneurial spirit, highly educated professionals, and the world's most talented students. Companies inspire each other and make optimum use of each other's expertise. Here too the collective interest of a successful Valley trumps the individual interests of each company (Hoek & Jonker, 2012: 38).

3 Joining the competitor

New economy businesses also see competitors as potential partners. By using the instruments previously described, they look for opportunities to expand the total market share and improve the final product. Both parties ultimately profit from this approach since the result is the enlargement of their potential market.

During the patent war between Apple and Samsung, Steve Wozniak, Co-Founder of Apple made a plea for the two companies to work together. He said, "I would love to see all the parties in this sector reach an agreement to share their patents so that each company could work towards making the best possible product."[74]

4.4 Intellectual property, back to Venice

Unilever,
EUROPE | **ENGLAND, THE NETHERLANDS**

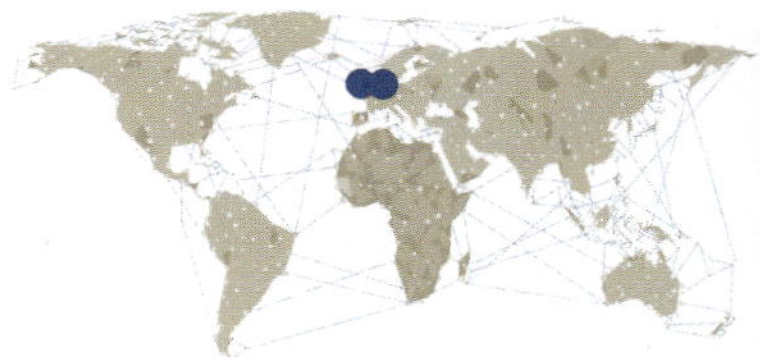

In addition to traditional in-house R&D activities, Unilever, the third largest producer of consumer goods in the world, also operates a broad range of external innovative activities. Examples of this are joint ventures and acquisitions as well as participation in public-private partnerships.
By participating in fundamental research and working together with other companies, scientists and institutes, Unilever has access to valuable technological knowledge sooner than if they would develop everything themselves.
Furthermore, Unilever invests in promising start-ups, and helps in the acquisition of governmental subsidies. Unilever not only provides financial support to the start-ups, but also offers the necessary business coaching by doing market analyses as well as sharing experience and contacts. Unilever centralizes these activities in their business units Unilever Technology Venturing and 'Unilever Foundry'.

Intellectual property in the new economy holds a different kind of value and has a different function. The question is no longer: Do I have the knowledge within the four walls of my organization? But rather: Do I have access to the knowledge?

In the traditional economy, businesses earned revenue from their IP and from the sale of their patents. But as shown earlier in this chapter, in the new economy businesses are no longer building fences around their intellectual property. Instead, IP has a supplemental value and function. It is not primarily a legal instrument anymore but a means of exchange. The thought behind this is simple: IP gains real value once it is cashed in.

The interesting thing about intellectual property is that the first instance of registering IP was initiated for that very goal. One of the first patents was granted in the 15th century in Venice. It was an instrument used to persuade individuals to share their knowledge and make it available for societal use. In exchange, IP rights were obtained. In the very beginning, intellectual property was a means to advance the exchange of knowledge (Schippel, 2001).

However, in the traditional economy, companies would choose to keep their innovations or innovative ideas on the shelf or on the back burner if a concrete application was not readily available. The thinking was, if we hold on to it, then others can't get their hands on it.

Businesses that are strategically designed for the new economy realize all too well that 'keeping it to yourself' by definition means 'getting less'. The size of the pie using the traditional economy rationale remains the same and even all the pieces of that pie are ultimately less lucrative than a few pieces of a bigger pie.

With an open approach, it can even prove to be a good thing when a discovery is made by accident or when innovators do not see an opportunity to create a tangible product or service from their IP. With open innovation, intellectual property is a new asset classification which contributes to gaining extra income and even helps to create entirely new business models.

General Electric,
NORTH AMERICA | **USA, CONNECTICUT, NEW YORK**

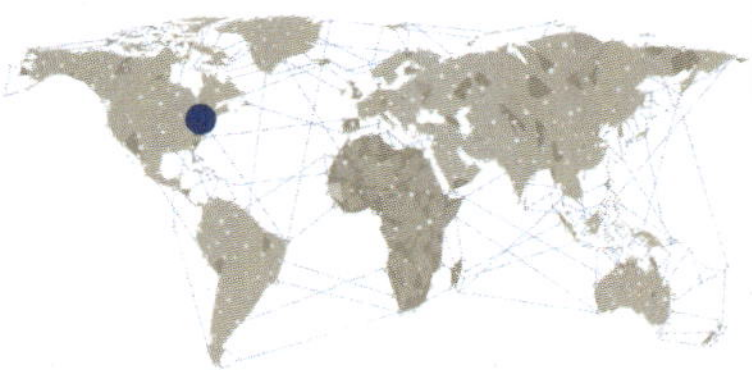

The American companies General Electric and Quirky (Quirky is a company involved in the field of social product development) launched a platform in May 2013 in which General Electric makes thousands of patents and technologies available to the global community. This platform challenges developers and innovators to work together to develop app-controlled products for homes, health, safety, water, and air quality. General Electric and Quirky hope that the patents will inspire the community to come up with new ideas and that the platforms will give new life to the original idea of what patents should be used for: A source of inspiration, instead of limitation.[75]

Businesses can earn revenue from intellectual property in different ways. They may donate it to a collective pool for mutual benefit (as presented earlier in this chapter, for the purpose of creating a bigger market), or put it on display and conduct a selection process to choose who they want to work with to move the innovation forward (creating partnerships). The cash value of the IP is determined during the negotiations and innovators profit from their IP when another company commercializes it. To sum up: IP rights are no longer being used to withhold innovations from others but are being used to control who does what with the innovation.

Illustration 19

Intellectual Property

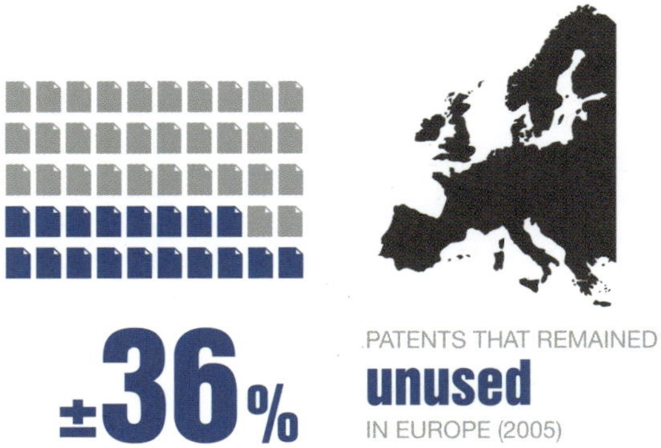

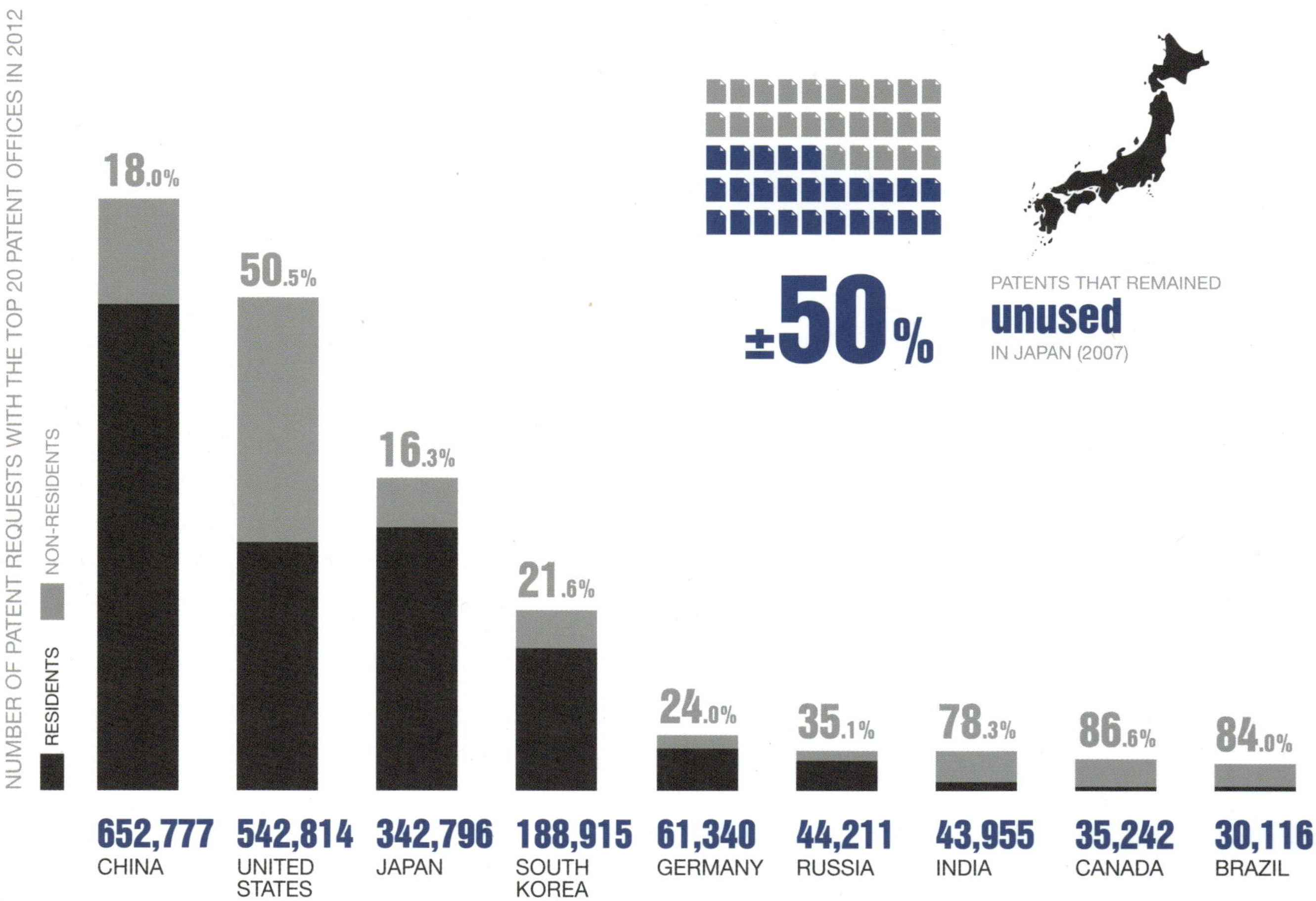

Focused on threats and protection

Intellectual property primarily offers protection against copying. Bear in mind, though, that this inadvertently promotes internally focused, protectionist behavior when it comes to innovation. It also inspires distrust and the presumption that competitors will try to steal successful products, services, and business models. Additionally, IP offers opportunities for abuse. Under the IP rights, a particular innovation can be withheld from the public on purpose. Another drawback is that IP can lead to a monopoly of a specific innovation that offers a societal benefit.

A company's success in the new economy is largely determined by the extent to which they are prepared to exchange knowledge. The "not invented here" syndrome is rapidly losing ground to the "invented there, but we make it work" motto. Wouter Kersten of the crowdsourcing platform Enviu expands on this concept, "An organization should not worry about whether or not the innovation came from their own offices but whether they are in a position to make the most of the innovation and turn it into reality. The new economy is not centered around the survival of the fittest but on the survival of the most adaptable. Most innovations today are not inventions of something brand new but are combinations of elements that already exist – only not yet in that combination."

Due to the growth in collaboration of innovative efforts, there is more collective social and intellectual capital. This stimulates further sharing of Intellectual Property and thus creates a positive spiral in the new economy. Although IP retains its status as the best way to develop innovative products and services, innovation managers in the new economy are acutely aware of the IP portion they are willing to share, especially since it is the value of that shared IP that strengthens their negotiating position. This gives IP an active, rather than passive role.

Wrap up

Innovation is key to substantially accelerating economic sustainability. Continual, collective and transparent innovation leads companies to the frontline of the new economy. As discussed in the previous chapters and in the following chapter: Business Case, a collaborative approach is at the core of successful business endeavors and innovation in the new economy. This collaboration sometimes goes against the tide of the closed, in-house innovative model of the traditional economy. Therefore, it requires a paradigm shift towards transparency and cooperation. This shift can be seen in examples from pioneering companies such as General Electric and Quirky. The current trend in this direction is gaining momentum. Collaborative and transparent innovation is becoming a movement.

New economy business cases are dynamic and adaptable.

Chapter 5

WINDOW OF OPPORTUNITY:

Business case

The focus is on sustainable, comprehensive value for the ecological, social and financial assets of the economy.

Businesses continually search for creative ways to generate income rather than focusing on cutting costs.

Entrepreneurs think long and broad. This expanded view literally gives the business case the space to reduce risks and increase opportunities.

IKEA's OptiLedge

EUROPE | **THE NETHERLANDS, SWEDEN**

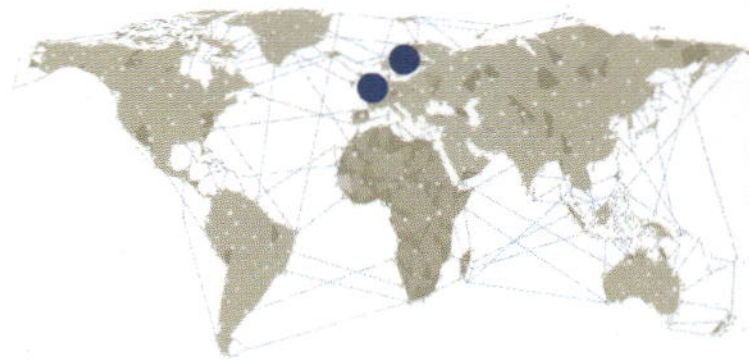

The OptiLedge is a completely recyclable alternative for the standard wooden pallet. The product was initiated by the furniture giant IKEA who was looking for an alternative for the relatively heavy, bulky, wooden pallet.

The OptiLedge is a more compact and lighter product than the wooden pallet. A set consists of two plastic beams on legs. When a load is placed on the OptiLedge, it is enclosed by the raised sides and fastened using a strap. The set weighs approximately two pounds (less than one kilo) which makes it very compact and extremely easy to store. In one pallet storage space of three feet (one meter) high, one hundred and fifty OptiLedge sets can be stored.

According to Ben Beckmann, the European Distribution Director of OptiLedge, "Using the OptiLedge is, in terms of initial investment, rather inexpensive. But the most significant savings is achieved by the reduction in transport costs. For air freight, the cost reduction is due to the fact that our pallets weigh approximately 20 to 50 pounds (approx. 10 to 25 kilos) less than wooden pallets. For road shipping, our pallets can be more efficiently loaded and therefore, more cargo can be transported in one truck. This results in enormous savings in transport costs and also decreases the amount of CO_2 emissions. In a space big enough for 20 wooden pallets, a total of 182 OptiLedge sets can be placed. In addition to space efficiency, the number of times a truck would need to drive back with empty pallets is also reduced by 90 percent. While 500 wooden pallets fit in a typical transport truck, the same vehicle can hold 5,000 OptiLedge sets." IKEA uses more than thirty million OptiLedge sets per year.[76]

Introduction

Constructing a good business case has been the Achilles' heel for sustainability pioneers in the traditional economy: nice plan, but too expensive; pretty picture, but too risky; substantial investment required with too long a wait for a return. The list of objections goes on.

Staunch protectors of the traditional economy would gladly use such arguments and as such, innovative and sustainable business cases would, one after the other, be thrown to the wayside. Entrepreneurs striving for sustainable solutions would – with their cup of fair trade coffee in hand – raise their crestfallen heads to the heavens and breathe a sigh of despair after their encounters with unwilling bankers and profit thirsty investors. There were the rare few who managed to scrape together enough cash by applying for subsidies and rounding up some crowdfunding, but it was never enough to make it into a big business.

Although the previous paragraph may seem a bit exaggerated, it clearly shows the essence of the problem; namely, there has been no fertile ground in the traditional economy for sustainable business and value creation. It simply did not fit the mold.

Sustainable business cases did not easily fit in the traditional economy for an obvious reason. The traditional economy has a very different starting point than the new economy. Doing business in the new economy means: a sustainable relationship with the ecological, social, and financial assets of our economy; innovative use of interacting trends in our economy; and incorporation of the revenue and expenses related to the assets mentioned above. This last point is elaborated on in Chapter 6: Financing which shows that a significant change to the entire system is needed.

A new approach to revenue and expenses is crucial in order to understand the true value that is created. And innovative use of trends as well as the incorporation of revenue and expenses are essential to the success of a business case.

Sustainable business cases often fail to get off the ground because not all of the costs – and therefore not all the revenue – are incorporated. Moreover, the business case is being rolled out in a non-conducive context. Many 'external' costs are not or hardly translated into fiscal calculations.

Even viable sustainable business cases often need to yield to more traditional business cases as they frequently deliver a slightly larger profit margin. This is to be expected though because the financial benefits related to the social and ecological assets are not incorporated into the calculations, and therefore left out of the evaluation and comparison of the different business cases.

Consequently, it is not valid to measure sustainable business cases by the same yard stick used in the traditional economy. Does this mean that cost or risk analyses have no place in the new economy? No, of course not. Risk and cost are still relevant parameters to analyze, however, the starting points are much more dynamic, innovative, broader and longer.

A business case in the traditional economy is oftentimes rather static in breadth (stakeholder diversity) and in length (time span) and there is little room to maneuver. Entrepreneurs would develop a business case from their own perspective. From there, they would look for financing, partnerships and customers. Based on this one-dimensional, linear view of costs, revenue, and risks the business case would get a 'go or no go'. Innovation in the traditional economy is not the leading motivation but functions as an additional feature that would improve the chances of success. Innovation is rarely used as the basis for the successful introduction of the business case (Boons & Lüdeke-Freund, 2013).

However, innovation is an overriding ingredient in creating ecological, social, and financial value. Here is an example of what it means to place the business case, and not the organization itself, as the center point in the new economy.

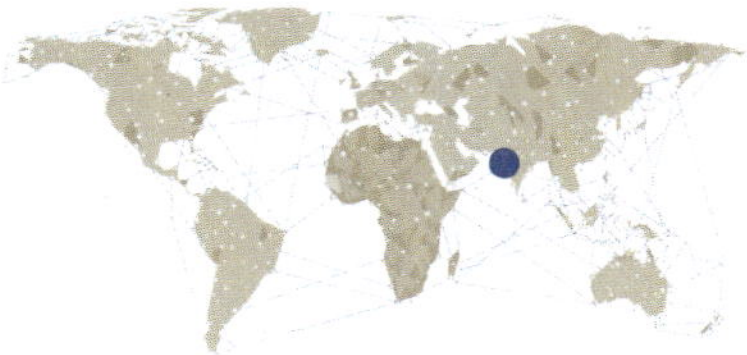

Mahindra: out of the boardroom, on to the farm

ASIA | **INDIA**

To the north of Mumbai, in a large Indian factory, countless red tractors roll off the production line. The factory is owned by Mahindra, one of India's largest conglomerates. Senior Vice President Sanjeev Goyle told *The Guardian* how the company went through a significant transformation over the last decade.[77]

In 2005, Mahindra declared that its goal was to become the world's largest tractor manufacturer. Two years later, the achievement of this goal was already in sight. "But continuing to be the world's number one just isn't that motivating," joked Sanjeev. "We realized that we had a very inside-out kind of vision. We asked ourselves, why not try to have a vision that is outside-in?"

In order to give this 'outside-in' vision credibility, the manager embarked on a mission to meet the farmers who their company wanted to serve. Sanjeev reflected that "Although I worked in a tractor company, I realized what an urbanite I was." The majority of Indian farmers worked small plots of land consisting of a couple of hectares each. Farming the land is hard work. It takes the farmers days to plow it, days to sow the seeds and days to harvest the crops. It was a wake-up call for Mahindra.

It became clear that the tractors that Mahindra produced were far too expensive for these farmers. This realization led to the development of a one-cylinder tractor called the Mahindra Yuvraj. It is fifteen horsepower and compact enough to use on the small plots of land but strong enough to relieve a lot of the heavy workload from these farmers. Sanjeev is proud to say that the Yuvraj soon became an indispensable part of farm life in the rural areas of India.

Although the Yuvraj was a very popular addition to their product range, it still did not provide the sense of satisfaction that Mahindra was looking for. It seemed that despite the power and compact stature of the tractor, there were still many farmers who were not able to use the tractor efficiently. The problem was that many of the farmers did not have enough knowledge and understanding of irrigation, planting, and other basic farming techniques. Consequently, Mahindra chose to expand their business endeavors. "We started to think differently. Our ultimate goal changed from selling as many tractors as possible to improving the well-being of the Indian farmers and the Indian economy, which to a large extent relies on the agricultural sector. The company supported the farmers step by step, not only with products, but with knowledge as well."

Overview

To achieve a tenable, high quality and sustainable business case, entrepreneurs in the new economy do not reason from their own perspective. This would be one-sided, inefficient and would lack the overview needed to signal and utilize the business case opportunities. To illustrate, let us suppose you have two map makers. One of them gets a view of the west coast of the United States by driving from Seattle to San Diego. The other one gets into an airplane and sees the coastline from a bird's eye view. The overview that the second map maker gets is crucial. He sees the connections and lines that the car driver missed. Using this analogy, entrepreneurs in the new economy are choosing the pilot's vantage point rather than looking out of a car window. They are building their business case from the perspective of the business case itself and are not taking their own organization as the starting point; they are analyzing the foundations of the business case in accordance with the foundations of the new economy. Innovative leaders have the ability to rise above, look around and ascertain with which parties they can create real value.

With the business case in mind, entrepreneurs continually strive towards creating the ideal combination of main ingredients, namely: cash flow, partnerships, and content. Organizations tailor these ingredients by connecting the content to several funding avenues and several parties while creating opportunities for 'economic cross-pollination'. By bringing together multiple parties from inside and outside of their own sector, they generate new cash flow opportunities (we call this 'broadening' the business case). In addition to developing cross-sector connections, they allow themselves more time to create a positive business case (this is called 'lengthening' the business case). In this way, maximum innovation, long-term value creation, and a positive rate of return can be achieved for all parties involved. Because these connections are sought from a broad and long perspective, a myriad of combinations and possibilities are available, some of which offer surprisingly unique added value. They enhance the business case by providing more time and space to the revenue model. Partners, investors, and financiers are willing to take on more of a risk when the time parameters for the business case not only offer the room for a return on the investment but also allow for the quality of the business case to improve, thus increasing the overall yield. For example, take a business case for the construction of an apartment building: the business case does not end after the last brick is laid, it continues over the entire period the building is used.

Business case old economy

- PROFIT OVER CONTINUITY
- SUPPLY-ORIENTED
- PERSPECTIVE: OWN ORGANIZATION
- PARTNERSHIPS BASED ON NECESSITY
- BLUEPRINT
- STATIC
- COST-ORIENTED
- FRAGMENTED BUILD UP OF BUSINESS CASE
- LOW INVESTMENT COSTS, HIGH EXPLOITATION COSTS

Business case new economy

- LONG-TERM CONTINUITY
- DEMAND-ORIENTED
- PERSPECTIVE: COLLABORATION
- PARTNERSHIPS BASED ON VALUE CREATION
- TAILOR-MADE
- VARIABLE AND DYNAMIC
- REVENUE-ORIENTED
- COMBINATION OF CONTENT, CASH FLOW AND PARTIES
- HIGH INVESTMENT COSTS, LOW EXPLOITATION COSTS

Illustration 20
From old to new business case

The essence of the new business case is the dynamic approach to the content, parties, and cash flow that is facilitated over the entire period of time by broadening and extending the business case (Hoek & Jonker, 2012: 75-77). This can be seen in illustration 20: From old to new business case.

The ingredients, conditions, and tools needed to form a successful, sustainable business case are explained in the following section.

Ingredients of a business case

- **Content**
  Content stands for the value proposition of the business case. An approach that is business case-oriented requires knowledge and competencies that many entrepreneurs do not have. Therefore, they bring in the necessary knowledge and abilities from external parties who contribute to the strength of the business case and attract new funding.

- **Funding**
  Organizations fund their business cases using the Trias Pecunia paradigm (See Section 6.1). The interaction among the various parties and the value proposition results in an optimal approach. The business case is made

broader and longer which allows for greater possibilities as well as the opportunity to transform costs into revenue.

- **Parties**
  The business case comes to fruition by forming collaborative relationships with private (and public - if value is added) parties inside and outside the given sector, including individual consumers as well. Organizations distinguish between location-specific and location-independent parties. The local, location-specific players are vital because of their knowledge and presence in the local area, and the large location-independent parties are needed because of their size, liquidity, and leverage.

Framework of a business case

Horizontal expansion
A broader approach to the business case gives a boost to its quality and consequently a boost to the organization as a whole.

Long-term horizon
The quality of the business case is not measured by short-term profits, but by long-term assurance. The duration of the business case is often based on how long the product is used.

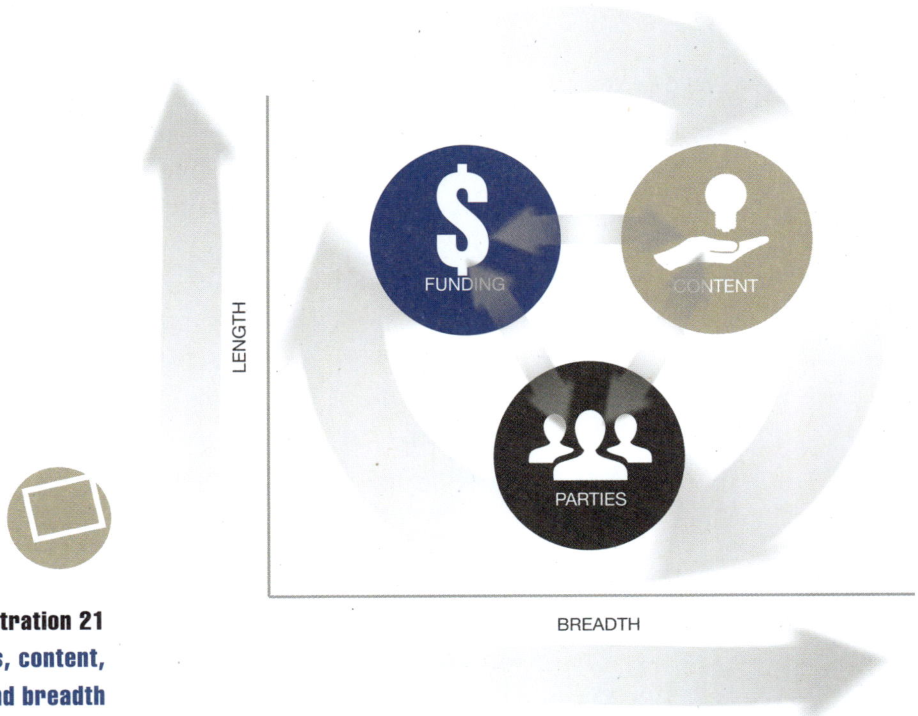

Illustration 21
Funding, parties, content, length and breadth

Length X breadth = sustainable innovation

A business case in the new economy always includes funding, parties, and content. The builders of the business case maintain a large scope in terms of the parties involved (the breadth) and the duration (the length). Moreover, the business case remains adaptable during the entire time that it is valid.

Bavaria beer and the *tenderos*

SOUTH AMERICA I **COLOMBIA**

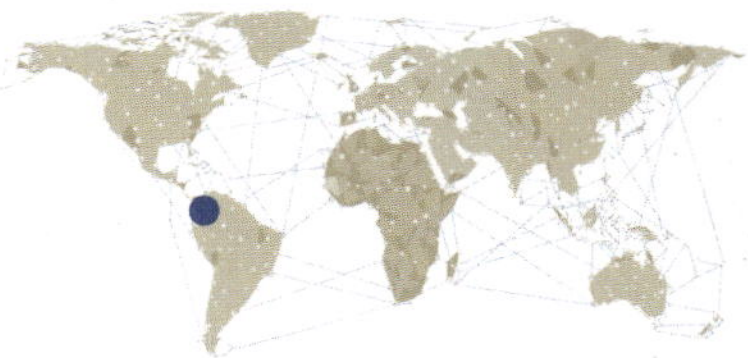

In Colombia, approximately 95 percent of all the companies there are micro-businesses. These are businesses that are no more than one small store where the retailers – the *tenderos* – and their families must do everything they can in order to make a living. The average monthly income from the approximate 400,000 *tenderos* varies from 130 to 315 dollars. 375,000 of them also sell Bavaria beer products. The parent company SABMiller saw an opportunity to contribute to the government's aim to create more jobs by introducing the project "Oportunidades Bavaria." With this initiative, the company works towards creating a more conducive environment for these businesses to thrive and improves the standard of living for the families involved in these micro-businesses. Bavaria focused on a group of 230,000 *tenderos* who would be able to meet their expenses by selling three to seven bottles of beer a week. This is also made possible by working closely with small local banks to provide micro-financing of between 100 and 1,000 dollars including related services. In addition to the local banks, Bavaria also worked with local governmental agencies in order to improve some of the regulations. They reached out to technological companies in order to make electronic payments possible, and they made agreements with some large wholesalers from which the *tenderos* buy their products. In 2013 alone, Bavaria reached 10,000 tenderos with a total loan amount of 15.6 million dollars. The goal is to reach 17,400 *tenderos* by 2018. Bavaria has also begun to provide marketing and sales training. This should lead to a rise in income for this target group as well as an increase in the amount of Bavaria products being sold.[78] According to Bavaria's CEO Karl Lippert, the economic success of the local population and that of Bavaria goes hand in hand: "If societies thrive, business also thrives."[79]

5.1 Ingredients for an adaptable business case

Although there is still no set model for a business case in the new economy, extensive research has led to a large number of business cases from which we can glean the common denominators. *Case-based reasoning* leads us to a model that is a dynamic combination of content, funding, and parties. It is dynamic because the combinations that are made are subject to continuous change and the businesses anticipate potential opportunities time and time again. A business case in the new economy continues to develop so that businesses can learn from each other's best practices, integrate new insights and knowledge about sustainability, and keep track of the strong and the weak elements of the business case. Such a business case is therefore never set in stone, but is open to improvement and remains adaptable.

Content

The content, or the value proposition of the business case, measures the value for the ecological, social and financial assets (Boons & Lüdeke-Freund, 2013). Together, the parties involved in the business case look for the right balance. With adequate knowledge and know-how, a solid foundation can be built for collaborative efforts and these collaborations can be modified over time as the business case remains *adaptable*.

For instance, when a highway is developed you would naturally think of the following parties being involved: engineers, project developers, tar and cement suppliers, and so on. However, in the exchange between content, parties, and cash flow, and in the variation between length and breadth, space is created for innovative ideas. For example, it may appear that an interesting proposition would be to lay a new form of asphalt that produces energy. If this were the case, it would then create the necessity to involve experts in the field of solar cells. Or perhaps the idea of creating mobile work spaces at the gas stations along the highway would be a value creating proposition. In this case, it would be wise to involve an office specialist. An example of an adaptable business case is the new building that was developed for the Dutch company Carglass. It was designed so that it can use the heat byproduct from the neighboring DSM paint factory for its own heating needs. Patrick Niemeijer, the Operations Service Manager at Carglass says, "We always try to find partners on a local level with whom we can work efficiently and innovatively."

The continuing variation and dynamic interactions that are shown in the previous examples require broad, flexible constructions for the business case.

Funding

Entrepreneurs in the new economy are viewing financing and cost management in a whole new way. This is to be expected as business cases in the new economy tend to involve a high level of investment but incur low costs. In the traditional economy this was often the other way around.

In order to drum up the initial investment capital, entrepreneurs are becoming more creative with funding. When possible, for example, they are involving financial backers for the entire duration of the business case. The financial approach has shifted in the new economy. The focus is no longer on the cost per item but on the cost for the finished product. That is to say that the concentration is on fulfilling the customer's needs instead of selling the customer a certain number of goods (Johnson, 2010).

Invariably, the question arises of whether costs can be transformed into revenue. Entrepreneurs in the new economy are not cost-oriented but revenue-oriented. A revenue-oriented approach differs from the way in which business cases are built in the traditional economy. This is a necessary shift because when the same old requirements of the traditional economy are applied, namely: return on investment, pay-off period, net present value, internal rate of return, and other common financing constructions then we see that sustainable projects are often difficult, if not completely unable, to be financed.

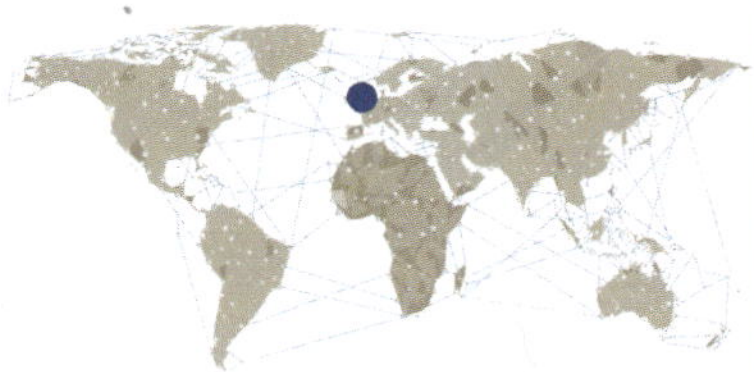

Naked Wines, no overhead

EUROPE | **ENGLAND**

Businesses in the new economy put conventional business case principles to the test in order to create maximum value. Sometimes that requires minor adjustments and sometimes more rigorous ones. A perfect example comes from the British company Naked Wines who, together with a brand new combination of partners, funding, and content managed to create an award winning entry into the wine market. According to Naked Wines, "When you pay 50 dollars for a good bottle of wine from Napa Cab, you are paying approximately seven dollars for the wine and 43 dollars for sales, marketing, and other business expenses that you do not taste." Naked Wines believes that this does not need to be the case, but how can it be changed? By taking the overhead out of the process. "You would rather buy wine from a wine maker than from a salesman, wouldn't you?" Naked Wines' strategy is a mixture of crowdfunding, a 'wine club' idea, and selling wholesale. Clients, or investors (Naked Wines calls them *angels*), pay approximately 30 dollars (25 euros) per month for as long as they want to continue. There is no minimum contract period. They do not receive any dividends or shares, but they do get a 40 to 60 percent discount when they buy wines from the Naked Wines website. Naked Wines works with hundreds of small, independent wine makers in thirteen countries with whom they have exclusive arrangements. This business model allows their clients to directly share in the startup or the financing of a wine maker. Naked Wines stimulates the wine producers to experiment and develop new wines. The farmers do not run any risk by doing so because Naked Wines pays for the grapes. The wine makers are paid the same for every bottle of wine that is sold.

The company has grown by 50 percent in recent years and currently ships 25,000 bottles per day to 150,000 customers. The total revenue in 2012 was 50 million dollars (41.2 million euros). The founder, Rowan Gormly, shared 1.7 million dollars (1.4 million euros) from the profits with his employees (Hurley, 2013).

Parties

In order to build a successful business case, entrepreneurs in the new economy create a 'dream team': the ideal mix of parties who, together, contribute maximum value. This includes private and sometimes public parties as well.

An example of this is the American cable manufacturer Southwire, located in Georgia. Some of their technical personnel had retired. At the same time, a local school was battling the issue of a 40 percent dropout rate. The factory recognized that they could not expect to gain much from the students if so many were dropping out. So they decided to come up with a creative solution that would benefit all parties. They set up a factory near the school and offered well-paying part-time jobs to kids who might be heading in the direction of dropping out. They also offered school-work assistance and school guidance. This resulted in a 100 percent graduation rate among the students who participated in this program with a third of them starting a career at Southwire. Not only did the children benefit by staying in school, Southwire benefitted by attracting better educated, better trained personnel which ultimately resulted in an additional yearly profit of nearly one million dollars (Kramer, 2012).

Equality
Although one of the parties in a given business case would most likely take the lead, all participating parties are seen as equal. This is not dependent on the amount of capital they each invest but based on the value they contribute towards making the business case prosper. The added value that the respective parties offer ranges from financing to specific expertise about markets, products or processes.

Because many business cases are location oriented, a winning team for new economy business cases often consists of location-specific and location-independent parties. A location-specific party would be, in the case of constructing a new residential neighborhood, a local paving company. A location-independent company would be one who is active regionally as well as nationally and internationally. Following this example, it could be a producer of pre-fab houses that delivers worldwide.

The combination of location-specific and location-independent parties offers many advantages. Location-specific parties contribute their specialized expertise to the project and the location-independent parties develop

Illustration 22
Location-specific and location-independent

Location-specific	Location-independant
LOCAL OR REGIONAL	OFTEN REGIONAL OR GREATER
KNOWLEDGE OF THE LOCAL MARKET	CONCEPTUAL KNOWLEDGE
COMPACT, FAST	EXTENSIVE, BIG BUDGETS

the business case further and roll it out in multiple areas. This makes participation in a business case more attractive for diverse parties. In some cases, though, it is not feasible to transform a location-specific business case into a location-independent concept. In that case, new economy businesses look for opportunities to expand and engage their area as much as possible.

Consumers are also an important part of business cases in the new economy. The interface between businesses and customers in the new economy is such that customers are stimulated to take responsibility for their use of the product and for the effect it has on the other stakeholders involved. But businesses are not expecting the consumers to take on the task of creating value for the business case, what they are doing is developing a relationship with the customers so that they can better meet the market specific challenges related to value creation (Hart & Milstein, 1999) and the company-specific challenges that come from their own supply chain (Boons & Lüdeke-Freund, 2013) (See Chapter 2: Value cycle).

Interaction
The three business case ingredients described above do not stand alone. Businesses endeavor to find the ideal combinations. They maintain a holistic approach in order to create maximum value overall.

5.2 The business case parameters: Longer and broader

Extending and expanding the parameters of a business case is part of the comprehensive approach to value creation that has been described in this and other chapters of this book. In the traditional economy, many businesses would approach value creation from a frightening perspective. They used the guiding principle of optimizing the short-term financial results, without much consideration of the customer's needs and the broader influences that determine the long-term success of the company (Porter & Kramer, 2011). They would attach too little importance to the welfare of their clients, the depletion of natural resources that are crucial for their business, the viability of their suppliers, and the economic unrest of the communities where they have their production facilities and market their products (Porter & Kramer, 2011). Businesses in the new economy, however, fundamentally keep a broad view and a long-term approach to their business cases.

Renting the land from the people

EUROPE | **SWEDEN** ASIA | **LAOS**

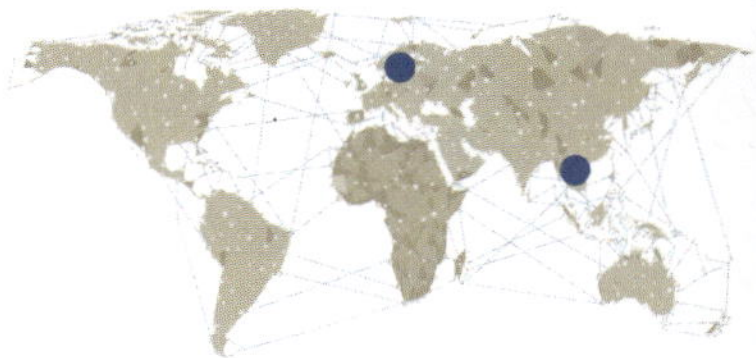

Burapha Agroforestry, a subsidiary of the Swedish company Silvi Nova AB, is a good example of stretching the parameters of the business case. The company consists of a lumber mill, wood processing plant and twelve thousand hectares of land. As the Swedish company and many of their clients, including IKEA, are interested in sustainable, high-quality wood, they only use valuable wood sorts. Burapha Agroforestry has set their business up in such a way that the local population profits from the company's endeavors. As a consequence, the company has gained access to unique financial resources such as loans, of approximately 1.65 million dollars from the World Bank and from IKEA. Since the total investment amount needed was 2.9 million dollars, they easily secured over half of the financing required to reach their target.[80] The core of their business model is that they only use trees that they have planted themselves, therefore sparing the natural rainforest. Additionally, 400 hectares of land are shared with local farmers to grow crops. The farmers that participate in this project do not own the trees but they do generate additional revenue through the work that they do on the plantations. The additional revenue means that the families that participate in this program earn approximately 4,800 dollars a year while the average family in Laos must get by on less than 4,380 dollars per year. Current plantations cover 6,000 hectares but the goal is to expand this to 60,000 hectares with the project stopping after 30 years. At that time, the intention is to return the rented land to the local inhabitants.[81] This new business model heralds a growing trend in Laos to preserve the rainforest, while at the same time, the quality of the wood that is generated allows the company to export the lumber to Europe and sell it to their main customer base at market prices.[82]

Extension

Business cases in the new economy have ample time frames. This is advantageous for the participating parties as they profit from the long-term security, not from short-term profit margins. Businesses in the new economy know that time is on their side. With this assurance, new doors are opened. After all, the longer you have, the more room there is to create a sustainable earnings-model. Within the context of a long-term business case, the risks are also diminished for the investors because there is more time given to generating a return on the investment.

An extended business case requires a different starting point, namely beginning with the end in sight. Where should this business case have led to in 20 years' time? How adaptable is my business case if there is a change of participating parties, funding, or content? An example is given by Paul van der Wijk, Director of the Martini Hospital in Groningen, The Netherlands. He explained, "Our hospital has been built to be flexible for the long term. It did entail higher building costs to achieve this but it allows us to use the spaces for a variety of purposes. It even presents the possibility of someday using the building for something else entirely."

By approaching the business case in such a way – not from the starting point but from the end point – the organization spreads the risks and does not put all their eggs in one basket. Moreover, they put themselves in a position to create value which will ultimately produce profits – if not today, then in ten, fifteen or perhaps twenty years' time. In this respect, it is a long-term investment which means that businesses do not focus their cost analysis based on the initial investment but on the costs related to the entire life cycle; the 'Total Costs of Ownership' or in other words, the 'Total Costs of Use.'

Expansion

Expanding one's view when creating a business case implies finding new ways of collaborating in order to create higher value. It requires a collaborative effort to bypass private and public obstacles. And collaboration also contributes by adding to each organization's insights, expertise, and resources.

Therefore, a company's success greatly depends on their willingness to collaborate. Companies who isolate themselves, rather than forming clusters

or partnerships will not be in a position to create shared value.
Large companies are also not shying away from collaborating with competitors, especially if they can help to create pre-competitive conditions. This has rarely been the case in the traditional economy. Successful collaborations in the new economy are data and knowledge driven. They are connected by the expected outcomes and the stakeholder targets, and managed by using a clear matrix (Porter & Kramer, 2011).

Expansion: from retail to freetail

As mentioned earlier, a broader view of business cases leads to greater innovation. But innovation can sometimes result in a blow to an entire sector (See Chapter 3: Scale). For example, the retail sector took a hit from the unstoppable technological advances (See Chapter 0: The New Economy, Section 2: Interactive trends) and the growth of shopping online. As a result, retailers have had to do their best in order to protect themselves from obsolescence.

The digital cash register from the Dutch company Sweebr.com is an innovation for the retail industry that is symbolic of the movement from retail to 'freetail'. Retailers who let go of time and location constrictions become complementary to online retailing and the other way around as well. Sweebr.com launched a digital cash register system last year. With this system, retailers are able to use a 'cloud-based' cash register at any time and from any location. They can access this system by using any computer, smartphone or tablet, and with any operating system. The web-based software can function independently or by using the router connection which is also compatible with existing cash register hardware. "By using your iPad, you can open your cash register," explained Bart Jaspers from Sweebr. "This can save a company with twenty stores an investment of twenty times seven thousand euros because an average cash register can easily cost thousands of euros."

Additionally, with the online Cash Register Dashboard, the retailer can see – in real time – the reports and the inventory. Jaspers goes further to explain that "If a retailer is interested, there are additional apps that can be downloaded which can connect to the administration, to the printer, and can also be used for music streaming so the retailers can choose the music they would like to play in their stores. For a mere ten euros more, they can also opt to connect to their online store. From retail to freetail."

The Sweebr cash register application illustrates the developments towards a much more dynamic retail sector that is independent of location and time. Retailers in the traditional economy have been strictly dependent on time (store hours) and on location (physical premises). However, in today's society, consumers do not want to be bound by these factors. They want to be free to shop whenever and wherever they want.

Given the technological developments and the changing consumer shopping behavior, non-food retailers are frequently choosing to turn their stores into showrooms. Consumers are able to get personal advice and choose their purchases with the help of the retail assistants and have the item delivered to their homes. As a result of this altered consumer proposition, retailers are hiring experienced sales people rather than cheap personnel with little knowledge of the products and the sector. This is because the contact with the consumer is precious and is an essential aspect of the sale. By paying attention to the significance of this moment of contact, retailers can prevent the problem of the consumer gaining information from their specialist and then buying the item from a cheaper competitor online.

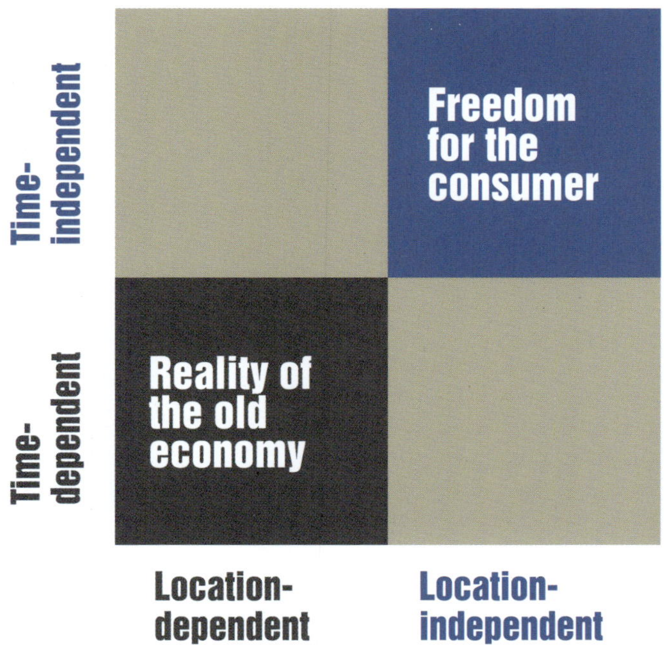

Source: Bart Jaspers (2012)

Illustration 23
From retail to freetail

Wrap up

Creating a business case in the new economy involves a dialogue between business and value creation. The word *dialogue* implies a kind of interaction that inspires learning and that is precisely what it is all about. As shown in this chapter with numerous examples, this interaction is necessary and stimulating for the development of the best possible business case content, cash flow, and connections. When creating a business case and striving for the optimal return on investment, entrepreneurs in the new economy do not go it alone, they share their knowledge, expertise, clout, innovation capabilities, and vision. This approach allows them to look further and have a broad view which results in the ability to break through old patterns and open up a brand new way of doing business.

Ultimately, in the words of Mark R. Kramer, author and co-founder of FSG – a consulting firm for social change, the new economy revolves around "good business." In that respect, it is not different from the traditional economy. However, the intense collaboration and rigorous focus on value creation for the primary assets of our economy has put businesses in the new economy in the position of going a step further: "doing good business better."

Money and real value are reunited in the new economy

Chapter 6

WINDOW OF OPPORTUNITY:

Financing

The Chief Financial Officer (CFO) is evolving into a Chief Value Officer (CVO) with far greater impact.

A new breed of investors has emerged. Crowdfunding, shared risk and long-term commitment are the order of the day.

Entrepreneurs are financing their businesses according to a new paradigm: The three principles of the Trias Pecunia.

Introduction

Over the last few decades, the financial sector has created a chasm between the economic and real value of money. For the last twenty years, maximizing the return on investment has been the name of the game. It has been an adrenalin rush and this rush has surged through the entire financial sector resulting in a self-righteous approach going so far as to become self-declared judges of right and wrong. This unbridled acceleration has created even more distance between the lender and borrower.

In the meantime, risks have been accruing for which no one seems to be accountable. 'You make money with money' is the accepted credo. But the real value of that money and the products or services it represented, is often obscure. Definitions and parameters of the economy, such as the gross national product (GNP) and share prices have not been reliable reflections of the state and value of the real economy. Therefore, the conclusions that we connect to it are based on a weak foundation. Although the financial sector has run wild with adrenalin it recent years, it was not solely responsible for the financial and economic crises. The failing economic system as a whole is to blame. This is described in Chapter 0: The New Economy, and we are confronted every day with the ramifications of this failing system.

In the new economy, money and real value are close companions again. They have reconnected to each other. Money is regaining its original function. It is again a valuable commodity that makes it possible to create long-term, sustainable value. This approach fits well with the broader definition of the economy which we describe in Chapter 0: The New Economy. Financial worth is not the only measuring stick being used in the new economy to determine the state of the economy; *all* assets are integrated into the picture. Ecological and social assets are also given a financial value. In this way, the sum of the costs and revenue for all the assets can be calculated, therefore providing a more accurate reflection of the overall health of our economy. Furthermore, this value application changes the basis of a financial analysis and redirects the focus towards value rather than money.

As previously argued, by defining the economy in broader terms, more room is given to the creation of value and more opportunities present themselves for economic growth.

Businesses are recalculating their positions in relation to the financial sector.

They are realizing that their dependence on financial service providers and lenders must be reduced if they want to provide positive influences to their business cases. New and varied building blocks are necessary in order to break away from a position as a follower to become a leader. In the traditional economy, organizations would finance their business case with separate blocks of the same financial color. Now they are building their business cases on a broader foundation which provides a stronger base.

Innovative entrepreneurs build that foundation according to the *Trias Pecunia* principles, a pyramid with three layers (See illustration 24).

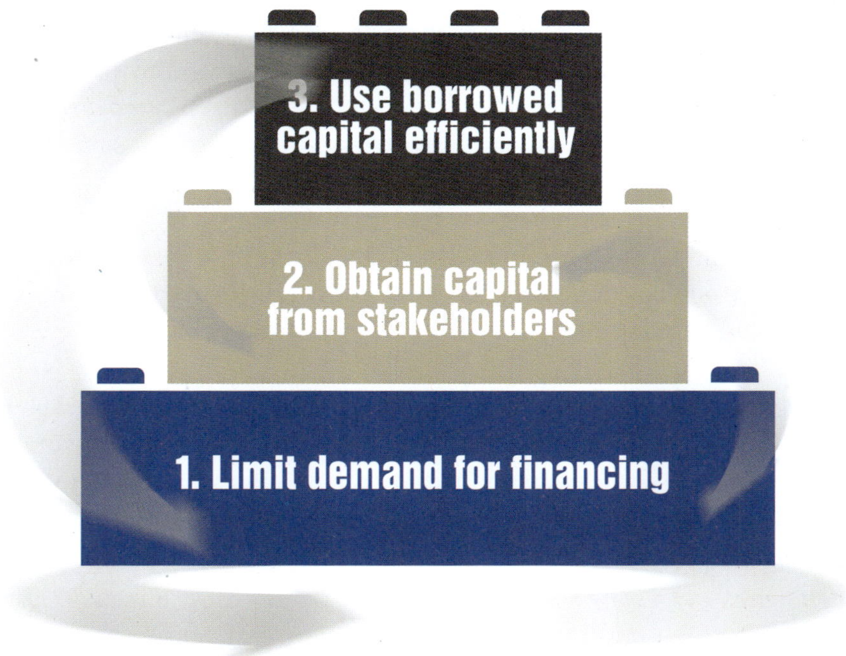

Illustration 24
The Trias Pecunia

The cement for the foundation, *the bottom layer*, is not the product of borrowed capital, but of value creation. This means that businesses do not immediately approach banks to provide the funding for their endeavors, but look for opportunities to limit their financial need. Obtaining borrowed capital in the early stages of a company or business case takes more time, effort, and money than it actually delivers. Entrepreneurs can limit their financial need by creatively collaborating with other parties. Parties who contribute to making the business smarter, guarantee a market, or parties with whom products or services can be exchanged. They build connections that reduce their financial need, give the business case a quality boost, and increase their financial independence.

The *second layer* of the pyramid primarily consists of financing gained by equity capital. Financiers invest their own money as well as their knowledge, expertise, and network in order to strengthen the quality of the business case. Financiers share the risks of the business and reap the benefits when the business excels. Building blocks connect the business objectives and the results. In other words, they are stakeholders that are intrinsically involved in the business case and have an interest in the success of the company. Due to this involvement, they are willing to share the risks and the opportunities, and because they contribute financially, their interest and involvement grows. It is this cycle that builds a connection to the financing so that not only the financial capital of the company increases but also the social capital, the network, and consequently the strength of the entire business. In fact, the second layer complements the first and curtails the explicit question of financing.

At the *top* of the pyramid, entrepreneurs can get an overview of the traditional economy's pile of blocks. Which of these blocks connects to the business case? Which parties should they attract in order to add specific value?

Business owners in the new economy are making carefully considered choices regarding how quickly they want their business to grow, says Juriaan Ruys, a Partner at McKinsey & Company. "If they choose to grow quickly, then they must consider the need for a larger portion of borrowed capital. If they prefer a more balanced volatility, then they choose slower growth but less debt."

New role

The financial building blocks in the traditional economy acquire a new role in the new economy. Banks, pension funds, and investors are no longer the leaders but are taking on a more supportive role. They are looking for – much more so than in the traditional economy – opportunities to support the interests of the business as well as their own. They are working together with their clients and realizing that they need to not only provide capital but also value. The new task of the financial sector is not to steer businesses towards increasing short-term profits, but to increase overall value and impact. Ultimately, this is - even from a purely financial perspective - the only stable and sustainable path for the long term. In this regard, the financial sector fulfils an indispensable role in the new economy.

This attention to value rises above the going market price because this often does not reflect the real cost of the product or the *total costs of ownership*.[83] Just think of the negative effects that business can have on social and ecological assets. Entrepreneurs in the new economy are conscious of that potential impact and therefore maintain a broader understanding of value creation. They examine and define the negative and positive effects of their business endeavors. By expanding the definition of value creation, the business playing field is amplified, new markets open up and new opportunities are created. Businesses are now building a solid pyramid comprised of shared risks, guaranteed markets and long-term value creation. It is a sturdy pyramid that allows the financier to easily reach the top.

In this chapter, we will look in depth at the question of reuniting money and real value. In order to do that, we will zoom in on:

1. The concept of the Trias Pecunia and how entrepreneurs combine the three principles in order to give maximum meaning to the financing of their business. Also, which financial innovations can be sustainably refreshed by their sector?
2. The financial sector. How can banks, pension funds, investors, and other financial players bring meaning to their roles in the new economy?
3. The shift from financial management to value management. This shift means that non-financial value related to social and ecological assets, can also be expressed monetarily. For this, integrated reporting plays a significant role. At board level, this requires a transformation of the CFO (Chief Financial Officer) to CVO (Chief Value Officer).

6.1 The Trias Pecunia, effective financing

Businesses in the new economy are looking at meeting their financial requirements in an entirely new way. They are conscious of retaining the leading role in their business case. In order to show how this manifests itself, we have come up with a new model called the Trias Pecunia. It will show how entrepreneurs are embedding their financing into their businesses. The Trias Pecunia is based on the Trias Energetica which was developed in Europe in the 90s as a guideline for sustainable energy efficient development and design.

The first step in the Trias Energetica is to limit the demand for natural resources such as raw materials, water, and energy. The idea is to use renewable resources as much as possible (See Step Two – expanded on further in this section). If that proves insufficient, then the last resort is to use some finite resources, but use them as efficiently as possible (See Step Three).

Although money is inexhaustible, as opposed to energy and natural resources which are obtained from exhaustible sources, the principle behind the Trias Energetica is also applicable as a guideline for sustainable and effective financing. The Trias Pecunia also consists of three steps:

1. Limit demand for financing
2. Obtain capital from long-term partnerships with stakeholders who are directly involved with the organization
3. Use borrowed capital efficiently

This approach to financing is essentially different than that of the traditional economy, where borrowed capital was often secured to finance the lion's share of the business case. Entrepreneurs in the new economy are financing their business cases by going around the traditional financial channels. This is proving to be hugely advantageous. There are lower costs and risks, and better partnerships with stakeholders and suppliers. But above all, approaching financing according to the Trias Pecunia principles leads to a better business case.

Step 1: Limiting demand for financing

In the new economy, business cases are being set up in such a way as to limit the need for financing. The less capital needed, the quicker the business can see a return on investment and the lower the risk profile is for the business case. A low risk also makes a business case more interesting to additional financiers. Furthermore, when a business does not borrow money they also do not need to pay interest which of course saves them money. How do businesses go about this? And which principles can we yield from this? In essence, they are working towards increasing the viability of their business case and improving the certainty of it.

Case-based reasoning shows how this can work:

- By guaranteeing years of marketability; businesses look to engage parties who are interested in buying their product or service over a long period of time. This provides income security which in turn reduces the need for financing and the risk profile.

- By arranging long lasting agreements to exchange services; businesses and organizations work together and connect based on other values besides money. In fact, money is not seen as the only source of capital. Knowledge, networking, services, and attention are integrated into the core logic and strategy decisions for the company. By using these other types of capital, organizations are generating added value for themselves and for their environments.[84] Additionally, this results in more security and less risk.
- By contributing products or services to an affiliation of parties; in exchange for this contribution, a company may utilize the products and services within the consortium.

Time/bank

EUROPE | **THE NETHERLANDS**

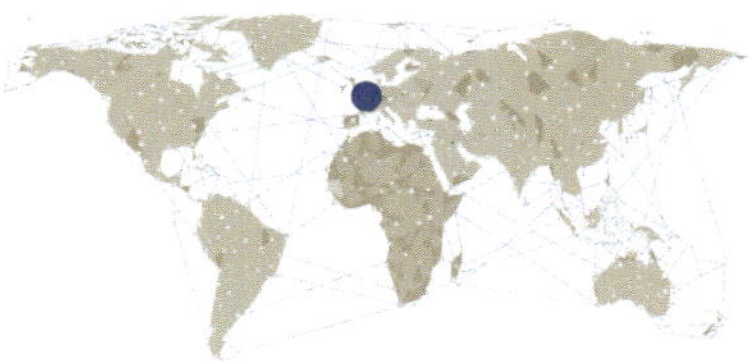

An example of the first step, on a small scale, is Time/bank; an international initiative born in the cultural sector. Members sell, or rather, *exchange* their time with others. One hour of your time is worth one hour of someone else's time. Members pay for services using the "hour note" and can build up credit at the *bank*. The website Time/bank connects the supply and demand which consists of a wide range of categories including 'handy works', art, transportation, research, and more. Time/bank has established locations worldwide, an international currency, and a parallel micro-economy. Their philosophy is: "Time is time, no matter where you are".[85]

What the three methods listed above have in common is that the financiers have a vested stake in the business case. They directly benefit from its success. When a party guarantees business to a particular supplier, it is of course in the interest of that party that a high-quality product or service is provided. So entrepreneurs who exchange their services can only do so if there is a mutual exchange of quality. Therefore, those that choose to contribute their services to a consortium will naturally ensure a high caliber product or service.

Bartering

Bartering fits into the Trias Pecunia very well. In the wake of the crisis we have experienced in recent years, this form of exchanging products and services has seen a significant boost. Bartering is of course, not new.

In 1990, Pepsico and the Soviet Union struck a bartering deal to exchange cola for vodka. The deal was worth a whopping three billion dollars. Although this deal was quite sensational, it did not inspire many others to follow suit. However, in recent years this has been changing. Bartering is booming business on every level.[86] In America, the number of bartering companies has risen by 8 – 12 percent.[87] In 2012, the sum total of goods and services exchanged by bartering totaled 12 billion dollars![88] Bartered exchanges take many forms and transcend all sectors.

Large scale examples come from the Asian car manufacturers Honda, Kia and Subaru who exchanged their cars for advertising. And Haymarket Exhibitions reduced their advertising budget by bartering with several media outlets as well as electronic appliance companies. They arranged that excess appliances or older models would be placed in hotels in exchange for media credits. Moreover, this arrangement gave way to acquiring the hotel chain as a new client. Lufthansa also bartered for advertising by offering property, and even bartered the use of their airplanes for fuel.[89]

Bartering knows no limits and can lead to surprising situations where new value is created. Kia is another example. They arranged a deal with the bartering company Miroma and an advertising agency. Kia took car models that were not selling very well and exchanged them for advertising space for its newer model. The advertising agency used the cars as prizes for a contest they conducted which resulted in them being shown in television advertisements and on the cover of a magazine. This of course had the pleasant consequence of free advertising for Kia on top of the advertising they received in exchange for the cars themselves.[90]

In the new economy, entrepreneurs are becoming savvy about bartering. They look for added value for their companies. For example, products and services that can benefit their cash flow, increase their customer base or market, advance their brand recognition and credibility, or help launch a new product or service.

Step 1 in the Trias Pecunia naturally leads to the relationship between financiers and businesses growing deeper and more extensive. At the same time it results in substantial risk reduction and decreases the need for financing (and interest payments, transaction costs and the potential financial perils that go with it).

To sum up: The first step in the Trias Pecunia of limiting demand for financing delivers a significant boost to the quality of every business case.

Step 2: Long-term, sustainable financing

To find a solution for the remaining financial requirements once step 1 has been implemented, businesses are seeking funding from investors who have a long-term interest in the business case. An added benefit of this is that companies can often tap into the knowledge and expertise of these intrinsically involved investors as well. The financial relationship is such that the risks and the profits are shared. Albert Fischer, a venture capitalist from Yellow & Blue gives an example of this kind of arrangement: Locamation, a company from Yellow & Blue's portfolio developed 'smart-grid' technology together with Alliander, a potential client. After Yellow & Blue invested, Alliander became the launching customer which meant that Locamation had no further need for funding in order to grow.

Crowdfunding - in the broadest sense of the word – is a perfect example of this sustainable method of financing. New economy businesses secure funding by approaching their extensive network of stakeholders. In the traditional economy, this group is hardly utilized even though they usually have a vested interest in the success of the company or the product.

Liquor store

EUROPE | **THE NETHERLANDS**

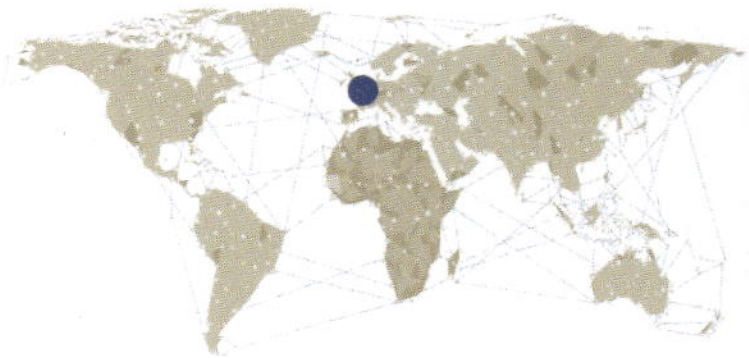

Petra de Boevere, entrepreneur and social media expert, financed the cost of moving her liquor store without having to approach a bank. Although the move would cost hundreds of thousands, she offered investors the following deal: for every thousand euros they invested, they would receive twelve hundred euros' worth of vouchers for future purchases at her store. Not only did she reach her target, she ensured future clientele.[91]

Crowdfunding is no longer a new phenomenon. It is a recognized method of financing not only for entrepreneurs looking for starting capital or relatively small amounts to achieve a specific goal, but it is also a valid source of funding for companies with serious liquidity issues. There have been many examples over the past few years in the United States where crowdfunding endeavors have produced millions of dollars in financing. By the end of 2014, it was estimated that crowdfunding had been responsible for pumping approximately 65 billion dollars into the world economy and facilitating over 270,000 jobs.[92] Crowdfunding has now made its way to many Asian countries as well. FlyingV is the largest platform in Asia. Although it is only two years old, this platform already hosts many multi-million dollar projects.[93]

What is crowdfunding?

Crowdfunding is a form of financing that allows entrepreneurs to tap into the fund-raising power of the masses. Anyone can go online and find products or services to invest in. Crowdfunding platforms, unlike micro-financing, are not connected to any financial institution and are solely dedicated to providing capital. Crowdfunding started in the United States and grew so popular it expanded to Europe and recently to Asia. Crowdfunding rose in popularity when it was used by Barack Obama in his first election campaign to raise over 500 million dollars for his campaign fund. Remarkably, this enormous amount was raised by many donations of less than one hundred dollars each.[94]

Crowdfunding platforms come in all shapes and sizes. A familiar form which is often used by the American platform Kickstarter is the pre-sale of a product based on the prototype. For example, suppose an entrepreneur needs a hundred thousand dollars to develop a product that will ultimately cost fifty dollars in the stores. If there are 2,000 buyers in the crowd then the production can be financed. These initial buyers are often rewarded by the company with the deluxe version once the product is manufactured.

Other platforms offer investment opportunities using another kind of arrangement. 'Lending crowdfunding' or otherwise known as 'Equity crowdfunding' which is a form of risk capital. Equity crowdfunding offers shares and falls under legal regulations in some countries. It became officially permissible in the United States on January 1st, 2013.[95] Although to date only four percent of all the money generated by crowdfunding comes from this form,[96] it is predicted that in the near future upwards of 184 million dollars will be collected through this type of crowdfunding in America alone.[97]

New economy businesses embrace crowdfunding because it offers a whole range of advantages, such as the elimination of transaction costs and making financing accessible to everyone. Prior to crowdfunding options, entrepreneurs were often forced to seek capital from institutions that predominantly dealt with large organizations that had substantial collateral and excellent credit reputations.[98] Additionally, crowdfunding facilitates more than funding, it allows start-ups and established companies to get in contact with their target market.

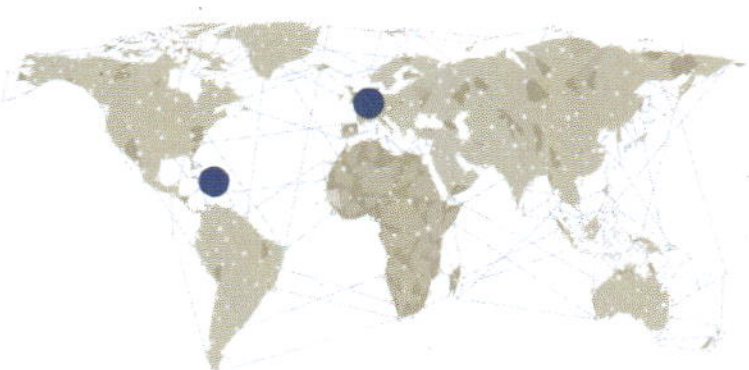

WakaWaka Light for Haiti

SOUTH AMERICA | **HAITI** EUROPE | **THE NETHERLANDS**

WakaWaka Power set up a crowdfunding campaign when it introduced its revolutionary device – a solar powered LED lamp combined with a charger for smartphones and tablets. The company even combined their fundraising with creating value for the greater social good. For every WakaWaka Power that was sold, a WakaWaka light was donated to Haiti. This was especially important at the time when Haiti had just been hit with a devastating earthquake and more than fifty thousand Haitians were left without electricity and only flammable, poisonous and expensive kerosene lamps to use for light. In one month's time, a half a million euros was raised from more than seven thousand crowdfunders using several different crowdfunding platforms. Many people participated because they wanted to be the first ones to have this efficient solar lamp and charger, others wanted to contribute towards making a difference in Haiti and get this 'cool gadget' as a bonus.[99]

By investing in a product or service, there is an intrinsic interest in the success of the end product. As a result, investors are likely to tell their friends and family about the product. This natural consequence, in fact, also turns crowdfunding into a marketing tool which in turn makes crowdfunding especially interesting for larger parties in the new economy.

Crowdfunding also facilitates a new form of market research. When a company attracts interest and manages to gather the necessary investment capital within a short amount of time, they are in a stronger position to approach a bank for further funding if need be. They can show this track record to demonstrate the market interest in their product or service. It is also a good way to present their company to business clients and retailers.

The role of the stakeholders changes with the second step of the Trias Pecunia. They become long-term ambassadors for the company.

Joint venture

EUROPE | **IRELAND, GERMANY, SWITZERLAND AND THE NETHERLANDS**

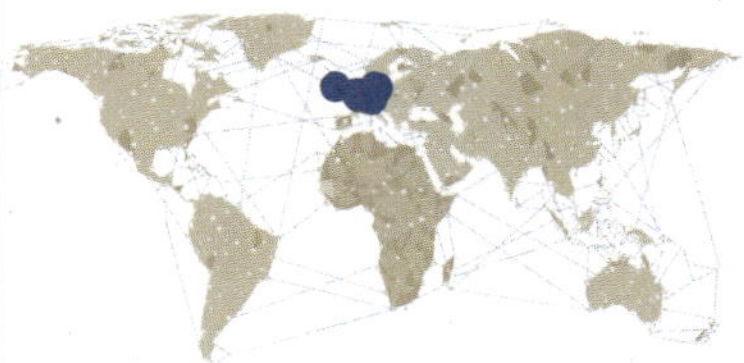

Public-Private Partnership (PPP) is a joint venture between a government service and a company from the private sector. An example of this kind of partnership is the collaboration between the Royal BAM Group (involved in building and infrastructure) and the pension fund PGGM. In 2011, they formed a joint venture in which PGGM contributed their know-how and became a long-term investor, and BAM brought in their expertise as developers.

The joint venture, which was the first of its kind in Europe, is interested in investing 390 million euros in the growing PPP markets in the Netherlands, Belgium, UK, Ireland, Germany, and Switzerland. The focus would be on the development of roads and public buildings such as schools.

Through this joint venture, BAM, who is responsible for the maintenance of the project, ensures a long-term source of capital which is needed for growth in the European PPP market. For PGGM, revenue is guaranteed because of the collaboration with the government which makes it a very attractive proposition for them, and they benefit from a stable cash flow. Furthermore, the development of roads and schools fits in well with the ESG factors (Environmental, Social, Governmental) that PGGM is committed to.[100]

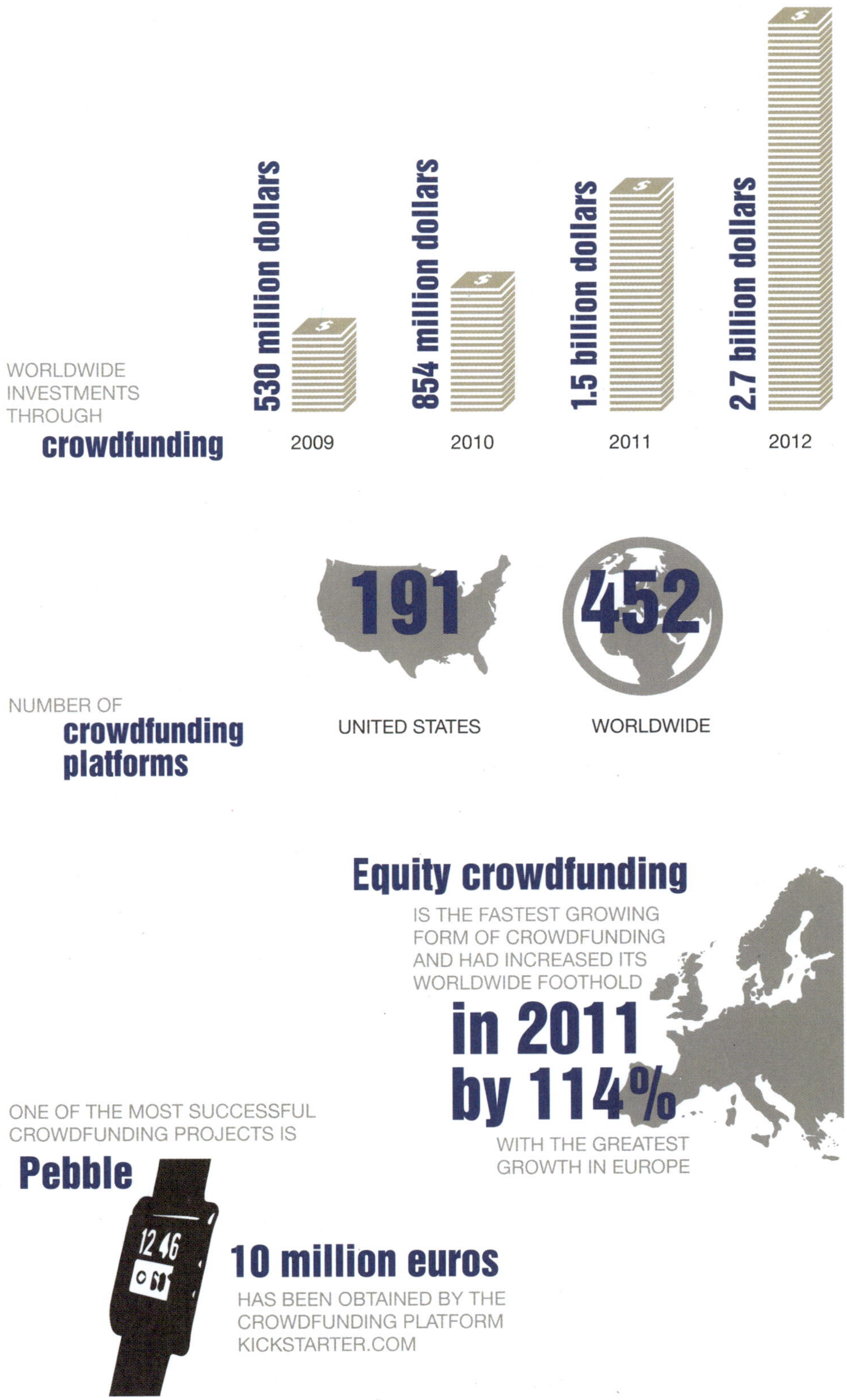

Illustration 25
Crowdfunding

Cooperation

A cooperative business model is another way to limit the need for borrowed capital. There are many such cooperative ventures that take a variety of forms. A popular construction is the transfer of ownership to the employees. [101] The idea behind it is that if employees invest in the company by buying shares, they not only get a say in the company but also increase their interest in the success of the company.

In England, there have been a lot of experiments with this type of cooperation. Currently, cooperative businesses have a total of 15.4 million members. The John Lewis Partnership is a very successful cooperation in which the profits are shared with the employees. This is also popular in Scotland and has produced visible results in productivity and profit compared to the competition.[102]

Step 3: Effective borrowed capital

Borrowed capital is utilized for specific goals. It is not drawn to finance the lion's share of the business case, but to specifically cover a particular gap or to expedite the upscaling from regional to global level.

As a result of steps 1 and 2 in the Trias Pecunia, the use of borrowed capital becomes cheaper and more solid. The financing rests on a sturdier foundation. A foundation that spreads and reduces the risks and involves the investors, stakeholders, and customers. This security is important for banks and investors.

Credit unions, worldwide, will do well in the new economy. In many countries they already play a large role. In the United States, credit unions control ten percent of saved capital. Their engagement has led to good financial results.

When entrepreneurs look for growth capital in the traditional economy, they make themselves beholden to big investors. However, by pursuing the Trias Pecunia financial route of risk reduction, they present a strong and sound impression to investors. Small meets big in an optimal capacity. Not only does this approach strengthen the position of the small start-ups, it prevents them from having to hold their hand out to banks in order to upscale their business. It also presents a new opportunity for larger stakeholders to benefit from a small but strong external R&D department.

Systematic

The Trias Pecunia is not a comprehensive model. It is a supportive paradigm for innovative entrepreneurs who would like to strengthen their business case and their financial basis. Consequently, the trias is not static. Steps 2 and 3 do not necessarily follow step 1. Sometimes, for example, a small initial investment is needed to secure a long-term partnership and the partnership in turn helps limit the financial need.

The trias stands for a repetitive approach to the financial construction of the business case. Entrepreneurs continually search for the best combination of building blocks for a solid foundation. As shown in the examples given, no set pattern is defined. Innovative entrepreneurs allow the different layers of the Trias Pecunia to interact depending on the unique characteristics of the business case.

To measure the success of this approach, entrepreneurs count the points where the three layers of the Trias Pecunia touch. There is a lasting association between value creation and the costs of capital. How does the financing construction influence the liquidity of the business in the long term? Does the financial burden affect the value created for the customer? Entrepreneurs in the new economy continually keep an eye on the added value of the financial construction. In other words, the financing is there for the business case, the business case is not there for the financing.

Governments

Entrepreneurs who want to shape their business cases using the Trais Pecunia benefit from the governmental policies which are put in place in the areas they are interested in doing business. In the new economy, local, regional and national governments facilitate the multi-layer financing of sustainable business cases. Sustainability ‘from the bottom up’ can only exist if the economic conditions allow for it.

The government can use all sorts of instruments at its disposal. For example, it can have guarantees depend on the degree to which the initiative contributes to sustainable objectives or participates in consortia. In this way, the government supports the feasibility of sustainable business cases and helps the market step in at a lower interest rate and with lower risk.

The government can also offer simple guarantees to banks which offer benefits in addition to a reasonable security premium if the initiative performs better than expected. In this way, all parties are adequately compensated for taking risks and enabling the bank financing (Hoek & Jonker, 2012).

The 'Feed-in Tariff' (FIT) programs are the most effective financing format worldwide for governments to advance investment in sustainable technologies. These programs consist of a contract between a local governmental agency and a supplier of clean energy. The government agency pays a premium, above market price, for the energy and thus subsidizes the clean energy initiative. In 2000, there were only 14 FIT programs. By 2012, this number had grown to 90 FIT programs in 65 countries. Germany is the leader in sustainable energy and has been utilizing FIT programs since the 90s.[103]

The biggest obstacle standing in the way of successful FIT programs is that oftentimes small businesses – especially those located in poorer parts of the world – do not manage to secure financing from a bank. This is usually because they do not have access to banks. Therefore, crowdfunding platforms offer a good alternative for this problem. An extra advantage of FIT programs being combined with crowdfunding, instead of involving traditional bank loans, is that crowdfunding provides opportunities to extend the length of the loan giving the business more time to turn a profit from the business case. Additionally, traditional payment terms take immediate effect and follow a linear trajectory, whereas crowdfunding platforms can be more creative such as paying the loan back at the end of the term and paying the accrued interest at that time as well.[104]

6.2 Renewal of the Financial sector

There are a large number of active players within the financial spectrum. Each with their own role and each playing their part in the collective. Although the new role for each party varies, it is clear that the financial sector has undergone a significant metamorphosis.

The financial needs of businesses in the new economy are less often satisfied by only one party. Instead the demand is covered by a variety of parties who differ in size and leverage. When you put it in the perspective of the various building blocks in the Trias Pecunia, it is understandable that there are fewer parties who carry the entire financial risk alone. Spreading the risk is a key principle in the new economy. Therefore, financial institutions and service providers that anticipate this shift, maintain and achieve a competitive edge.

These developments imply new forms of cooperation within the financial sector. Financiers, investors, and pension funds no longer operate as stand-alone entities, but form a financial value cycle. This value cycle serves to ensure that viable business cases can be realized and money can be made through innovative cyclical constructions within the financial sector. For example, a private equity party or a given bank may bundle a number of small initiatives, then involve the investment of a pension fund to share the risks and round it off with additional financing and other innovative financing methods.

This type of risk sharing is different from the traditional method of index investing. Although index investing involves the conscious choice to spread the risk, it is done without being in contact with the actual economy and without examining the market in depth.

The following paragraphs explain the different roles of the various parties in the financial sector.

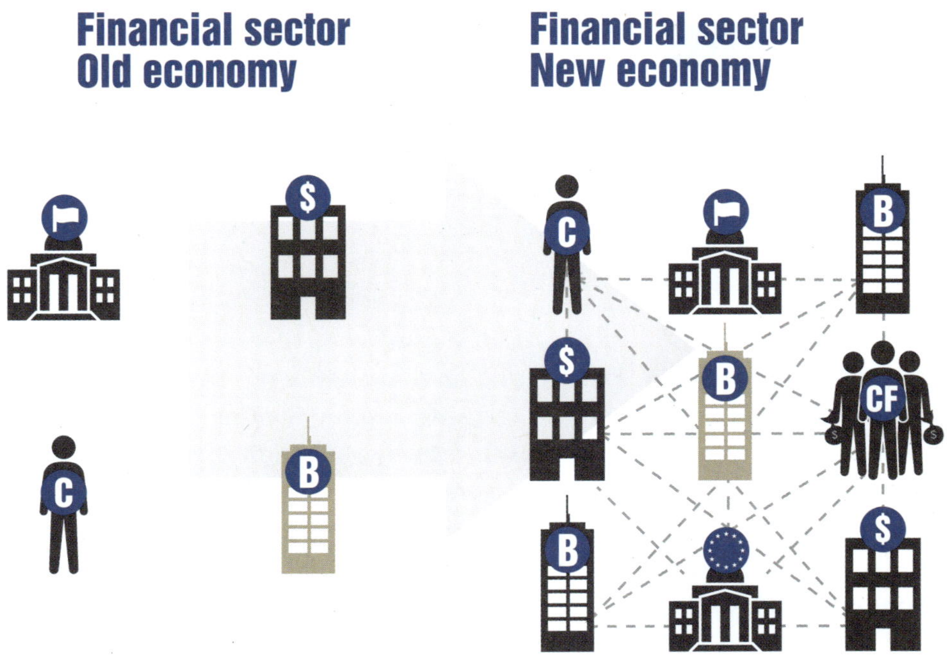

Illustration 26
The new financial sector

Banks

Are banks irrelevant?

Scratch, a subsidiary of the American media giant Viacom conducted a three year long research project related to 'millennials' (also known as Generation Y; people born between the early 80s and early 2000s). Upon the conclusion of their study in 2014, they had come to some remarkable discoveries about the views these 18 to 33 year olds had about banks.[105]

Since the bank crisis exploded in 2008, banks have been taking a place on the sidelines. According to a survey by Forrester, only 29 percent of Europeans believes that the banks have the best interest of their clients at heart.[106] Businesses feel the same way, especially small and medium sized companies. They blame the banks and figure, "if you need credit, don't bother going to your bank, it's a waste of time."

70%

OF THE 500 PEOPLE SURVEYED **did not notice any efforts** BEING MADE BY BANKS TO WIN BACK THEIR TRUST AND CONFIDENCE

52%

STILL THINK THAT THERE IS **no better alternative** THAN CONTINUING TO USE THEIR CURRENT BANK

Illustration 27
Banks

Banks are in a difficult position. On the one hand, they are bound by strict restrictions related to liquidation, and on the other hand, they must comply with equally strict regulations regarding capital lending. This position, however, does not release the banks from their obligation to innovate so that they can break away from the old business model of moving money around, covering risks and charging interest. But so far this process has barely started. This contrasts sharply with what we see in the business world. When businesses are faced with liquidity issues, they respond with fast, effective innovations in order to continue doing business. Some of these innovations may actually make banks unnecessary in the future. A development that has become rather commonplace in the new economy is called 'supply chain finance'. Buyers and sellers look for opportunities within their chain to arrange financing. They have a vested interest in ensuring enough working capital for their supply chain partners.[107]

Another interesting alternative is the creation of other types of currency allowing specific parties to do business with each other. The most well-known example is that of the Swiss WIR franc. It was established in the 1930s and over the years has accounted for billions worth of turnover for over ten thousand companies. Especially in times of economic crises, an adjunct financial avenue offers a welcome alternative. Another example is the Bristol Pound which is a successful currency that is only accepted in the British city of Bristol. The Bristol Pound was created to keep revenues in the city of Bristol and to stimulate the local economy. This initiative has since been copied in other parts of the United Kingdom.

Banks are starting to reinvent themselves in the new economy. New, often small scale, financial innovations incorporating technological developments, crowdfunding, digital currency, and other initiatives are reactions to the clear indications that customers are no longer strictly dependent on banks, and that banks need to be much more service oriented towards their private and business customers.[108]

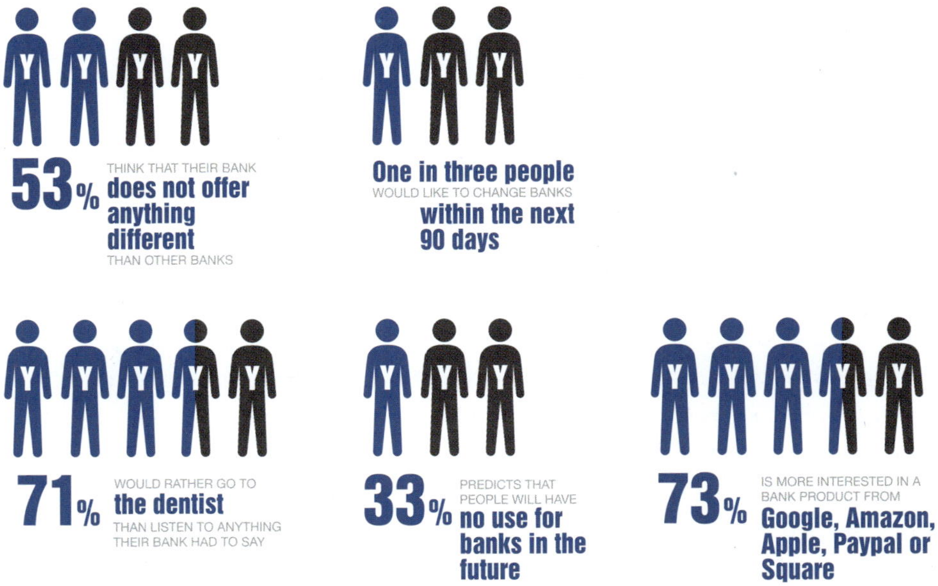

Illustratiion 28
Are banks irrelevant?

Zweite Sparkasse

EUROPE | **AUSTRIA**

The ERSTE Stiftung, Austria's largest savings bank came up with the Zweite Sparkasse, the epitome of a banking *service*. The project gained ground thanks to a number of participating banks and credit institutions. This program aims to help people who, for whatever reason, are not eligible to open a regular bank account. Zweite Sparkasse gives them the opportunity to open an account at their bank with access to all the usual banking facilities including a bank card. For people who have found themselves in unfortunate circumstances, this opportunity allows them to get back on their feet. Over 400 staff and managers all work on a volunteer basis to help over 40,000 people in Austria who would not otherwise have access to a bank account. Ten thousand people have already been helped by this initiative.[109]

The following examples show how technical, financial innovations are transforming the banking world. Analysis shows some drastic changes on the horizon for financial institutions. Experts foresee how Google Bank, Apple Bank and Facebook Bank and countless 'fintech start-ups' are pulling the rug out from under the established banking order.[110] Young, 'social disruptors' are transforming financial services by introducing new companies that change the way we save, borrow money, and transfer funds.

Transaction costs

EUROPE | **ENGLAND** NORTH AMERICA | **USA, NEW YORK**

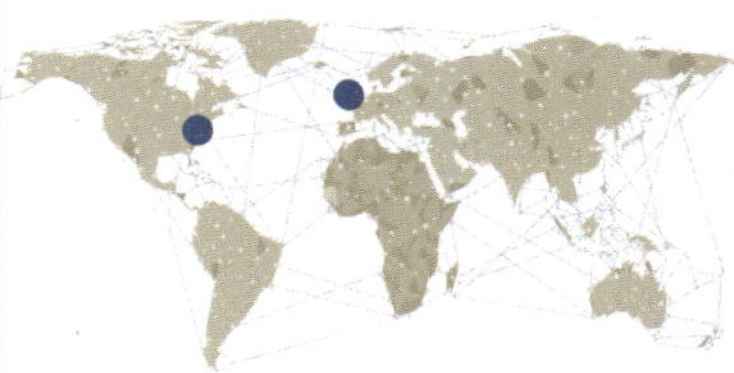

How is this changing? TransferWise shows how. This British company just couldn't bear it any longer to idly sit back and accept the exorbitant transfer fees the bank was charging. According to TransferWise, a hidden fifty euro fee for an international transfer of a thousand euros was utterly unnecessary. The company offered an alternative for this 'unfair ' bank practice. On their website, they declare that banks use another exchange rate for international transfers. On top of that, they charge a 'service fee' for these unfair practices. TransferWise uses a clever peer-to-peer system that functions outside of the bank's grasp. They promise transparency and for a one thousand euro transfer like the one just described, they only charge a five euro administration fee.[111]

Another example is given by the British company Iwoca who noticed the enormous growth of small businesses but at the same time, an inability for banks to finance these companies due to high administrative costs. Iwoca came up with a data based approach to measuring credit worthiness. They analyze a company's sales performance on eBay, Amazon, and other e-commerce platforms. This approach enables Iwoca to provide quick, flexible but well-considered credit lines to promising young businesses.[112]

These kinds of new approaches, together with 'disruptive' innovations encourage the banking sector to become more closely connected to the value that is created by the business, and to utilize parallel developments taking place in IT and mobile technology.

In the new economy, banks are starting to connect money and value again. They are letting go of the 'investment risk-return-reward' model. And are operating from a sustainable business model based on a shared value strategy: the creation of long-lasting value for all stakeholders.

Marcel Jeucken, the Director of Responsible Investment at PGGM, sees examples of this in Europe (Jeucken, 2002). Swiss banks as well as the Norwegian Den Norske Bank have made a cautious start with targeted premium differentiation. "It is not so much about evaluating or limiting environmental risks, but about purposefully shaping a direct contribution to a sustainable society. After all, for investors, strong financial securities or a healthy company can be a compensating factor for environmental risks."

Jeucken sees another example with the Co-Operative Bank of England. This bank developed a risk analysis method called "Natural Step" to check a company's contribution to sustainability. Companies that score well qualify for a lower interest rate. The total savings can amount to as much as thirty percent compared to regular bank rates (Jeucken, 2001).

Social Media Banking

EUROPE | **GERMANY**

One of the most prominent innovations in the banking world has come from Germany. At the Fidor Bank, you can open an account and log in using Facebook Connect. In one overview, you can see all of your accounts, investments, savings, and even virtual currencies such as World of Warcraft-gold. Furthermore, it is the first bank to let its interest rate be influenced by the number of 'likes' it receives on Facebook. The minimum is a half percent but it can increase by up to one and a half percent. Every month they calculate how many likes there are and adjust the interest rate. If there are 22,000 likes then the interest rate goes up by one and a half percent.[113]

The clever thing about this construction is that customers know that by 'advertising' to their Facebook friends, they can get a higher interest rate. Customers sharing with their friends like this also benefits the bank because it means that the bank can reduce their advertising budget. From the year they were founded in 2010 until 2012, Fidor has only spent one hundred thousand euros on marketing. This works out to less than one and a half cents per client. As a comparison, for a bank to advertise using Google Adwords, it costs an average of seven euros per click. Fidor also partners with other kinds of financial services on the web, such as peer-to-peer platforms where individuals can lend money to each other using crowdfunding. Additionally, they are utilizing hyperWALLET which is an international payment service, and Smava – a German classified advertisement listing for money instead of products.[114]

Facts & Figures

- The market for social banks is expected to rise 13 to 15 percent as opposed to 3 percent for traditional banks.[115]
- A survey of 5,300 bank customers showed that 70 percent would like there to be a physical bank location nearby so they can go there for whatever financial services they need.
- 22 percent of those surveyed said that closing these bank facilities are reason enough for them to switch banks.[116]

Micro-financing

Traditional banks attach high demands to their loans, such as a short-term return on their investment and having enough collateral to cover any financial risks. For small innovative businesses, these requirements are often difficult to meet and therefore, micro-financing can sometimes offer an alternative.

Micro-financing or micro-credit is the provision of a relatively small amount of money to people with low incomes. This type of financial arrangement is common for people living in countries without access to even the basic necessities such as clean water or electricity. This kind of financing, however, is not interesting for most banks because the return is low and the risks are high. Small businesses are therefore often directed to other financial institutions.

Micro-financing and crowdfunding platforms are not mutually exclusive. The Danish company My C4 is an example of a combination platform that uses crowdfunding to gather money from individuals and then micro-finances small businesses in Africa by lending them money at an attractive interest rate.[117]

Private equity

Private equity firms often receive similar criticism from the public as banks do. They are seen as 'blood sucking leeches' that attach themselves to a company, bleed it dry, then go on to the next victim.

Without diving into whether or not private equity firms brought this reputation on themselves, they are, nonetheless, giving themselves a makeover in the new economy. It is especially their rigorous focus on the return on investment that leads them to the conclusion that investing in sustainability delivers high returns. David Rubenstein, Director of The Carlyle Group, the largest private equity firm in the world states simply, "If you are prepared to put time into making your company sustainable, you will invariably earn more money."[118]

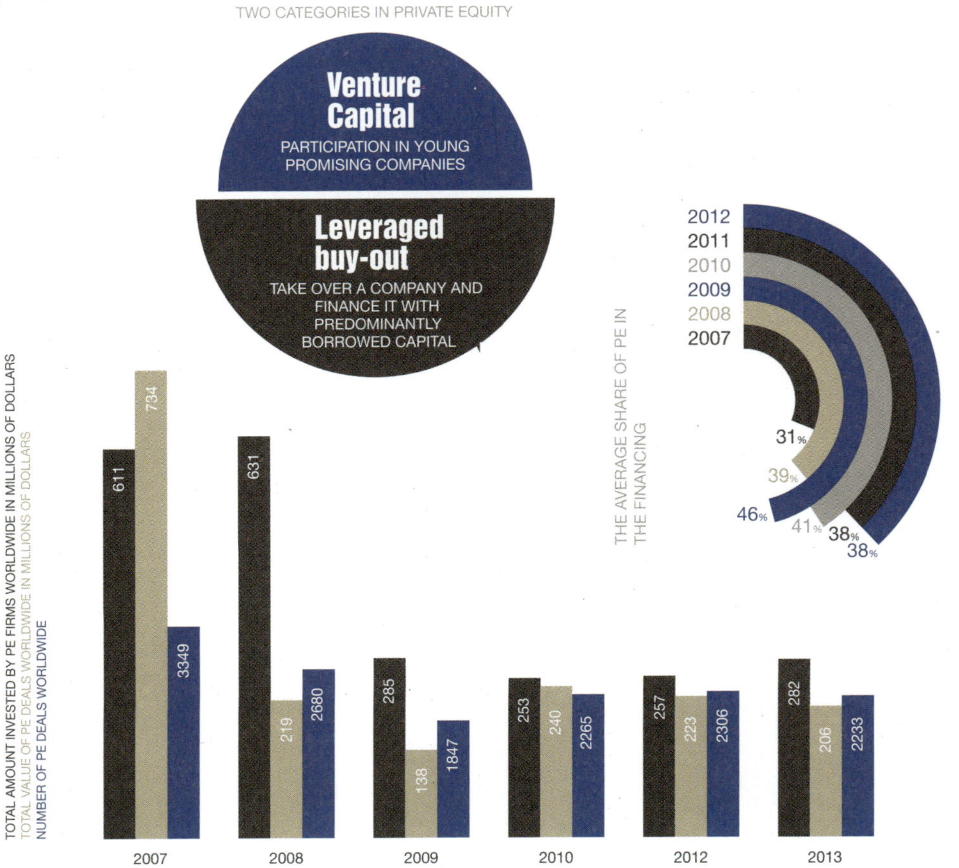

Illustration 29
Private equity

A recent study conducted by Malk Sustainability Partners and the Environmental Defense Fund dived deeper into the private equity firms and their application of sustainability, also known as *Environmental, Social and Governmental issues* (ESG). The result of the study showed that 54 percent of the firms in the United States views ESG as a lever for creating value. More than 90 percent predicts that their focus in the coming years will be on sustainable issues. Important contributors to this transition are the rising prices of raw materials and the opportunities for higher profits from energy efficiency.[119]

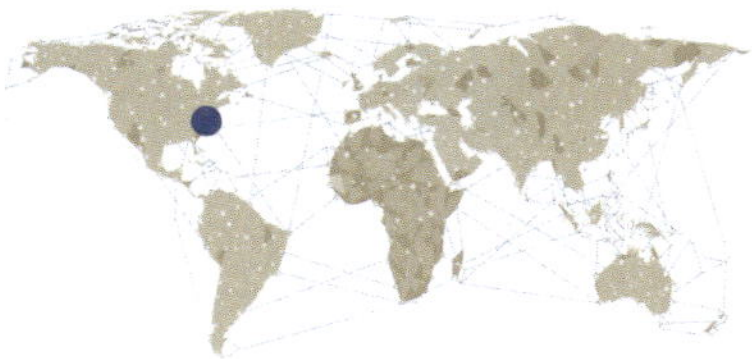

Private equity firm, Kohlberg, Kravis and Roberts (KKR)

NORTH-AMERICA I **USA, NEW YORK**

A successful example comes from the reputable American private equity firm Kohlberg, Kravis and Roberts (KKR) that launched the 'Green Portfolio Program' several years ago. This initiative was a collaboration with the Environmental Defense Fund. It began small but since 2008 it has expanded rapidly. KKR took twenty-five companies into their green portfolio and by doing so brought costs down by 644 million dollars. At the same time, these sustainable companies were able to reduce their CO_2 emissions by 1.2 million tons, their waste by 3.4 million tons, and 13.2 billion liters of water were saved.[120]

The study also showed that American companies, more so than their European counterparts, approach the integration of sustainability from a financial point of view. European firms are aware of the advantages that sustainability offers in the areas of risk management and image, but have yet to recognize that investing in sustainable companies delivers hard cold cash. In the new economy, a different perspective is emerging. Investing in the combination of cost savings on the one hand and ecological and social benefits on the other hand is resulting in private equity firms being promoted to top players in the financial sector.

Pension funds

The visible shift within the banking and investment sectors can be seen in pension funds as well. They are looking for opportunities to create sound and sustainable value for both their investment policy and the pension holder. Pension funds are replacing the passive *index investing* with a sense of involvement in the company. This comes from the conviction that investing in sustainable activities will pay off in the mid-term, which should cover the return on investment.

Pension funds are setting clear parameters for sustainable investing. PGGM offers a good example: In 2012 they launched the Responsible Investing in Private Equity Policy. This policy states that all companies that PGGM invests in must have a sustainable agenda or at the very least, they must be working on creating one. This is not only because of an ideological standpoint but also because a sustainable investment policy is profitable as well as cost and risk reducing. The French fund, the Réserve pour les Retraites, the American CalPERS, the Brazilian PREVI and the Norwegian governmental pension fund are all applying sustainable criteria more often.[121] In the new economy, funds are not only shutting the back door on unsavory practices such as weapons trade and child labor but they are opening the front door to active shareholders who stimulate companies to create positive, sustainable value.

Promising companies involved in sustainable activities such as green technology have not been attracting much attention from pension funds in the traditional economy. "Pension fund investors won't even get out of bed for an investment of less than a hundred million," or so they say. In the new economy, however, these small green companies are making themselves more interesting for pension funds. They are leaving their green island and rather than complaining about unwilling capital investors, they are seeking opportunities to collaborate with other promising start-ups. In this way, they increase their leverage and reach a more attractive scale for the pension funds.

Managing such a consortium requires a financial chain. Institutional investors, banks, and pension funds can cash in on the sustainable and financial potential of promising companies by forming a collaboration. There is a particular approach to pensions in the new economy that advances the creation of value. PGGM changed their course three years ago to make use of this. Frido Kraanen, Director of Cooperation and Sustainability explains, "A pension was originally created as a kind of postponed income. When you get to a point in your life that you are no longer in the workforce, then at least you will still have an income; you'll have the means to enjoy your retirement. Today you often see, even in large organizations such as ours, that the means is slowly but surely transforming into the goal. As PGGM is a cooperative, a direct line to our members is a crucial element to bringing that goal into perspective."

Therefore, PGGM decided to talk to their members to find out what was considered an enjoyable retirement. They expected that the conversation would mostly be about their pension. However, to their surprise, people hardly talked about it. According to Kraanen, "They mostly spoke about vitality, social surroundings, and a nice living environment. These were the things that were most important to their members. Money? Yes, well you need that to live of course."

As a result of their findings and through some self-searching, PGGM concluded that they should choose a different track. "That is why we said: at our essence, we are not about pensions, but about a valuable future." Kraanen draws the parallel between their shift in focus and that of a funeral service company called Dala. Dala had taken out a full page advertisement in the newspaper with just one word on the page: "Dear," It was the beginning of a letter to a loved one. Kraanen explains, "Dala does not say: 'We are excellent at burials and cremations. Oh, and we also offer you a nice cup of coffee and a piece of cake at the end of the funeral service.' No, instead, Dala says: 'We are a company that helps you bid farewell, because this is of value to you in this time of grief.' Of course they take care of the funeral arrangements, but the broader perspective is their leading message."

With their focus on value creation, pension funds are not simply paying out money at the time of retirement, they are forming partnerships with housing corporations, care facilities and insurance companies so they can issue their pensions together with more buying power and better living environments and care, and thus deliver to retirees the things that they truly value.

6.3 Shift towards value management

Financing, according to the blue print of the Trias Pecunia, means a shift from financial management to value management. As described in the introduction of this chapter, value is defined in the broad sense of the word and covers the ecological, social and financial assets. Entrepreneurs in the new economy strive to create value for these three assets. In order to make this manageable and comprehensible, it is necessary to put a price tag on the value. This is not happening often enough in the traditional economy.

"There are a lot of companies that do something with sustainability", says Peter Bakker, President of the World Business Council for Sustainable Development (WBCSD). "They have a Sustainability Manager and a Sustainability Report. However, in the capital market, sustainability carries less weight than the financial report. This can only change if we treat natural capital as scarce commodities and bring it into the reporting."[122]

Integrated reporting

New economy businesses attach a financial aspect to value management by using integrated reporting. This method of reporting integrates the social and economic value in the traditional annual reports and associates financial weight to it where possible.

Businesses scrutinize their entire valuation cycle related to the new economy model, from project plans and annual reports to business statements and multi-annual programs. In other words, it should be transparent how and where value is being created or associated on every level. It is about being one step ahead instead of two steps behind.

This method of valuing is not only meant to measure risks and external factors, it also measures the social and ecological value creation that would have been ignored in the traditional economy. This leads to environmental and social profit and loss statements.

It is important that there is an unambiguous value association and categorization. There must be an appropriate value associated with the social and ecological assets but also the processes within them. As seen in the examples below, this is already being done in many parts of the world.

Creating social value is the most unchartered aspect of this spectrum. Recent developments, with a fair amount happening in my country, the Netherlands, have made clear that social profits can be transparent and well implemented. The People+ Program from DSM is a good example of this. DSM, the global science-based company active in health, nutrition and materials, has developed their own framework to make social value creation transparent. For instance, just think of the positive effects that vitamins and healthy nutrition have on consumers.

Integrated reporting that clearly shows the positive value being created for social and ecological assets is very attractive for companies in the new economy. It is also used as an instrument to lay the connection between the strategy, management, and financial performance of the company and the ecological, social, and economic context that the company functions within. However, it can be difficult to make value creation noticeable and transparent. Carola Wijdoogen of the Dutch Train Service (Nederlandse Spoorwegen) says, “The reported quality of our services - public transportation - needs to be put in the perspective of the experienced performance. To put it more clearly: we are proud to be in the top three of the international benchmark when it comes to punctuality versus track occupancy, but this achievement does not mean anything for the individual traveler who experiences a delay.”

One of the hurdles that sustainable companies had to overcome in the traditional economy was the lack of a key ratio. Integrated reporting can, in due course, eliminate these hurdles because, as opposed to the prevalent sustainable annual report, value creation goes hand in hand with commercial company goals. Wijdoogen agrees, "In 2013, we made our first steps to monetize our impact, especially our environmental impact.[123] The primary reason for us to go in this direction was to better manage our impact and to make better informed, integrated decisions."

Puma,

EUROPE | **GERMANY**

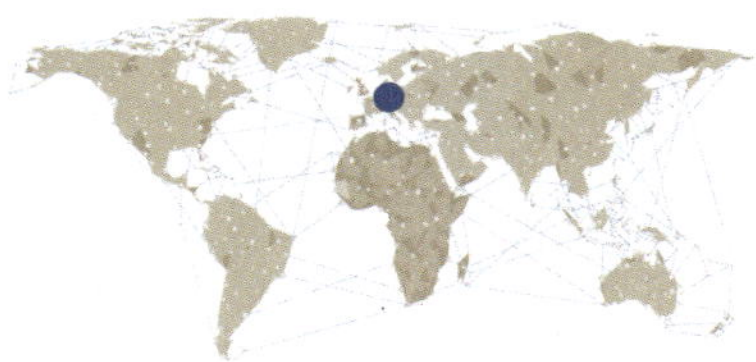

The German shoe and clothing manufacturer Puma shows how they have introduced integrated reporting into their environmental profit and loss statement (EP&L). Puma wanted to use this type of reporting to give an honest impression of the financial consequences of their ecological footprint. In 2010, the company calculated the footprint of their entire supply chain with the help of accountants at Trucost and PricewaterhouseCoopers. It turned out that the ecological costs amounted to approximately 170 million dollars which Puma then deducted from their profit. The use of leather was especially detrimental to the environment. Consequently, Puma is now looking for an adequate replacement for leather. [124]

Puma now puts 'environmental price-tags' on many of their new products. Puma has already introduced biodegradable shoes and T-shirts. The environmental impact of their new InCycle shoes is calculated at three percent of the sales price (approximately $3.50). That is a third of the environmental footprint resulting from the production of most shoes. For their T-shirts, the environmental cost was much higher at twelve percent, but that is compared to seventeen percent for the traditional cotton versions.

Puma also currently integrates social aspects in their reports. Parameters include fair wages for their workers, good living and working conditions, safety and stability, race and gender equality protections, and health.[125]

The development of knowledge about integrated reporting is essential, says Johan Piet, a Dutch accountant for social responsibility. He has defined over five hundred social areas that should be taken into account in an integrated report. "If you cluster these, there are approximately one hundred areas to consider. Therefore, it will take decades before we can reliably quote integrated reporting."[126] Wijndogen has experienced this hurdle at the Dutch Train Service as well, "This year, we want to further develop this way of thinking and reporting, especially related to quantifying the societal costs and benefits of the organization. It is challenging, however, because for the most part, it is unpaved territory. There are various methods to quantify and to monetize, but there is no generally accepted method for the consistent application to the social impact."

New economy businesses are following Puma's example from the perspective of risk management. The depletion of natural resources and the continuous usage of fossil fuels always come at a price in the long term. By making the costs visible and internalizing them at an early stage, businesses can reduce their ecological and social impact more easily and become better prepared for the future. As Peter Bakker, President of WBCSD, points out, "What is measured is also managed." [127]

From CFO to CVO

New economy businesses recognize the transformation to value management and understand that it requires a fresh approach to the organizational and leadership structures. The latter is expanded upon in Chapter 6: Leadership, and the former can best be described by stepping into the C-suite. The C-suite is where the Chief Executive Officer (CEO), the Chief Financial Officer (CFO), the Chief Innovation Officer (CIO) and the Chief Operations Officer (COO) reside. Over the last few years, some new Cs have arrived. There is the Chief Ethics Officer (another CEO), the Chief Learning Officer (CLO), the Chief Marketing Officer (CMO), the Chief Sustainability Officer (CSO) and the Chief Knowledge Officer (CKO).[128]

As companies in the new economy are reconstructing their value proposition based on social, ecological and financial assets, they are making the transition to a holistic management style that enables and promotes value creation. While this requires a new approach, it also calls for the introduction of a Chief Value Officer (CVO). This is not an additional 'C' in the suite, it is the same CFO but with a broader perspective.

The reasoning behind this is that value creation, also on the social and ecological levels deserves a financial representation, as argued in the Chapter 0: The New Economy. Chris Ballinger, CFO and Senior Vice President of Toyota Financial Services explains: "The differentiator between the finance department and other departments in the organization is the matrix that we use: the value matrix. The targets of the sales department, for example, are expressed in units. If we sell X amount of units, we have Y percentage of the market share. But these units often do not mean anything to the other departments. The finance department, on the other hand, uses a value matrix which is understood by the entire company." [129] In other words, everyone understands when it is about money. And that makes the CFO the most appropriate candidate to become the CVO.

Illustration 30
CFO to CVO

The CVO is in a position to express values such as labor conditions, ecological effects of production, and transport in monetary terms and steer the company towards maximizing these values. Doing business in the new economy is more than achieving the maximum financial return, it is based on networking, cross-sector connections, thinking beyond the supply chain, and multiple value creation. The CVO does not just concern himself with the financial value but with the total value of the company. In short, he cares about the creation, evaluation, and management of value.[130]

This is a very different approach than what is seen in the traditional economy. For years there has been a certain definition of profit that did not include any financial connection to the social and environmental impact the organization or their partners had.

Associating value to social and ecological assets was rarely seen before the digital and mobile revolution, says Melle Eijckelhoff, Director of the management training institute Alex van Groningen. " Thirty years ago, no one knew what the consequences were of their business activities up or down the supply chain. Business owners were not aware and neither were their customers." However, the feedback loops have gotten shorter over the years and business owners are being held accountable which makes them, and their entire chain, more vulnerable.

The CVO sees this development as an opportunity, not a threat. By broadening the value definition within his organization, he expands the field of vision and consequently the potential market. In the words of Eijckelhoff, "If you make choices in your production process that will reduce the environmental impact in India, for example, or if you ensure that your labor policy and your use of cheap labor creates value for the communities where these people live, then you develop a situation where the people living in those areas will one day become your customers as well."

Value management, far away and close by

As value management is not only about limiting negative effects, but also focused on the creation of value, this can be applied to the direct surroundings of the organization as well, says Eijckelhoff. "For instance, you can create value for the area surrounding your office building. You could, for example, have a look at the parking pressure that is caused by your company, or check whether there is sufficient lighting at night? Are you causing noise pollution? And in a positive sense, what are you doing for your environment? For instance, you may have a canteen that is busy at lunchtime but is empty the rest of the day. Perhaps there is a school nearby that might be interested in using the space for supplemental lessons. If you can provide this space to the school, you will help them out and moreover, you will bring the community closer to you. This is advantageous for all parties involved and contributes to a better society. The ripple effects of a value creating approach are sometimes unforeseeable but are often positive and worthwhile."

In other words, by stretching the parameters of the value proposition, CVOs expand the reach of their organization and deliver a new range of opportunities for the short and the long term. Such an approach demands new competencies from the former CFO turned CVO. He or she needs to include long-term calculations and convince shareholders to accept long-term returns, sometimes looking at five, ten or fifteen years before they will see a profit from the investments.

A Chief Value Officer is also responsible for making sure that the entire company and all the organizational processes are focused on the same goal: creating maximum value. Additionally, risk management in the new economy is focused on what the company, and the CVO *do*, not what is omitted. This is due to the fact that the value created by an organization does more to reduce or eliminate long-term risks than the avoidance of value associations. The CVO sets organization-specific values and connects these values to company targets and guides the appropriate departments to develop strategies to reach these goals. The CVO is the pivotal figure in value management within the organization.

Wrap up

New economy businesses are connecting real value to money once again. They are including social and ecological factors into their calculations and looking at the financial picture from a holistic viewpoint. This approach gives a truer insight into the real revenues and expenses of the company and allows sustainable activities to count towards the company's worth. Financing is no longer controlled by powerful banking institutions. Various funding solutions such as crowdfunding and other creative forms of financing are providing a broad pallet of opportunities for sustainable initiatives. The development of financial solutions that create value also boosts the quality of the business. Businesses are using the principles set out in the Trias Pecunia, which is a dynamic yet stable paradigm that outlines the emerging perspective of financing in the new economy. Companies are limiting their demand for financing, drawing capital from long-term partners and vested stakeholders, and using borrowed capital frugally and efficiently. With value creation as the main driver, the Chief Value Officer is the natural evolution of the Chief Financial Officer, as financing in the new economy is based on a comprehensive vision including all assets.

Leadership roles in the new economy are redefined.

Chapter 7

WINDOW OF OPPORTUNITY:

Leadership

New leadership is transformational, not transactional.

Successful leaders and organizations live and breathe social, environmental and financial sustainability.

Leadership revolves around added value. The leadership role is shared accordingly.

Introduction

In the previous chapters, I have described a new perspective of doing business in a sustainable economy - a radical new economy that is sustainable in itself; an economy where entrepreneurs create value with the focus on our three primary assets. We have looked at the different management areas – from innovation to financing – and explored the frontline of the economy and saw how pioneering companies are approaching business from an innovative, sustainable vision.

The trailblazers on the frontline are showing courage and vision, but sometimes they stumble along the way. This is understandable. After all, it is the frontline that gets hit first. But ultimately, they all (each in their own way) reach the forefront and reap the rewards of their courage. They profit from the acquired knowledge, innovative business models, and competitive advantage. It goes without saying that the pioneers of the new economy are showing real leadership in the true sense of the word. These leaders are, in the words of the late leadership guru, Stephen Covey, "beginning with the end in sight." They dare to let go of the old principles and have the courage to take an unknown road. At the same time, they are able to convince not only themselves but also the people that work with them and are able to mobilize others with their authentic enthusiasm. They share their vision, expertise, and enthusiasm but they also share their leadership. They are empowering their people and breaking away from short-term performance indicators.

The above description awakens some questions, including: Why and how do leaders share their leadership? Wouldn't they need to let go of established structures if they did this? How does one know that 'beginning with the end in sight' will lead to success? And which competencies are needed for this?

While most CEOs these days place sustainability at the top of the agenda, there are many who still find it difficult to actually shift their business model to become fundamentally more sustainable. Many claim that a lack of financial latitude is to blame for not moving forward with sustainability. This also leads to another obstacle, namely a limited scope. The way to true sustainable transformation requires an approach that is not limited to only one sustainable activity, such as the reduction of CO_2 emissions or a sustainable purchasing policy. An organization needs to focus on creating sustainable value in all its economic activities: financial, social and ecological. Sustainability is not a sideline, it is a concerted shift in the portfolio in order to achieve real results. Sustainability needs to be part of the heart and soul of the organization. Sustainable thinking needs to permeate actions within the entire organization and be an integral part of KPIs, integrated reporting, bonuses, and promotions.

As the CEO of the Sustainable Business Association, I work with leaders from all over the world on a daily basis who choose, from a sense of conviction, to be pioneers in their field of expertise. So before we go any deeper into these questions, it is important to realize that many of these leaders were faced with the same questions when they decided to start doing business in the new economy. They ventured into the new rules of the game even though they had yet to find the answers.

So why did they make this choice? Why did they choose to let go of the old structures and set a course for the new economy? In essence, it comes down to the following: leaders in the new economy take responsibility. They take responsibility for their own organization, but also for their surroundings and for the environments where they operate and where their suppliers operate. They have come to the same conclusion that we talked about in Chapter 0: The New Economy, namely that the world is not here for the economy, the economy is here for the world.

Paul Polman, CEO Unilever

"If we reach our goals of sustainability but nobody follows us, we will have failed."[131]

This is an entirely new principal than that of the traditional economy where leadership, to a greater or lesser degree, revolves around the achievement of a competitive price quality ratio. For example, to this day laborers in low-wage countries are underpaid, following the corporate motto, “better underpaid than unemployed.” We justify our leadership this way, but at the same time we do not contribute, with any sense of conviction, towards the wellbeing of these workers or their economy.

The leadership of the traditional economy tends to have an exploitive nature and is often primarily focused on the creation of value for the organization. Leaders in the traditional economy walk a path of value extraction. This has been going well for a long time because the amount of value that could be obtained seemed endless. However, we now know it to be finite. Think of the unrestrained extraction of fossil fuels and raw materials that has resulted in environmental and food crises, but also of the unbridled speculation and money creation that has resulted in catastrophic financial and economic hardships. This approach has led to much social misery. There used to be sweatshops in Manchester, England. Although they no longer exist there, the same business practices are being used in other parts of the world. There are still places on our planet that are ridden with child labor, underpayment and exploitation.

Entrepreneurs who are genuinely driven to explore sustainability, lead the way towards value creation for all assets. They empower the value of the earth, the value of people, and the value of money. To achieve this, they are prepared to let go of the path to efficiency and apparent effectiveness, and to tight controls and management of cost calculations, volumes and margins, as well as business based on scale.

Before I took on the leadership of the Sustainable Business Association, I was an entrepreneur. I know from experience how difficult it is to let go of patterns that dominate the economic context in which you operate. You need to be headstrong. You need to be able to step away from the current conservative context and welcome renewal. As a leader, you must be able to give others the assurance they need so they can follow your path. You should also share your own doubts and uncertainties but without burdening others with undue concern.

Authentic sustainability leaders are lonely at the moment. That is why they seek connections with other like-minded leaders in communities and networks. But their mission surpasses these networks and they take on the role of leading others in the transition to the new economy.

7.1 Profile: From transactional to transformational leadership

A leader in the new economy has the qualifications to translate the potential of the sustainably driven economy into real business models. In comparison to the traditional economy, this is a movement, a shift from transactional to transformational leadership. Authenticity, intrinsic motivation, networking, and sharing are the most important tools in the tool kit.

Transactional Leadership is by definition 'old leadership'. It is focused, to a large degree, on the short-term success of the company. In order to achieve short-term successes time and time again, an employer motivates his employees to complete transactions, by either offering rewards or penalties.

Leaders use principles of exchange to appeal to the extrinsic motivation of employees, such as salary raises, bonuses, or gifts - such as the latest smartphone or a company car. Transactional leaders reward good performance and 'punish' bad performance. Transactional leadership is, by definition, based on hierarchy and domination.

Consequently, transactional leadership creates limited sustainable value which is one important reason why this approach is not desired in the new economy. This is not to say that rewards such as salary rises should be relegated to the wayside, just that it should not be the leading factor. Employees that receive a pay rise see it as a confirmation that they are doing well. By receiving this form of appreciation, they will most likely continue doing what they are doing and maybe go about it in a slightly more efficient way, but this kind of stimulus does not inspire them to do things from a whole new perspective. However, it is exactly this radical change in perspective that is needed. The path to the new economy requires a transformation and a complete paradigm shift. Intrinsically, rather than extrinsically, motivated employees and a dedicated focus on the creation of sustainable value for the whole ecological, social, and financial context of the enterprise is essential in the new economy.

This was illustrated earlier with the example of Zappos, the online clothing store. They ensure that only intrinsically motivated people join their company by giving them a choice at the end of their training period. They offer them either 4,000 dollars or employment. The trainees that opt for the employment contract rather than the quick cash are motivated to work for Zappos.[132]

Ricardo Semler, CEO Semco SA

"What it comes down to, of course, is that when people make their own decisions, they are more dedicated to everything that follows."

New leaders are, at the core, transformational leaders. They lead by tapping into their workers' intrinsic motivation as well as offering extrinsic incentives.

In other words, they manage their people by offering the rewards that are still appreciated, like higher salaries, but they specifically pay attention to the process that leads to the rewards. Transformational leaders exchange old principles for a new focus on the development of capacities as well as norms and values of their employees. They set up their internal hierarchical structure as a dynamic network that is based on trust. Employees are granted far-reaching autonomy as opportunities to excel. Uwaygo, a Dutch mobility service which is an initiative of the Royal HaskoningDHV and Technolution, presents a good example of this new setup. Coen Jager of Royal HaskoningDHV explains, "Uwaygo gives employees complete freedom when it comes to how they travel and how they spend their mobility budget." The employer and employee have full insight into the mobility costs and the impact of the CO_2 emissions. This results in the employees being intrinsically motivated to make more efficient and responsible choices (which also results in financial benefits). In this way, the employer uses positive incentives to steer the company in a sustainable direction. The result is an effective balance between supply and demand, less traffic jams, and less CO_2 emissions.

Transformational leadership also means that the decision making power is decentralized. In other words, new economy leaders allow others to occasionally take the leadership role while they take a serving role. Giving others an opportunity at the helm allows them to develop, and ultimately strengthens the innovative power of the organization.

New economy leaders are accountable and conscious of their added value. Provided they can deliver added value based on their capabilities, their vision, their ability to think in long-term perspectives, and their power to outline a broad view, they take the reins and lead the company with authority. However, if they cannot add value in a particular context or situation then they pull back and take a place in the background.

In his *Harvard Business Review* article, "Level 5 Leadership" author Jim Collins called this the 'blend' between personal humility and a deep rooted professional will. Collins referred to one of the most famous American presidents, Abraham Lincoln, as a "quiet, peaceful and shy man who never let his ego get in the way of his ambition to build an enduring, great nation." Collins' five-year study showed that the paradoxical combination of *humility* and *will* is what it takes to transform a company from 'Good to Great' (Collins, 2001).

Will Day, Chairman, Sustainable Development Commission (2010)

"Sustainability works best when an organization's leadership gets it, wants it to happen, and enables it in such a way that everyone from the person who sweeps the floor to the finance director feels part of that mission."

Transformational leadership is therefore the essential foundation for intrinsically driven leaders striving for sustainability, maximum value creation, and no waste.

The human factor is often overshadowed when talking about a new sustainable economy. There seems to be little attention to broken families, burn-outs, and overworked or overstressed employees. According to Harry Starren, former CEO of the Dutch top management institute De Baak, "We have come to accept these things as a natural part of the working world. It's the old adage, *no pain – no gain*." However, leaders in the new economy reject such a trade-off. They embrace the new circular leadership which calls for a radical change in behavior. In a circular driven organization, success no longer depends on the qualities of an individual, but the interaction among those individuals.

In the traditional economy we would compliment managers by saying: "He's a good one! He knows how to get the best *out* of people!" In the new economy, a leader distinguishes himself by getting people to *rise* to their highest level. This way the employee is given the opportunity to create value instead of having the value extracted from him.

Hotel Botanique

SOUTH AMERICA, **BRAZIL**

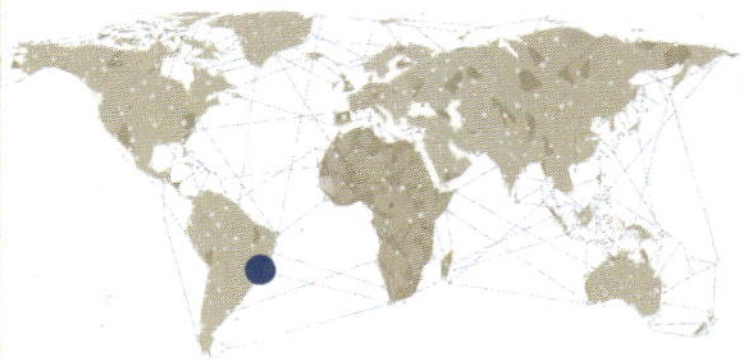

The renowned Brazilian businessman Ricardo Semler is a good example of this kind of leadership. He caused a sensation in the nineties by fundamentally transforming his organization. Semler radically reduced his management team and shifted many responsibilities to his staff. He applied the same democratization in his new hotel Botanique, as he explained in a recent interview.[133] "We wanted to eliminate everything that bothered us about hotels. Therefore, there are no check-in or check-out times, the rooms are cleaned multiple times a day, the guest can even have his bag unpacked for him and his clothes ironed and neatly hung up in the closet. From the moment you book a room, there is one person responsible for you which means that you do not have to continually deal with different hotel employees all the time. Before we started with this, everyone said it was logistically impossible. However, we made the wise decision of recruiting people who lived near the hotel and who therefore had an interest in staying on in our company. Although none of our employees had ever worked in a hotel before, we won the Tatler award in our first year, making us one of the top 5 hotels in the world."

7.2 New Leadership: Six key characteristics

New economy entrepreneurs are approaching their businesses and management in a totally new way. This has been expanded upon in the previous chapters and is outlined in the following summary of the six characteristics of new economy business. This chapter on leadership is intentionally placed as the last chapter in the book. Leadership is the wrapping around all business activities. Leaders steer the way in the new economy to create value for all our assets.

Leaders need to possess specific characteristics in order to pave the way to new economy business. Intrinsic motivation is the most important. Sometimes leaders need to take certain actions related to sustainability when the results are uncertain, making intrinsic motivation a prerequisite. Leadership must also be authentic; leaders should dare to follow their own moral compass and should be convinced that the transformation to sustainability is essentially their responsibility. Only then will they be able to cope with the pressures from stakeholders. Sustainable leadership must be long term, consistent, and formed over time. Research has shown that it takes at least three years for an intensive sustainable policy to yield demonstrable financial results. Short-term results and profits, therefore, should not be the motivating factor. The route to true sustainability in the new economy is not a sprint, but a marathon.

A summary of the six characteristics of new economy business

Customers
Access and performance are consumers' main interests in the new economy. Businesses are adapting to the new customer proposition by developing services to accommodate the total needs of the customer. Automobile manufacturers, for example, produce cars but sell mobility. Short-term sales transactions are being replaced by long-term service agreements.

Value Cycle
The Value Cycle is the dynamic creation of maximum value on a large scale for all assets: social, ecological, and financial. Global challenges, long-term thinking and innovation are key factors. Collaboration and a circular approach to production shares the risks, forges new profit channels and creates sustainable value. Circular 'satellites' are designed to replace the linear supply chain allowing new economy businesses to close the loop. Recycling, reuse, and upcycling are becoming more commonplace, easier, and more profitable.

Scale
Companies are creating strong, decentralized markets. As a result, local, regional and global businesses are developing different, interconnected relationships with each other. Globalization is giving way to 'Glocalization'; a global perspective with a local interest. The development of renewable energy also plays a crucial role. Businesses recognize the strength of a decentralized economy and are exploring, primarily on local levels, possibilities to connect with each other to become more efficient and more profitable. For example, they are creating industrial ecosystems to efficiently use residual resources.

Innovation
New economy businesses are choosing *collective* innovation rather than *isolated* innovation. Sharing knowledge supports competitive advantages.

Entrepreneurial innovation means innovating in networks, not according to hierarchal positions. By working on business innovations together with suppliers, consumers, and even competitors, companies are expanding their knowledge, strengthening their financial leverage, increasing their profit, and promoting the viability of their innovations.

Business cases

Companies are setting up their business cases in an entirely new manner. They are not reasoning from their organization's perspective but from the business case. In this way, they stop thinking in a linear fashion and the parameters fall away. Their search for partners is not based on first looking at themselves but rather by using the business case as the starting point and asking, "With which partners can I create value?"

Financing

Businesses are reconciling the real value of capital. They are avoiding short-term financing options with high risk profiles and opting to operate according to the Trias Pecunia principles. This means that they are viewing borrowed capital with a critical eye to the real added value. Financial institutions are starting to ask what the societal aims are and putting these targets into their equation. The question "What can we earn from this deal?" is no longer the predominant determiner, but is rapidly being replaced with, "What opportunities are we contributing to by providing this financing?"

So, what characterizes leadership in the new economy? There are six primary skills that leaders must have in order to steer their businesses in this new arena. These skills are crucial for adequately positioning oneself within the interactive economic variables that were described in Chapter 0: The New Economy. Those variables are: disruptive technology, new customer values, globalization, fluctuating geopolitical relationships, growing connectedness of businesses and consumers and the associated mobile and digital revolution, and the consumer demand for full transparency and sustainable business practices.

Peter Bakker, President World Business Council for Sustainable Development

"*Shared values* calls for a shift in focus. *Shareholder value* is no longer the driving force for businesses, shared values means looking at employee interests and the interests of society as well. This requires a deviation from the purely shareholder-driven capitalist model." [134]

The new leadership model can be best described as: guiding the optimal integration of business objectives in a rapidly changing economic playing field in order to create maximum ecological, social and financial value. The leadership skills required for this can be qualified in the following six essential characteristics.

1 Open and uniting

New economy leaders are convinced that working together with partners delivers better results than 'going it alone'. Consequently, a successful CEO in the new economy has the ability to create connections with partners who can contribute value through innovations, dynamic business cases, or minimizing the financial burden.

As was shown in previous chapters, connections need to be made cross-sector and cross-market. Knowing your own sector thoroughly and focusing only on your own arena is becoming less important and less relevant. The ability to connect knowledge and qualities to your organization is of higher significance in today's economy. Therefore, it is crucial in this regard to also be prepared to share knowledge and expertise. Keeping it all behind closed doors ultimately means less gain. Close-fisted leaders lose their positions because they do not add value.

Sharing and connecting goes beyond the four walls of the company. Global issues such as pollution and climate change are perfect examples of problems that affect us all. Leaders need to understand the extent of these challenges and not only put their own time and energy into it but also rally their networks.

New economy leaders approach business relations as a player in a network. This is a more dynamic position than in the traditional economy where companies are often just parts of a linear chain with fewer partners. These dynamic networks also differ in that consumers play a role as co-creators, innovators, and financiers.

2 Curious and interested in collaboration

Maximum value is created through connections and collaborations. In order to achieve this, leaders need a broad overview. The fast-paced technological developments that we face today require a cross-company, cross-sector approach. CEOs that are not primarily concerned with internal company politics are in a better position to see the big picture. They have more room to ask, "What is happening in the outside world?" And, "How does my company relate to the developments taking place out there?" Given this perspective, the leader is better able to identify any shortcomings of the organization, circumvent problems, and find solutions. Collaboration is also crucial for an effective innovation strategy which, in contrast to innovation processes in the traditional economy, no longer takes place in-house only, but also in open relationships with large and small partners.

3 Focused on the long term

From the perspective of building relationships and laying connections, CEOs are looking more at the long term. They realize that real value creation gains stature in the long term. Additionally, the new client proposition (the transformation from *ownership* to *access* and *use*) necessitates the skill to build enduring relationships with customers. The 'point of sale' is falling by the wayside, and it is being replaced by sustained relationships with customers. Because of this new approach, CEOs need to build their company's performance levels rather than concentrating on the maximum price-quality ratio. Customers in the new economy are not looking for the best product anymore, but want the best overall experience.

4 Fully transparent

Transparency within the organization and outside is a requisite in today's digital world. Businesses and individuals are subject to global public exposure. But leaders in the new economy see this as an opportunity not a threat. It is because of this wide-spread exposure that they can make their value known. A new economy leader is in that respect a *communicator* who is ready to spread the word about his company's endeavors. The CEO should be able to motivate, stimulate, and activate. There is no such thing as too much communication in this day and age. However, the message needs to be authentic if it is going to be effective. Leaders who are transparent towards their employees, customers, partners, as well as towards themselves possess a high level of self-awareness and authenticity. Good leaders know and understand their own motivations and those of others as well. Because of this, they are able to stimulate and activate the intrinsic motivations of their employees. Consumers are also calling for more transparency and more sustainability in the production process. Therefore, it is not only crucial that CEOs achieve more transparency within their own organizations but also that their entire supply chain, or rather the entire value cycle, is transparent as well. To reach this objective, value cycles need strong leadership that can persuade and guide all the parties involved. The leadership cannot be based on hierarchy alone, but should be self-aware, authentic, and intrinsically motivated.

5 Globally present, locally rooted

Strong roots in local markets is now being recognized as an essential element in the new economy. It is in the local communities and local ecosystems where innovative collaboration is grown. Local presence is vital because the relationship with the consumer has become more important and more involved. At the same time, entrepreneurs are keeping a close eye on the developments and opportunities in the world around them. With the advent of the mobile and digital revolution, borders are diminishing rapidly in the international business arena. The global spread of information is bringing the frontline of innovation to the front door of every business regardless of their location. New economy leaders are able to connect the strength of the local communities and the endless opportunities presented by the global economy. This approach allows the company's leaders to think small and think big at the same time. It is becoming simpler to take innovations that are created on a local level and upscale them to a global level but it requires the ability to think on a collective level. The world is behaving as a collective organism and no longer as separate companies, markets or countries.

6 Facilitators of innovation

It may seem to be a given that CEOs should be facilitators of innovation, but unfortunately it is not. In the traditional economy, an innovative company would fund their own internal R&D department. In the new economy, however, innovative leadership is interpreted as the capacity to attract innovative talent. Leaders are also keeping an eye out for small and creative innovators but resisting the inclination to incorporate these innovators. Instead, they are giving them a place outside the parameters of their organization.

As facilitators, they insist on significant innovation, not incremental improvements. The amount of capital investment is not the leading determiner, it is the way in which the capital is invested which is the most important consideration. The new leadership understands that developing a truly innovative company is a cultural endeavor. They need to encourage all members and partners of the organization to contribute to the innovative process and allow them the room to express their creativity. Innovation is not limited to the R&D department. Innovation is being initiated, inspired and supported by the leadership and leaders are also "letting go" to a certain extent in order to create a conducive environment for creativity. This comes down to the shift from *management by decision* to *management by design* (Kumar, 2012).

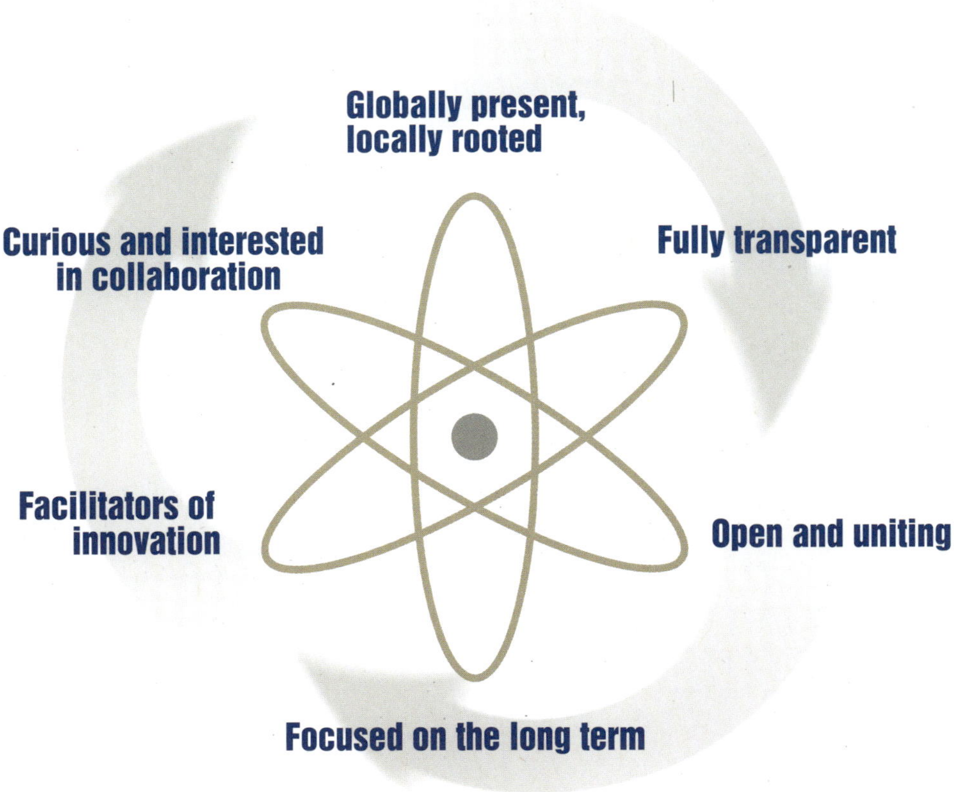

Illustration 31
Leadership atom

Illustration 31 shows the six characteristics of the new leadership. They are complementary characteristics and each one is important in order to create maximum value in the six management areas of new economy business.

Herman Wijffels: Professor Sustainability and Societal Change at the University of Utrecht, The Netherlands and former CEO of Rabobank, The Netherlands.

"Leadership will become more of a reflection of the feelings within an organization. Leadership in this context refers to the capacity to inspire and persuade others to enter unknown terrains."

7.3 New definitions for old roles

Leadership in the new economy is conducted on different levels and fulfills a variety of roles. As mentioned earlier in this chapter, leaders are sharing their leadership and the hierarchal lines are being replaced by network structures. CEOs, managers, professionals, and supervisors are fulfilling their roles based on their added value and they are being held accountable. Leadership also means evaluating when you should come to the forefront and when you should take a step back to either assert your authority or allow others to take the lead.

CEO (Chief Executive Officer)

CEOs in the new economy are convinced that their organizations contribute value to society. This is their firm starting point and from this perspective they can see how their business plays a role and creates value. They can also recognize how things should change and what improvements are needed. CEOs are charged with the important task of maintaining an overview. They look *horizontally* for new partners (small and large) to innovate with, build connections, and create value either by receiving input or sharing their own expertise or value network. They also look *vertically* because – in contrast to many CEOs in the traditional economy – they do not live and operate from quarterly report to quarterly report, but instead focus on the long term. CEOs think about their legacy. In the words of Paul Polman, CEO of Unilever, "Short-term focus does not benefit society. By following this course, we are stealing from our children and grandchildren."[135]

In the transition towards an economy driven by sustainability, CEOs know their part to play. They do not wait for governments to take action. They establish themselves at the forefront and continually search for opportunities to bring about change and communicate the need for this change. CEOs are the ones who are in a position to achieve significant impact for the long term. They are also often able to stay at the helm longer than their political counterparts.

CEOs in the new economy operate from the conviction that businesses that are led towards creating value ultimately create better business. This approach requires vision and courage. When Unilever's CEO Paul Polman was asked by a journalist from the *Harvard Business Review* if he could prove that sustainable business actually led to greater bottom line profits, he answered: "I'd rather turn that question around. How can you prove that non-sustainable activities do not damage society and humanity? Because that is what is now happening. This approach to business has brought us many of the problems we face today. It is crystal clear that if organizations set up their business models with sustainability in mind that they will accelerate their growth."[136]

CEOs approach the people in their organizations in a similar way. They recognize that control and hierarchy does not inspire employees to develop their own vision and aspire to be of value to the organization. To achieve the desired goal, leadership and responsibility should be shared. CEOs realize that they do not need to be good at everything, but they do need to excel in the right things. And what are those things exactly? We will describe the six essential skills of a CEO in the following section but there is one thing they all exude and that is *clarity*. Clarity about their goals, their value, and their business model. In other words, they make crystal clear: What are we trying to achieve?; What values do we use to pursue that goal?; and How do we ensure that the organization remains financially sound and competitive?[137]

Six essential CEO skills

Based on a study involving over twenty thousand CEOs, researchers of the Harvard Business School found six crucial skills that help CEOs to think strategically and navigate through the unknown.[138]

1 Anticipate

Many organizations are not good at seeing the threats and opportunities that appear on the periphery of their organization. The beer company Coors, for example, missed a major business opportunity because it did not notice the demand for a low calorie alternative in time. CEOs in the new economy are keenly observant. They speak with clients, assess client satisfaction and if they lose a client they find out why this happened and what they can improve. They also keep an eye on fast growing competitors and visit conferences and events related to other industries and they look at various scenarios in order to be prepared for the unexpected.

2 Challenge

CEOs challenge themselves and others to test and refine patterns and assumptions. Only after careful consideration and examination from various points of views do they make a decision. They are patient, courageous, and open minded. When approaching a problem, they focus on the cause and not on the symptoms. To achieve this, they hold 'safe-zone meetings' in which open dialogue and discussion are encouraged. When making a decision, "naysayers" are involved to question problems quickly. CEOs in the new economy also cherish the input of people who are in no way affected positively or negatively by the decision.

3 Interpret

Leaders - even those who challenge their organizations in the right way - will sometimes be confronted with complex and contradicting information. CEOs must therefore have the ability to interpret the information. They do not respond instinctively but they analyze, investigate and uncover hidden implications. They zoom in on the details and zoom out to get the big picture. They look for new information and arguments that might disprove their hypothesis. They test their final observation using quantitative analysis. And they occasionally take a step back to get a fresh perspective. They go to museums, play tennis or take a walk in the park to open their minds.

4 Decide

CEOs in the new economy prevent hasty and simplistic 'go or no-go' decisions based on incomplete information. They consistently look for the right balance between acceleration and consideration and they pay attention to both the short-term and long-term effects. In order to improve their decision making capabilities, CEOs in the new economy take the following measures: they explicitly ask their team about possible options; they divide their decision into parts to get a better idea of the content and the implications; they share their state of mind and do not avoid debate; and lastly, they consider whether pilots and experiments would be suitable. This method of decision making serves as a nuance to the Angelo-Saxon model of the almighty CEO that makes all the decisions. The new leader surrounds himself with people who actively think together with the CEO and dare to speak up against him if need be. By doing this, higher quality decisions are made and the decisions have more support. Some of these aspects can also be seen in Rhine capitalism which is the predominant economic model in countries like Germany, France and the Netherlands. In the transition to 'management by design' as mentioned earlier, these elements are incorporated.

5 Steer

It is crucial that CEOs have the ability to find common ground for their course of action and that they create unity amongst parties who may have different agendas and views. Success depends on communication, building trust, and frequent involvement. CEOs in the new economy communicate a lot and often. They identify the most important stakeholders inside and outside their organization, gain an understanding of their views and ascertain whether there are any hidden agendas or coalitions. They conduct structured discussions in order to get any misunderstanding or dissatisfactions out in the open and they show understanding towards any pushback or concerns.

6 Learn

CEOs in the new economy promote a learning organization and draw lessons from successful and unsuccessful results. They study their own mistakes and those of others in an open and constructive way. To further expand the learning capacity, CEOs research and communicate the lessons that can be drawn from failed or canceled projects. At the same time they reward managers that have tried something praiseworthy, even if they have failed. They create a culture where mistakes are seen as learning opportunities and people feel free to try.

Human Resource Director (Human Value Management)

The most valuable assets of any organization are the human assets. Although they do not show up on a balance sheet as assets, it is important to recognize that it is the people of the organization that deliver the real value of the business. New economy organizations are therefore changing from human *resource* management to human *value* management (HVM). They are implementing a personnel strategy that develops their employees rather than depleting them. Individuals gain and maintain a place within the organization based on their added value rather than based on their function or title. This is a radical shift which also means there is less room for control and hierarchy. In fact, when added value is the main criteria instead of functions or titles, there is greater equality. Human value management is focused on utilizing this equality as a tool to maximize the value of the personnel. This is not related to the amount of time an employee contributes, or to a cost-benefit analysis, but is geared towards evaluating employees based on their ability to create value.

HR directors are therefore taking on a new role which entails the need to orient themselves to the new way of working. Outdated competency standards and management development programs should be scrapped in order to make room for *leadership interventions*. This supersedes classroom training. Research has shown that on-the-job training, peer-to-peer learning, action research, and training in self-awareness and reflection is much more effective (Gitsham, 2009). HR directors also deserve a place at the boardroom table, not as foot soldiers but as fellow leaders in the organization. Human Value Management belongs to the core business of the company. Each decision made by the Board of Directors should be examined by the HVM to determine the impact it will have on the motivation of the employees and on their ability to create value.

Board of Directors and Supervisory Board

The position and task of the Board of Directors and the Supervisory Board in the new economy is changing significantly. This is understandable because organizations as a whole are engaged in a revolution to create value for the essential assets of our economy.

A survey conducted by Deloitte[139] of over 100 Boards shows unanimous agreement that achieving sustainability is crucial. However, many Boards wrestle with incorporating sustainability into their business practices.

Although two thirds of the organizations have adopted sustainability into their strategic objectives, only one third of those incorporates a sustainability policy in their Key Performance Indicators (KPIs) even though 72 percent of those surveyed would want to do so. Moreover, 93 percent of the Board members recognize that consumers and society on the whole expect more oversight from them.

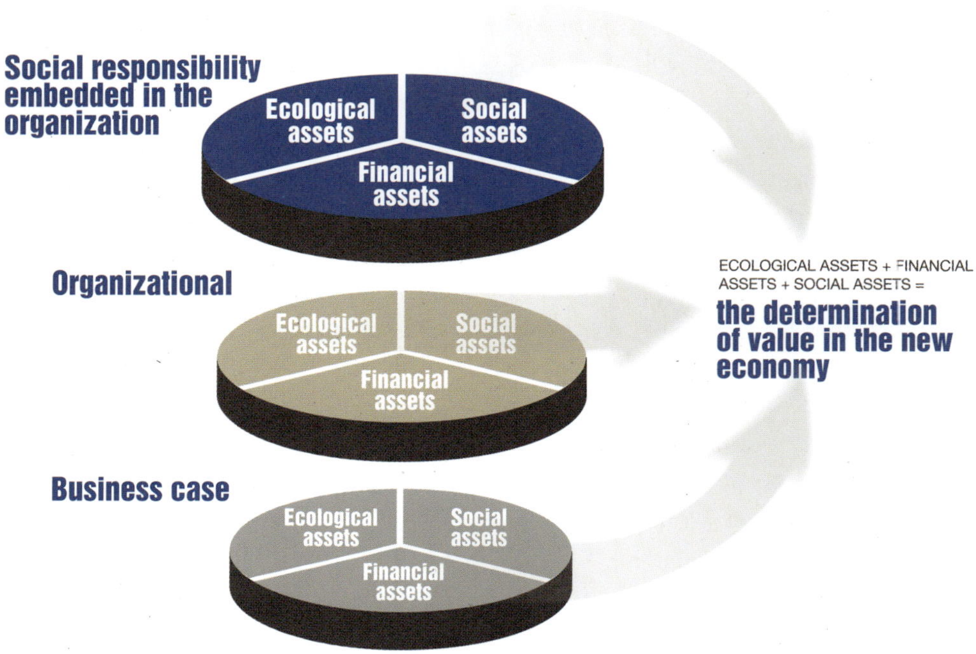

Illustration 32
The value driven Supervisory Board

In the new economy, the guidelines that the Board follows are determined by the company's financial, organizational, and societal objectives. The Supervisory Board is meant to articulate the company's goals, facilitate decision making, and ensure that those decisions are well executed. They are tuned in to the interests of the outside world as well as those of the stakeholders. They are, so to speak, the conscience of the CEO. Just as the Chief Value Officer (CVO) of the new economy differs from the Chief Financial Officer (CFO) in approach, the Supervisory Board is driven from the perspective of maximizing value.

From a business perspective, the new economy can be divided into three parts. The top level which is the macro-economic part; this is the total of the economic costs and revenue in which not only the financial, but also the ecological and social costs and benefits are included. The second part is the management level in which the same comprehensive approach is used. For example, *Integrated Reporting* (as is described in Chapter 6: Financing) is utilized to calculate not only the financial costs and revenue but also to assess the costs and benefits in a social and ecological sense. The third part is that of the individual business case. This is a broader approach towards costs and revenue but also towards parties, content, and timelines than what has been used in the traditional economy. This is further explained in Chapter 5: Business Case.

The Supervisory Board belongs to the top layer. The CEO and the CVO are positioned in the second layer. The Supervisory Board is not focused on the company's short-term targets, but keeps a sufficient distance in order to have a broad overview. The CEO may sit at the top of the tower, so to speak, but the Supervisory Board is in the helicopter. They have the overview and thus the ability to make connections that will create value for the organization and for the entire context where the organization operates.

Supervisory Board in the old economy	Supervisory Board in the new economy
1 X ANNUAL REPORT	ALWAYS ACCESSIBLE
CLOSED	OPEN
OLD BOYS' NETWORK	DIVERSE AND REPRESENTATIVE
ANONYMOUS	KNOWN
PASSIVE	ACTIVE
IN THE BACKGROUND	IN DIALOGUE
SUPERVISION	REFLECTION

Illustration 33
Old vs. New Supervisory Board

Competencies

Supervisory Board members possess expertise and extensive knowledge. They advise the Board of Directors about the general direction of the organization as well as the mission and strategy. They inspire the Board and the senior managers by working both 'backwards' and 'forwards'. When working 'backwards', they use their mandate and capacity as strict controllers to conduct relevant interventions based on the integrated reports (See Section 6.3). They can also work 'forwards' by working proactively to achieve even more value from their advisory position.[140]

The Supervisory Board members also have an external role in the new economy. They are not sitting in an ivory tower but are open to the outside world. The CEO or President is no longer the only spokesperson or point of contact. The Supervisory Board member is also in regular contact with the employees, the shareholders and other stakeholders such as government agencies and interest groups. From this perspective, the Supervisory Board members also act as ambassadors, opening doors and presenting themselves as accountable. We also encounter this kind of transparency in the traditional economy but a lot less.

The Supervisory Board member holds a mirror to the leadership of the company, thus protecting the integrity and transparency of the organization. Partly because of this, the time investment needed as a Supervisory Board member is increasing. The level of responsibility and the risk is also increasing. Therefore, courage, reliability, and integrity are core competencies needed to ensure that the company or organization achieves optimal, sustainable results.

This evolution demands more from a member of the Supervisory Board. It requires unique personal qualities including a good sense of timing to intervene at just the right moment, as well as empathy for society and sensitivity to internal and external motivations. A Supervisory Board member must have broad business savvy and the ability to see through complex situations and form well thought out judgments. And lastly, as the Supervisory Board is becoming more transparent and more visible, members should not be reluctant to take responsibility.

In order to fulfill their role and responsibilities, a Supervisory Board member must have a good overview and insight into how the organization is doing.

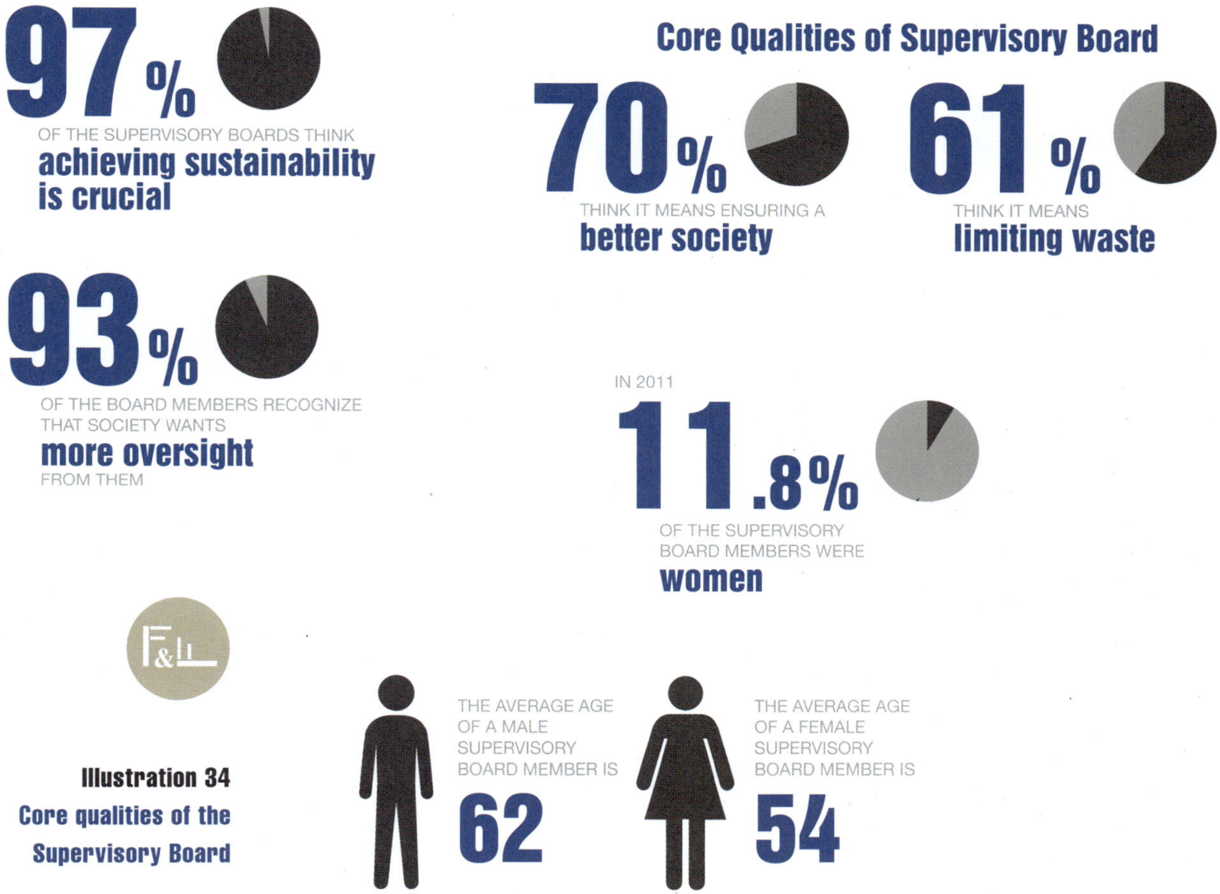

Illustration 34
Core qualities of the Supervisory Board

Blind approval of the annual accounts is no longer viable. They need to have an 'integrated dashboard' from which they can evaluate the qualitative and quantitative developments of the company. Through annual evaluations of the Supervisory Board members, their collective influence can be assessed. To stay sharp in relation to the organization as well as the outside world, a term of three years is preferred and the naming of Supervisory Board members should be based on experience and the right qualities. Diversity should also be a priority (male/female, expertise, education, cultural background). The *old boys' network* should no longer be maintained as it does not allow for the needed diversity and instead promotes excessive homogeneity. In the new economy, there is a critical need for a large scale renewal of the Boards.

The role and responsibility of the Supervisory Board depends on the nature, legal position and market sector of the organization. A family business is different, of course, than a public limited company and a bank is different from a corporation or a healthcare institution. However, the regulatory tasks of the supervisory board remain the same. For maximum value, the profile of the ideal Supervisory Board is determined by the interests and needs of the organization.

People become members or leaders of Supervisory Boards for different reasons: honor, desire to contribute to society or the organization, or a feeling of responsibility or connection to the organization. The tasks, as we have seen, have expanded considerably over the last few years, and laws and regulations are also increasing rapidly. Additionally, societal pressures on leadership is increasing public and media visibility. Participating in or leading the Supervisory Board is no longer an honorary title, it's a job.

Wrap up

The chapter on leadership is purposefully set as the last chapter in this book. Leadership is indispensable and is what ties the new economy together. Leaders give direction, they demonstrate the courage to go forward and pursue their vision even in the face of adversity. They are decision makers even in situations where the consequences are unforeseeable. The trailblazers that I talk about in the introduction of this chapter have a crucial function in the new economy and the value of this function is unabridged. The frontrunners of today lead the way to the economy of tomorrow. And tomorrow they point the way to the future economy. And so it goes, the economy continues to evolve and so do the leaders.

Epilogue

You have read in this book how the new economy is developing and why. You have seen business cases and gained insight into new paradigms. It has been expressed throughout that the underlying drive towards a new economy is to build an economy that is here for the world, and move away from a world that serves the economy.

And what are we doing this for? All economic facts aside, most importantly we want to leave the world a better place for our children, and their children to come. It is our responsibility to begin this process and it is our children's responsibility to carry on, and their right to be able to do so.

This is why it is crucial to invest in education, and why I have co-created a schoolbook for (and with) teenagers, teachers and school administrators, called NextGen (See www.neweconomybusiness.world). The book is written in accessible language and uses digital, innovative tools to teach teenage students and young adults about economic principles and new economy values and paradigms.

But it is not a one-way street. Adults are not the only teachers. Children can teach us too. Therefore, I would like to conclude with a story by Her Royal Highness Princess Laurentien van Oranje who, as founder and Managing Director of the Missing Chapter Foundation, embraces the strength and open-minded vision of children and brings them into contact with many international boards of directors.

She spoke to a group of children to hear what they had to say:

"When I asked a group of children - all about 11 years old - why adults often have a hard time solving complex issues, they gave three responses: 1) adults forget the first step, 2) the steps they take are too big and 3) they often forget why they do things. All three observations are as refreshing as they are logical. And they are, I believe, extremely relevant when thinking about new economy business."

Taking the first step towards change takes courage. Not easy, because courage requires a delicate balance between fundamental self-examination, and having a vision as well as confidence in the outcome without knowing what that outcome exactly looks like. Having the courage to change processes, systems and entire business models is easier said than done when we have been trained about the importance of being certain, not taking risks, and quick wins. It takes courage to realize that what we have been taught about short-term gains, competition and linear processes stands in the way of a new economy business based on long-term value, sharing and circularity.

Taking all the small steps needed to move towards new economy business requires determination and, yes, courage. One does not learn to think - let alone act upon it - circularly instead of linearly, overnight. Courage needs to be fed to be sustainable. One such source is curiosity about other ways of doing business. Without it, there might never be that first step either. As Walt Disney said: *"We keep moving forward, opening new doors, and doing new things, because we're curious and curiosity keeps leading us down new paths."*

Children are naturally curious because, as a 12-year old girl put it: "we haven't seen the world outside yet." They want to discover the world. They tell us: "just try" when the fear of failure stands in the way of taking that first crucial step. How to conduct a business without depleting our planet's shrinking resources - on land or in the oceans? How to design a product so that as many components as possible can be re-used at the dissembling stage, thus retaining their value? To children, circular thinking comes naturally. And children can teach us to be curious again, as a springboard to that first, vital step and all the small steps that follow. All we need to do is really listen to them.

And then there's the third observation: asking why. Should the 'why' behind doing business not be about making a positive impact on society, about creating value? The question is, against what criteria do we judge what is valuable or not? And for whom are we creating value? For ourselves or for future generations? New economy business is about the decisions that are needed now to make business and our economic and societal thinking, future-proof.

Educating future leaders: shared learning

What do future leaders need to learn so that they are driven by long-term value rather than immediate gains? In any case, they need the personal and professional authenticity and competences to continue the steps we are taking now. It means that teachers need to let go of the basic notions they themselves were taught when the world was organized linearly. And new economy principles and perspectives need to be structurally embedded in the way we train and educate young people, both in content, and form. Not just as a separate topic, but throughout a broad range of other subjects. We cannot predict the future and therefore do not know what they need to know exactly. What we do know is that no matter what the future holds, people need to be resilient, resourceful and respectful, both towards others as well as nature.

But there's more to youth than the future. We need their curiosity and thinking power right now. Apart from their curiosity, young people have the insights, imagination and open-mindedness that adult leaders, professionals and citizens have often lost on the path of what we call experience. So not only do we need to educate younger generations, they deserve the opportunity *now* to hold up a mirror to us. After all, learning is never a one-way street.

An increasing number of international and Dutch-based businesses are showing great leadership by bringing young people into their companies: some 40 companies now have a so called Kids Counsel, a board of advisors of 10 – 12 year olds. They examine a company's strategic dilemma according to a thoroughly researched in-depth six-step process. Children are no different from other advisors in that we should not expect them to solve the actual problem. But throughout the process, everyone wins: children learn to be leaders by thinking conceptually and creatively and feel empowered because "people finally listen to them," as they themselves put it; teachers are forced to be interested in business so as to be able to facilitate the child-led research. And by giving 'future-proof' a human face, company representatives get a much-needed push towards a new, future-proof way of doing business. I cannot wait for the Kids Counsel to spread its wings internationally and become a new standard for doing business.

Clearly, listening to young people is not a 'nice to have'. It's a 'need to have' for business to be truly future-proof. This does require leadership as defined by 12-year old Saiffedine, one of the six children with whom I wrote a chapter in the award-winning Dutch edition of this book: *"leadership is learning to let go of the idea that one always needs to be the best."* Just imagine the space this attitude creates for innovation and different ways of doing business.

Laurentien van Oranje
Founder and Executive Director, Missing Chapter Foundation

Young people will grow to be tomorrow's leaders and bring the new economy into full bloom. Read more on educational developments at www.neweconomybusiness.world

About the Author

MARGA HOEK is an internationally known trailblazing figure in the movement towards a new, sustainable economy and the transition to a new way of doing business. Her passion and clear vision are motivating and inspirational. Hoek has a strong business profile and extensive experience. Over the last 20 years, Hoek has held CEO and board positions in business and numerous positions on advisory boards in business, science, education and government sectors. In 2010 she founded and is the current CEO of The Dutch Sustainable Business Association, the Dutch representative for the World Business Council for Sustainable Development. She is also the founder and Chairman of the Dutch Sustainable Science Association, a network designed to unite scientists in the drive towards a sustainable future. Hoek has spent the last several years sharing her vision internationally and fulfilling many international advisory board positions at business schools and universities as well as international business networks. Hoek is also a frequent keynote speaker inspiring connections, synergy and co-creation between business, politics and science. She presents a new outlook on business by clearly showing what tomorrow's economy has in store.

Marga Hoek

References

Abbink, J. (2012). *Revolte en revolutie in de 'Arabische Lente'. Duurzame politieke klimaatverandering?* Amsterdam: FSW-VU (http://www.fsw.vu.nl/nl/Images/Talmalezing%2013%20januari%202012_tcm30-252366.pdf).

Anthony, S.D. (2012). The new corporate garage. *Harvard Business Review, 90*, pp. 49-53.

Boons, F. & Lüdeke-Freund, F. (2013). Business models for sustainable innovation: state-of-the-art and steps towards a research agenda. *Journal of Cleaner Production, 45*, pp. 9-19.

Bos, K. van den (2012). *Accessibility based business models*. Student thesis. Enschede: University of Twente.

Castells, M. (1996). *The rise of the network society*. Malden, MA: Blackwell Publishers.

Club van Rome (1972). *The birth of the Club of Rome: A quiet villa and a big bang* (http://www.clubofrome.org/?p=375).

Collins, J. (2001). Level 5 Leadership: The Triumph of Humility and Fierce Resolve, Harvard Business Review, July, pp. 66-67.

Ekekwe, N. (2012). The best global leaders are local leaders. *HBR Blog Network*, 25 January, 2012.

Elias, Chr.J. (2009). Diarrheal disease: Solutions to defeat a global killer, Seattle: PATH (http://www.path.org/publications/detail.php?i=1710).

Ellen MacArthur Foundation (2013). *Towards the Circular Economy*, Vol. 2 (http://www.ellenmacarthurfoundation.org/business/reports/ce2013).

Fisher, L. (2009). *The perfect swarm: The science of complexity in everyday life*. New York: Basic Books.

Gitsham, M. (2009) *Developing the global leader of tomorrow*, Ashridge University & EABIS Report.

Hart, S.L., & Milstein, M.B. (1999). Global sustainability and the creative destruction of industries. *Sloan Management Review, 41*, pp. 23-33.

Hawken, P. (1993). *The ecology of commerce. A declaration of sustainability*. New York: Harper Collins Publishers.

Hawken, P., Lovins, A. & Lovins, H. (1999). *Natural capitalism: Creating the next industrial revolution*. Boston: Little Brown and Company.

Hekkert, M. (2011). De muizen krijgen te weinig ruimte. NRC *Handelsblad*, 26 May, 2011.

Hoek, M. & Jonker, J. (2012). *Zakendoen in de Groene Economie. De 7 succesfactoren voor duurzaam ondernemen.* Den Haag: De Groene Zaak.

Hurley, J. (2013). Naked Wines shares maiden profit with staff. *The Telegraph*, March.

Jenkins, B., Ishikawa, E., Geaneotes, A. & Paul, J. (2010). *Inclusive business solutions: Expanding opportunity and access at the base of the pyramid*. Report of a Conference, October 7-8, 2010 in Washington. Washington DC: IFC.

Jeucken, M. (2002). *Duurzaam financieren & bankieren*. Assen: Van Gorcum.

Johnson, M.W. & Suskewicz, J. (2009). How to jump-start the clean tech economy. *Harvard Business Review, 87*(11), p. 129.

Johnson, M.W. (2010). *Seizing the white space. Business Model Innovation for Growth and Renewal*. Boston, MA: Harvard Business School Press.

Kasten, Ch. (2013). *51 Marketing strategies to dominate your competition in this new economy!* CreateSpace Independent Publishing Platform.

Kelly, K. (1998). *New rules for the New Economy. 10 radical strategies for a connected world*. New York: Viking.

Konz, W. & Thillart, C. van den (2002). *Industriële symbiose op bedrijventerreinen*. Proefschrift Technische Universiteit Eindhoven.

Korten, D.C. (2009). *Agenda for a new economy: From phantom wealth to real wealth*. San Francisco: Berrett-Koehler Publishers.

Kramer, M.R. (2012). Better ways of doing business: Creating shared value. *The Guardian*, April.

Kreijveld, M. (2013). *Samen Slimmer – Hoe de 'wisdom of crowds' onze samenleving zal veranderen*. Deventer: Kluwer.

Kumar, V. (2012). *101 design methods: A structured approach for driving innovation in your organization*. New York: John Wiley & Sons.

Levitt, Th. (1983). The globalisation of markets. *Harvard Business Review*, *61*, pp. 91-201.

Lier, H., Heiblom, R. & Waijers, A. (2009). *Van Experience naar Challenge Economy*. Groningen: Noordhoff.

Limpt, C. van (2012). 'Ik ben een vreedzame terrorist'. *Trouw*, 15 oktober.

Meyer, F. de (2011). *De impact van Megatrends op uw business*. Brugge: Die Keure NV.

Michel, S. (2012). *From product to service. Strategy and Growth* (www.ceoforum.com).

Michel, S., Brown, S.W. & Gallan, A.S. (2008). Service-logic innovations: How to innovate customers, not products. *California Management Review, 50*, pp. 49-65.

Mitchell, A. (2004). Environmental impacts of outsourcing. *E-commerce Times*.

Moss Kanter, R. (2003). Thriving locally in the global economy. *Harvard Business Review*, pp. 119-128.

Nimumolu, R., Prahalad, C.K. & Rangaswami, M.R. (2009). Why sustainability is now the key driver of innovation. *Harvard Business Review, 87*, pp. 56-64.

O'Neill, J. (2005). *The growth map*. New York: Penguin.

O'Rourke, K.H. & Williamson, J.G. (1999). *Globalization and history*. Cambridge, Mass.: MIT Press.

Olefson, S. (2013). *Financial fresh start: Your five-step plan for adapting and prospering in the new economy*. American Management Association. (www.amanet.org)

Pauli, G. (2012). *Blauwe economie*. Amsterdam: Nieuw Amsterdam.

Pine II, B.J. & Gilmore, J.H. (1999). *Welcome to the Experience Economy. Work is theatre & every business a stage*. Boston: Harvard Business School Press.

Porter, M.E. & Kramer, M.R. (2011). Creating shared value. *Harvard Business Review*, *89*(1/2), pp. 62-77.

Schippel, H. (2001). Die Anfänge des Erfinderschutzes in Venedig. In: *Europäische Technik im Mittelalter. 800 bis 1400. Tradition und Innovation.* 4e dr. Berlin: U. Lindgren.

Schwencke, A.M. (2012). *Energieke bottom-up in de Lage Landen* (http://www.asisearch.nl/wp-content/uploads/2012/08/ESSAY-Energieke-BottomUp-in-Lage-Landen-Schwencke-21082012-FINAL.pdf).

Shostack, G.L. (1982). How to design a service. *European Journal of Marketing*, *16*, pp. 49-63.

Stahel, W.R. (2006). *The Performance Economy*. London: Palgrave Macmillan.

Toffler, A. (1970). *Future shock*. New York: Random House.

World Commission on Environment and Development (1987). *Our Common Future, Report of the World Commission on Environment and Development*. UN Document (http://www.un-documents.net/wced-ocf.htm).

Notes / endnotes

Chapter 0 The New Economy

1 Robert F. Kennedy Jr. (Oct. 2, 2014). *Presentation at Elmhurst College: "Green Capitalism".* http://www.youtube.com/watch?v=zCyMEHcp5GM
2 At the time the first version of the book was printed, in 2013, these numbers were respectively 6,3 million and 2.500 book titles.
3 http://www.takepart.com/an-inconvenient-truth/film
4 http://www.ellenmacarthurfoundation.org/circular-economy/circular-economy/the-circular-model-brief-history-and-schools-of-thought
5 http://www.unep.org/greeneconomy/AboutGEI/WhatisGEI/tabid/29784/Default.aspx
6 https://trustcloud.com/blog/2011/09/20/the-sharing-economy-a-view-from-above.html
7 www.bostonglobe.com/opinion/2014/01/11/porter/XQHHPo1gDtuOjgNDOtzDMP/story.html
8 http://www.cbs.nl/nl-NL/menu/themas/macro-economie/publicaties/dne/economische-groei/archief/2014/2014-15-05-03-ne-e.htm
9 http://www.ren.pt/en-GB/quem_somos/missao_e_valores/
10 https://www.studioroosegaarde.net/project/smog-free-project/
11 John Elkington (1997). *Cannibals with Forks: The Triple Bottom Line of Twenty-First Century Business*. Capstone, Oxford.
12 Forum for the future, The Five Capitals Model – a framework for sustainability, (www.forumforthefuture.org/project/five-capitals/overview)
13 http://natcapsolutions.org/about/sustainability-defined
14 The current classification of ecological capital is not undisputed. The current economy sees them as financial capital with diminishing value. Treating them as ecological capital means acknowledging the materials as (renewable) resources, without equalizing them with natural renewable resources. A wooden bench is of less value then a living tree.
15 See reference 10.
16 This flaw in the economy does not only apply to ecological capital. Social capital, like volunteer work for the benefit of the community, is also not accounted for in a financial balance sheet.
17 Thomas Piketty, Le capital au 21e siècle, Editions du Seuil, 2013/ Capital in the 21st century, Harvard Business Press, 2014
18 http://www.intomobile.com/2012/10/11/itu-6-billion-cell-phones-worldwide-11-billion-gigabytes-data/

19 Bangladesh, Egypte, Indonesië, Iran, Mexico, Nigeria, Pakistan, Filipijnen, Zuid-Korea, Turkije en Vietnam. See also O'Neill, J. (2005). *The growth map*. New York: Penguin.

Chapter 1 Customers

20 http://www.thedailybeast.com/articles/2013/07/05/young-americans-are-abandoning- car-ownership-and-driving.html
21 http://www.treehugger.com/culture/japanese-trends-worth-watching-de-ownership-demonetization-de-materialism.html
22 http://www.wired.co.uk/news/archive/2012-07/13/end-of-ownership
23 http://www.apec.org.au/docs/2011-11_training/deloitte2006.pdf
24 http://offgrid-electric.com
25 http://www.forbes.com/sites/languatica/2012/05/31/delivering-happiness-why-at-zappos-its-your-birthday-every-day/
26 http://www.inc.com/welcome.html?destination=http://www.inc.com/articles/201105/small-business-success-stories-zanes-cycles.html
27 http://www.ellenmacarthurfoundation.org/business/articles/snapshot-ricoh
28 http://www.newdream.org/news/press-release-guide-to-sharing
29 http://neighborgoods.net/about
30 http://money.cnn.com/2011/10/13/technology/iphone_trade_in/
31 See reference 22.
32 http://www.strukton.nl/global/groep/documenten/nederlands/projecten/rotterdamse_zwembaden/besparen_zonder_betalen_esco_sept%202012.pdf
33 http://en.wikipedia.org/wiki/Upcycling
34 http://www.theguardian.com/sustainable-business/sustainable-fashion-blog/alternative-business-models-live-chat
35 http://www.schoolfacilities.nl/huisvesting/energiebeheer/3285-esco-ovvia-wil-financiele-blokkades-verduurzaming-scholen-opheffen
36 http://blogs.wsj.com/digits/2013/08/28/andreessen-horowitz-bets-on-car-sharing-for-corporate-fleets/

Chapter 2 Value Cycle

37 http://www.ellenmacarthurfoundation.org/case_studies/active-disassembly
38 http://www.ellenmacarthurfoundation.org/case_studies/wear2
39 http://www.env.go.jp/en/recycle/smcs/a-rep/2010gs_full.pdf
40 http://www.ellenmacarthurfoundation.org/case_studies/ecovative

41 See reference 37.
42 See reference 37.
43 https://www.cordaid.org/en/news/approved-proposal-sanitation-value-chain/
44 http://www.timberlandtires.com
45 http://www.duurzaambedrijfsleven.nl/70029/timberland-produceert-autobanden-voor-eigen-schoenen/
46 Intel and ASML Reach Agreements to Accelerate Key Next-Generation Semiconductor Manufacturing Technologies, 2012. http://www.intc.com/releasedetail.cfm?ReleaseID=690165
47 Reversed factoring is no panacea: revenues gained in the supply chain must be high enough to let it function properly.
48 Sometimes these entrepreneurs develop the programs together with banks and sometimes without them (see paragraph 6.1).
49 http://www.thenaturalstep.nl/wp-content/uploads/2014/04/TNS-NL-Success-Story-for-Interface.pdf
50 http://www.rtcc.org/2014/05/30/ghanas-bamboo-bikes-charting-the-path-to-sustainability/#sthash.rM1hvyjp.dpuf
51 http://www.nikeresponsibility.com/infographics/materials/
52 http://www.theguardian.com/sustainable-business/skanska-working-greater-good)
53 http://www.nespresso.com/nl/nl/pages/services
54 http://www.theguardian.com/sustainable-business/systems-ewaste-brazil

Chapter 3 Scale

55 http://www.documentairenet.nl/review/het-geheim-van-de-hema/
56 Institution of Mechanical Engineers (2013). *Global Food Report*. http://www.imeche.org/knowledge/themes/environment/global-food
57 SustainAbility (2007). *Raising our game, can we sustain globalization?*, p.10 http://www.sustentabilidad.uai.edu.ar/pdf/sde/Raising_Our_Game.pdf
58 http://www.economist.com/node/14031230
59 http://www.buzzback.com/blog/combining-glocalization-sustainability-to-attract-consumers/
60 http://www.newyorker.com/online/blogs/currency/2013/12/whole-foods-and-gentrification-in-brooklyn.html)
61 https://www.ser.nl/nl/publicaties/overzicht%20ser%20bulletin/2013/mei2013/fuji-innoveert.aspx
62 Zonnepanelen voor straatlantaarns. *Het Financieele Dagblad*, 3 December, 2012.

63 www.ceraa.be/uploads/annexes/journeesetudesjedd7/JEDDVII_orateurs/10_ROMBAUT-pps_en.pdf
64 Bangladesh, Egypte, Indonesië, Iran, Mexico, Nigeria, Pakistan, Filipijnen, Zuid-Korea, Turkije en Vietnam. See also O'Neill, J. (2005). *The growth map*. New York: Penguin.

Chapter 4 Innovation

65 http://nbs.net/wp-content/uploads/NBS-Executive-Report-Innovation.pdf
66 http://www.climate-kic.org/news/simgas-awarded-for-the-establishment-of-a-biogas-system-production-line/
67 http://www.simgas.com/newsandoffers/news/press-release-gesi550/item74
68 http://www.starbucks.com/blog/used-paper-cups-become-new-again/624
69 http://nbs.net/wp-content/uploads/NBS-Executive-Report-Innovation.pdf
70 *FastCompany Magazine* 2012. The 2012 Innovation by Design Awards. October, p. 105
71 http://www.veolia.co.uk/ren
72 Mezgebu W.T. & Firesibhat G.M. (2011). *Sustainability and Sustainability driven Innovation in case of* LEGO. Essay, p.41.
73 http://www.terracycle.com/en-US/products/capri-sun-drink-pouch-messenger-bag.html
74 http://bgr.com/2012/09/13/apple-samsung-lawsuit-steve-wozniak-iphone-5/
75 https://www.quirky.com/ge

Chapter 5 Business case

76 http://www.biojournaal.nl/artikel/14384/IKEA-pallet-verkozen-tot-Duurzaamste-product-van-2013
77 http://www.theguardian.com/sustainable-business/business-look-outside-reconnect-society
78 http://www.sabmiller.com/docs/default-source/sustainability-documents/harvard-kennedy-ecosystem-report.pdf?sfvrsn=4
79 http://www.fomin.org/HOME/FOMINblog/Blogs/TabId/628/ArtMID/8837/ArticleID/90/SABMiller-announces-commitment-to-support-small-retailers-in-Latin-America.aspx
80 http://chrislang.org/2000/11/25/laos-subsidies-for-swedish-profits-in-the-forestry-sector/

81 http://worldagroforestry.org/newsroom/media_coverage/private-sector-agroforestry-model-pays-farmers-laos
82 http://www.buraphawood.com/

Chapter 6 Financing

83 http://www.gartner.com/it-glossary/total-cost-of-ownership-tco
84 http://www.degroenezaak.com/upload/documents/WP%20Nieuwe%20Business%20Modellen%20Jan%20Jonker%20e.a.pdf
85 http://e-flux.com/timebank/about
86 https://hbr.org/2012/09/the-exploding-business-of-bart
87 http://www.amednews.com/article/20090112/business/301129995/4/
88 http://www.businessweek.com/articles/2012-04-26/rise-of-the-barter-economy
89 https://hbr.org/2012/09/the-exploding-business-of-bart
90 http://www.ft.com/cms/s/0/6da4934a-121a-11e2-b9fd-00144feabdc0.html#axzz3EPdcM5ux
91 http://www.omroepzeeland.nl/nieuws/2012-04-20/118063/slijterijmeisje-zet-banken-buitenspel-met-crowdfunding#.VGxiAvmG-7Y
92 http://www.entrepreneur.com/article/230912
93 http://www.crowdfundinsider.com/2014/09/50458-flyingv-largest-crowdfunding-platform-asia/
94 http://www.initialcrowdoffering.com/wp-content/uploads/2012/08/How_to_Raise_1_Million_Dollars-by_InitialCrowdOffering.pdf
95 http://www.funginstitute.berkeley.edu/sites/default/files/Crowdfund_Investment_Paper.pdf
96 http://socialstockexchange.com/wp-content/uploads/2014/05/Impact-Investment-Report-FINAL.pdf
97 See reference 80.
98 http://www.academia.edu/1484970/Peer-to-Peer_Financing_Mechanisms_to_Accelerate_Renewable_Energy_Deployment
99 http://www.allesduurzaam.nl/nieuws/nieuws_item/t/succesvolle_crowdfunding_campagne_wakawaka_zet_50_000_haitianen_in_het_licht
100 http://www.bam.nl/pers/persberichten/rijkswaterstaat-en-consortium-bampggm-bereiken-financial-close-voor-pps-project
101 http://www.ibtimes.co.uk/cooperatives-uk-economy-staff-ownership-john-lewis-482519
102 http://www.bbc.com/news/business-26560702
103 http://www.map.ren21.net/GSR/GSR2012_low.pdf
104 See reference 92.

105 http://thefinancialbrand.com/37787/millennial-banking-survey-viacom/

106 http://www.nu.nl/economie/2719034/vertrouwen-in-banken-gedaald.html

107 http://financieel-management.nl/artikel/nieuwe-fase-van-innovatie-in-financiering-verlaagt-kosten-in-de-totale-productieketen

108 These kinds of banks, often called social banks, link social trends with green entrepreneurship, crowdfunding, social media and their own supply of financial products and services.

109 http://www.erstestiftung.org/project/die-zweite-sparkasse/

110 http://financieel-management.nl/artikel/duizenden-banen-in-de-bankwereld-verdwijnen-door-talloze-fintech-startups

111 https://transferwise.com/blog/2014-04/watch-as-banks-admit-to-ripping-you-off-in-these-secret-recordings-video/

112 http://yhponline.com/2014/01/31/christoph-rieche-iwoca/

113 https://www.fidor.de/produkte/smart-account/like-zins

114 Skinner, Chr. (2012) Financial Services Blog, Fidor Bank: The most innovative bank concept out there. http://thefinanser.co.uk/fsclub/2012/06/fidor-bank-from-one-extreme-to-another.html

115 http://spice.fsi.stanford.edu/docs/european_answers_to_the_financial_crisis_social_banking_and_social_finance

116 http://blogs.cisco.com/financialservices/new-strategies-in-retail-banking-giving-customers-control-of-how-they-bank

117 http://www.academia.edu/1484970/Peer-to-Peer_Financing_Mechanisms_to_Accelerate_Renewable_Energy_Deployment

118 http://online.wsj.com/articles/SB10001424052702304636404577299652553219204

119 Http://www.act.is/ActisPDFs/ESG%20in%20Private%20Equity_A%20Study%20by%20MSP%20and%20EDF.pdf

120 http://www.act.is/ActisPDFs/ESG%20in%20Private%20Equity_A%20Study%20by%20MSP%20and%20EDF.pdf

121 http://www.theguardian.com/sustainable-business/public-pension-funds-sustainable-investment-pioneers

122 See reference 117

123 www.ns.nl/mvoberekeningen

124 http://www.theguardian.com/sustainable-business/blog/puma-scales-up-environmental-profit-loss-product

125 http://www.sustainablebrands.com/news_and_views/oct2011/measuring-eco-and-social-impacts-redefine-business-value-pwc-puma

126 Shortly after the conversation with Johan Piet about integrated

reporting, he passed away. He was 65 years of age. With the permission of his family it was decided to include his contribution in this book.

127 http://www.worldconnectors.nl/themes/green-economy-true-price/

128 http://www.treasuryandrisk.com/2011/02/10/chief-value-officer-debuts

129 http://www.leveragepoint.com/blog/does-your-company-need-chief-value-officer-0

Chapter 7 Leadership

130 http://www.sustainability.com/library/the-2013-sustainability-leaders

131 http://www.vno-ncw.nl/publicaties/Forum/Pages/Paul_Polman_Ik_wil_de_wereld_verbeteren_15934.aspx

132 http://www.forbes.com/sites/languatica/2012/05/31/delivering-happiness-why-at-zappos-its-your-birthday-every-day/

133 http://www.mt.nl/332/86790/business/ricardo-semler-het-tijdperk-van-wijsheid-is-begonnen.html

134 http://managementscope.nl/manager/peter-bakker/tnt-un-ambassadeur

135 http://www.vno-ncw.nl/publicaties/Forum/Pages/Paul_Polman_Ik_wil_de_wereld_verbeteren_15934.aspx (See reference 117).

136 https://hbr.org/2012/05/unilevers-ceo-on-making-respon/

137 https://hbr.org/2013/02/doing-the-right-thing-or-makin

138 http://www.thehindu.com/todays-paper/tp-features/tp-opportunities/strategic-leadership-the-essential-skills/article4409672.ece

139 http://www2.deloitte.com/content/dam/Deloitte/nl/Documents/commissaris/deloitte-nl-commissarissen-survey-dec-2010.pdf

140 http://www.nkcc.nl/files/files/hetprofielvandecommissaris_3_0_~_discussiepublicatie.pdf